Universities and Globalization

Universities and Globalization

Critical Perspectives

Editors
Jan Currie • Janice Newson

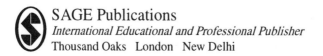

SAGE Publications
International Educational and Professional Publisher
Thousand Oaks   London   New Delhi

For information:

 SAGE Publications, Inc.
2455 Teller Road
Thousand Oaks, California 91320
E-mail: order@sagepub.com

SAGE Publications Ltd.
6 Bonhill Street
London EC2A 4PU
United Kingdom

SAGE Publications India Pvt. Ltd.
M-32 Market
Greater Kailash I
New Delhi 110 048 India

Printed in the United States of America

Library of Congress Cataloging-in-Publication Data

Universities and globalization: Critical perspectives / edited by
Jan Currie and Janice Newson.
    p. cm.
  Includes bibliographical references and index.
  ISBN 0-7619-1065-4 (cloth: acid-free paper)
  ISBN 0-7619-1066-2 (pbk.: acid-free paper)
  1. Education, Higher—Economic aspects. 2. Education,
Higher—Social aspects. 3. Education, Higher—Aims and objectives.
4. Universities and colleges—Administration. I. Currie, Jan. II.
Newson, Janice Angela, 1941-
  LC67.6 .U552 1998
  378.1—ddc21   98-9059

98 99 00 01 02 03 10 9 8 7 6 5 4 3 2 1

Acquiring Editor:	Peter Labella
Production Editor:	Diana E. Axelsen
Editorial Assistant:	Nevair Kabakian
Typesetter/Designer:	Danielle Dillahunt
Indexer:	Virgil Diodato

Contents

Preface

The germination of this book took place on two continents, North America and Australia. It came together when Jan Currie met Janice Newson in her house outside of Toronto, Canada, in 1995. We recognized instantly that we were talking with the same passion and urgency about the consequences of globalization for our universities. As feminists and unionists, we were seeing the implications of the way the work of academics was changing and the way female academics were often the first to be restructured out of their jobs or put into more exploitative positions in casual part-time jobs. But we also saw the broader implications for the function of universities in society and for the future of public sector organizations more generally in most societies.

We then discussed collaborating on a project titled *The Changing Nature of Academic Work.* Jan Currie had already received an Australian Research Council Large Grant for this project, specifically to undertake a study of three universities in Australia from 1994 to 1996. In this work, she collaborated with Anthony Welch (University of Sydney); Margaret Crowley (Edith Cowan University); Susan Robertson (Edith Cowan University), who subsequently moved to the University of Auckland; and Roger Woock (University of Melbourne). She also collaborated with colleagues in three American universities—Edward Berman (University of Louisville), Stephen Klees (Florida State University), and Sheila Slaughter (University of Arizona)—to carry out case studies in their universities. In 1993, an initial meeting for this project was hosted by Robert Lawson and Mary Ann Sagaria at Ohio State University, with Liz Gordon from Canterbury University, New Zealand, in attendance, along with some of the other colleagues mentioned above.

Our initial aim was to have a comparative study of how academic work was changing in four British-derived countries: Australia, Canada, New Zealand, and the United States. In the end, similar case studies were undertaken in Australia and the United States. In addition, a collection of distinct case studies, policy analyses, and related research projects were under way in Canada and New Zealand. This gave us a range of perspectives on the ways universities were changing.

The specific impetus for this collection of essays arose out of the World Congress of Comparative Education held in Sydney, July 1 to 6, 1996. Janice Newson and Jan Currie were chosen to organize a commission on globalization and higher education. This was publicized worldwide and drew the largest number of papers for any commission at the Congress. From this commission, we chose papers for this book to represent a wide range of issues related to globalization and higher education, and we asked writers who had been involved in similar research projects to contribute chapters on specific topics. Our underlying criterion for choosing papers was the development of a critical perspective on globalization. The significance of this topic was recognized by Peter Labella at Sage Publications, and we thank him for assisting us in publishing this book. We would also like to thank Diana Axelsen for her excellent editing of the book.

JAN CURRIE, Perth, Western Australia
JANICE NEWSON, Grafton, Ontario, Canada

From Jan Currie:

In addition to the colleagues identified above, there are many others I would like to acknowledge for their generous contribution to this book: first, the many academics and university administrators who were interviewed for her chapters in this book; Harriett Pears, who has worked as Research Officer on the project, Changing Nature of Academic Work, for the past 4 years and who excels in her use of NUD•IST, the software package used to analyze the interview data; Lesley Vidovich, Ph.D. student, research assistant, and coauthor,

Tallahassee in more ways than can be mentioned, during the case study of Florida State University; Ursula Thurgate, who did the final word processing of chapters to make all the references consistent; Bill Anthony, who did an excellent job of editing chapters; and James Bell and Carl Green, who did some of the initial interviews.

From Janice Newson:

I express my gratitude to The Association for Canadian Studies and the Social Sciences and Humanities Research Council of Canada's International Travel Fund for financial support in the research and writing of this book. I also acknowledge the contribution and influence of two particular colleagues. Professor Claire Polster, sociologist at the University of Regina in Saskatchewan, Canada, was a graduate student at York University in the early 1990s. I supervised her doctoral dissertation on the changing social relations of academic research. Our shared commitment to the university as a place of learning that should serve a broadly defined public interest transformed our relationship into a fruitful intellectual partnership and valuable friendship.

In the early 1980s, Professor Howard Buchbinder—now retired but formerly of the Social Science Department of Atkinson College of York University—and I became first political partners and then academic partners with a political purpose. We worked side by side in the leadership of the Faculty Union at York University, during a period of intense labor strife on campus. We subsequently decided to continue our struggle for a public, open, and accessible university by carrying out critically oriented research on managerialism and university-corporate links, both of which had begun to characterize higher education policy throughout the 1980s in Canada, Great Britain, and the United States. Initially, our research, along with our academic union organizing experience, provided the foundation for speaking engagements in Canadian and British universities, in which we tried to alert colleagues about the serious implications of emerging changes in the organization of academic work. Eventually, we published several articles and the book *The University Means Business: Universities, Corporations, and Academic Work* (1988).

Many other people whom I can't name here have contributed to the ideas, issues, and commitments that I have brought into this project: colleagues and students from my own department and university, but also from many other universities throughout Canada, the United States, Mexico, Great Britain, and elsewhere. I have become connected to them through our shared commitment to the university as an institution that should exist to serve the public good rather than to produce privately owned goods. It is to them and our struggle in common that I dedicate my share of the work in this book.

Susan Weinstein has been a superb research assistant and editor and a faithful emotional partner through it all. And finally, there is Otis, whose loss we had to bear but whose self-reliance, loyalty, and abiding presence always inspires us to reach for "the best there is."

CHAPTER 1

Introduction

Jan Currie

In 1997, a half-dozen conferences or symposia advertised in various parts of the world proposed to look at universities and globalization. It is apparent, as Waters (1995) declared, that globalization is the concept of the 1990s, as postmodernism was the concept of the 1980s. Although the term *globalization* began to be used in the 1960s, the first author to use it in the title of a sociological article was Robertson in 1985. When referring to globalization, the editors of this book go beyond the more neutral term of *globalizing* to designate processes that have made the world smaller. Such a definition is well described by Robertson (1992), who defined globalization as "a concept that refers to the compression of the world and the intensification of consciousness of the world as a whole" (p. 8). He and others describe the global world as one where time and space are compressed. It is important to distinguish between globalization as a process that has indeed made communication instantaneous and encouraged people to think in more global terms and a conception of globalization that combines a market ideology with a corresponding material set of practices drawn from the world of business. It is the latter definition of globalization that animates this book.

The contributors to this book, *Universities and Globalization: Critical Perspectives*, seek to understand how a globalizing political economy affects the way universities are governed and how the daily lives of academics have been altered by globalization practices. The authors look at managerialism, accountability, and privatization—practices that represent a shift toward business values and a market agenda for universities. Representing a wide range of political perspectives, the writers analyze what is meant by globalization and how its practices have come to influence so many nations and local institutions; and, more specifically, they examine how globalization practices have come to penetrate universities and why politicians and universities in some countries have chosen to shape globalization practices according to their own priorities. Are there alternative models to those that represent this ideology of globalization?

This book differs in three significant ways from most of the writing that has been produced to date on globalization and higher education. First, the writers do not unquestioningly assume that globalization, namely, the shift toward globalized economic, political, and social relations, has ever been uniform. There is considerable diversity in practices of globalization and in how countries have modified these practices to be more commensurate with their own economic and political philosophies. Second, the writers do not assume that, to the extent that these economic, political, and social transformations occur, they will be unproblematically beneficial to all citizens or groups within society. Instead, we not only attempt to expose some of the potential and already realized disadvantages of the present course of globalization, but also confront the possibility that the downside may not simply be a temporary stage in an overall process that, it is often argued, will eventually result in benefits to all citizens. We refute that assumption. Third, the writers do not view globalization as an inevitable process to which all accommodations must be made. Instead, we give centrality to the notion of choice and agency to allow modifications to the globalization agenda.

The editors have felt compelled to generate a deeper awareness of globalization processes because, as academics ourselves, we are living in universities that are rapidly changing, being restructured, and adopting practices that are more commonly found in businesses. We feel an urgent need to ask why universities and the governments regulating them are choosing this particular direction. Our daily lives have become and continue to become more distorted and twisted by the demands of ever-increasing workloads and by the intensification of our work, which leads to greater stress and a general sense of demoralization (Currie, 1996). We are fully aware that academics are not the only group affected by these processes; indeed, most other workers have felt the effects of globalization practices in much more dramatic ways than academics. This book, then, might be seen as just one case study of many but one that can reflect the experiences of other workers outside of academia in terms of the effects of specific globalization practices.

A major reason we are particularly concerned about the future of universities is that we believe a significant factor in their functioning is to encourage critical thinking within society. They are institutions where broadly based knowledge is supposed to be developed and disseminated widely, for social purposes. If the university is silenced, who will be able to maintain critical judgments within society and speak with a critical voice to the wider community? As the media, in so many forms, increasingly become controlled by vested interest groups, there is a growing need for universities to provide a space for a critical analysis of social issues. They must be more than engines for economic productivity and competitiveness. However, as Halsey (1992) has noted with respect to British universities, this is becoming increasingly difficult, as universities react to the pressures from government and begin to be molded in certain directions:

> Managerialism gradually comes to dominate collegiate cooperation in the organisation of both teaching and research. . . . Research endeavours are increasingly applied to the requirements of government or industrial demands. The don becomes increasingly a salaried or even a piece-work labourer in the service of an expanding middle class of administrators and technologists. (Halsey, 1992, p. 13)

Another example of the constraint on the university's capacity to be a vital, critical voice for society is examined in this book—the globalization practice of increased accountability, coming in the particular form of bureaucratic and financial accountability. Academics in many countries have complained about the ever-increasing amount of petty bureaucracy and form-filling that has accompanied this push to make universities more accountable, especially to external stakeholders, such as governments. This is well described by Miller (1995) in an article on the changing labor process of academics. He quotes an English academic about the changing decision-making style for universities:

> It's the ethos of the market, the language being used is the management style, completely market led, almost a profit driven type of

enterprise and we thought we were academics. The talk is of clients or consumers rather than students. But the management style is discredited, it uses techniques which are pretty naff [outdated and naive] in terms of modern business practice—the breaking up of academic community into a rigid hierarchical structure. We used to elect Deans! (p. 58)

In addition to the shift toward the market and managerialism, academics are coping with increased workloads. One Australian academic describes the situation of greater accountability coupled with the intensification of university work:

But what is stressful is that the magnitude of tasks just seems to grow with every couple of weeks. There are new things to be done and there is a sense of being overwhelmed by the fact that this will never end, it's just growing inexorably.[1]

GLOBALIZATION PRACTICES AND UNIVERSITIES

Not only is there a deterioration in the working conditions of academics, there is also a sense that the market is creeping into universities by stealth and determining the lives of academics to a much greater extent than it did a decade or two ago. The influence of the philosophy that "the market knows best" has also brought ideas from accountants and auditors and even their professional language into the quadrangle. Business practices have introduced greater and unrelenting competition for funds. Performance indicators are used to assess and measure individuals, departments, and universities against each other by the practice of benchmarking. Corporate managerialism and line management have replaced elected deans and marginalized faculty senates and academic councils, leading to a general decline in collegiality. These business practices have led to insularity among academics, greater closed individualism, and a loss of a sense of community.

The commercialization of research has led to much closer links with industry and, as a consequence, a move to more applied research agendas with the accompanying loss in curiosity-driven research and serendipitous discoveries. The privatization of universities has packaged research endeavors and led to the commodification of knowledge. In one of its guises, the "internationalization" of higher education, universities sell education to overseas students. In another guise, universities sell their intellectual work to industry. And in yet another guise, public universities outsource many of their services to create leaner institutions with fewer workers.

In almost all universities, the concept of "user pays" has spread like wildfire so that now, even inside universities, each individual and/or department has to pay for services from other sections of the university or directly from outside, such as library, postal, media, and graphic services; electricity; telephones; and heating, which used to be centrally budgeted services. It might be thought that there is nothing wrong with a user-pays system, but it is easy to see that certain sections of the university would be more affected by such a system due to economies of scale (for example, large commerce departments versus small philosophy departments). Students also have to pay for services that used to be free, such as interlibrary loans and course guides, and of course tuition fees are escalating in most countries.

National and international trends have led academics to work much longer hours. Not everyone has the time available to work the long hours that now seem required to advance one's career. Men and women without family responsibilities are able to devote themselves to the institution and their professional discipline, if they so choose. Women (and some men) with family responsibilities do not have the same choices. Another concept taken from the business world, labor flexibility, has infiltrated the universities, creating a small core group of academics who receive higher pay and benefits and, in turn, a much larger peripheral group of contract workers (more often women) who receive lower pay and have insecure appointments with no benefits.

These are a few of the globalization practices borrowed from business that have become part and parcel of the daily agendas of universities. There are a number of distinct globalization practices, which are sometimes overlapping, sometimes mutually reinforcing, but also at times contradictory. This book looks at the specific practices of managerialism, accountability, and privatization. It analyzes how the lives of academics have been modified by these practices. The book also reflects on the way many universities have been changed as a result of accepting the dominant discourse of the globalization agenda without sensible debate as to its consequences.

Many universities appear to be "moving with the tide" (some even actively promulgating or pre-empting changes) without consciously examining the long-term aims of the globalization agenda. The changes have not necessarily been imposed from the top; it could be that universities are modifying their practices along the lines of revised government policies and advice that flows to those governments from supranational bodies, such as the World Bank or the Organization for Economic Cooperation and Development (OECD). A question arises as to whether the managers of universities are becoming the knowing or unknowing instruments of supranational bodies.

Globalization has brought the free market into universities but with serious ramifications and significant costs. The frightening aspect of globalization is the subtle way the process infiltrates institutions so that resistance to its agenda is weakened. It takes a marathon effort to even question these practices, particularly when the daily work of academics is to fulfill their duty toward students and to continue with quality research. However, the warning this book brings to its readers is that unless there is more organized resistance to the globalization agenda that links universities to markets, the result will be a shift from scholar to entrepreneur. Academics are in a position to examine these globalization practices in depth within their own workplaces and to begin to understand the way in which many workplaces are being restructured and downsized. They are moving in a similar way to assimilate globalization practices, almost through unconscious osmosis. At the same time, the writers of this book recognize that it is important to identify those countries and institutions that are not moving with the tide—those that have consciously chosen to resist, negotiate, and transform these globalization practices.

THE INFLUENCE OF SUPRANATIONAL ORGANIZATIONS AND THE INTERESTS OF CAPITAL

The World Bank, in its 1994 report on higher education, urges countries to shift from dependence on just one source of funding—the state—toward multiple sources, with more money coming from student fees, consultancies, and donations. "In short, higher education should resemble the United States model more closely" (Hodges, 1994, p. 24). Some of the other reforms mentioned in the World Bank report are linking government funding more closely to performance and developing policies on quality and equity. This message has already been taken up in many Anglo American countries. In Third World countries, the World Bank can encourage these policies more forcefully through the imposition of structural adjustment principles that push them toward greater privatization of higher education. However, countries such as Australia, Canada, and New Zealand have more likely been influenced only indirectly by World Bank pronouncements and more directly by the OECD and movements in higher education emanating from the United Kingdom and the United States. The interactions among vice chancellors of the Commonwealth nations and among ministers of education in OECD countries have tended to see these globalization practices spreading quickly from one continent to another.

There are constant reminders suggesting to politicians that still more market forces can be applied to higher education. For example, in Australia, a report released in November 1995 by the Economic Planning Advisory Commission said, "micro-economic reforms embracing 'market incentives' should be extended to the education and training sector" (Armitage, 1996, p. 8). Then, the Hoare Committee in December 1995 found that work practices in Australian universities were "not keeping pace with the profound societal and economic changes affecting the sector and the Government needed to force universities to improve their management and governance policies" (Richardson, 1995, p. 1).

The neoliberal ideology of globalization has infiltrated the minds of politicians and managers to the point where it has become internalized and, alarmingly, normalized. It has become part and parcel of the new scheme of things; the new paradigm has linked local practices to globalized social relations. It is now the norm for governments to privatize social services in most Anglo American countries. It is the norm to mouth anti-statist rhetoric, which characterizes the state as bloated, wasteful, inefficient, and unproductive. It is the rare politician who challenges these assumptions because governments are now seemingly so dependent on the capital provided by international bankers to bolster their economies.

Santamaria (1996) claims that international financiers have become "modern potentates with the power to dictate policy to states" and that the Howard government in Australia is moving on virtually all of the specifics put forward by a group of 100 top executives of the world's biggest banks, which met in Sydney, June 7, 1996, and proclaimed that "more privatization, fewer subsidies, and smaller public payrolls" were the order of the day (p. 24). Or as one of Australia's public intellectuals put it,

> We live in a time when government is characterized as a bad thing, when governments do their best to abandon governing, or as much of it as they can get away with in their first term. We live at a time when bureaucrats, like welfare recipients, are characterized as bludgers, when citizens in need are characterized to have their 'snouts in the trough,' when people are expected to serve an economy rather than an economy serving the people. We live at a time when anything with 'public' used adjectivally is a target for neo-conservatism—whether it's a public space, a public broadcaster, a public defender, public education, the public health system, or the public good. Society is now seen as a business and, where possible, run by businesses. (Adams, 1996, p. 2)

The influence has come not only from international financiers and supranational bodies, but also from regional trade organizations. Academics and labor activists from Canada, the United States, and Mexico recently met in Monterrey, Mexico, to safeguard higher education from the North American Free Trade Agreement's (NAFTA's) so-called harmonization. A representative from Toronto remarked "Education is another institution our government has given away to the capital interests of North America" (Guerrero, 1996, p. 6). Buchbinder and Rajagopal (1996), writing about the impact of free trade and globalization on Canadian universities, identify the specific chapters of NAFTA—particularly Cross Border Trade in Services, Telecommunications, and Investment Services and Related Matters—that affect education. They also believe that the past 20 years of changes have "softened up" Canadian universities and left them "both vulnerable and to a great degree, acquiescent to the wide ranging influences of globalization" (pp. 289-290).

Under conditions of globalization, the state has not necessarily disappeared but rather restructured itself into the "competitive state" (Lingard, 1996). Pannu (1996) depicts the state as *remantled* or *reconfigured*, which means more management by experts; in Third World countries, this refers to the state's capacity to "successfully manage the prevailing capitalist economy of globalization, and notably to manage the resulting social tensions in such a way that the lid does not blow off and threaten the entire elite development regime of accumulation and legitimation" (Schmitz, 1995, p. 67).

Capital itself has changed as it moves freely across boundaries in our increasingly borderless world, at least as far as markets are concerned. This has enhanced the power of multinationals, bankers, and the media. The political mobilization of business has developed into a worldwide network of this capitalist class. These groups, in turn, have been influenced by particular think tanks, which have helped shape public opinion. The end result is that voting patterns have shifted to the right (Kim, in press). The main message of these "free market" think tanks is that American corporate practices should be adopted, economies should be deregulated, and the power of trade unions should be limited (Wheelwright, 1995).

IS THE GLOBALIZATION
AGENDA IRRESISTIBLE?

Many observers immediately respond to any questioning of these globalization practices with a surrendering and acquiescing attitude: We are all being swept along by these globalization trends (the Internet, e-mail, faxes, CNN, a global economy). How is it possible to stop what appears to be an inexorable movement drawing us into this particular type of a global world? The writers of this book assert that there is a significant difference between the globalization trends that draw us into a global economy and the globalization practices that hold that the market is the only factor to consider in structuring our lives and our institutions. This book examines the human costs of globalization practices (Rees, 1995) and asserts that there are other models, even given a global economy, that can and ought to be considered in shaping our institutions (Cox, 1995). There is no doubt that global communication systems have weakened national boundaries and ideas circulate more quickly around the globe; but one of the questions the authors of this book pose is, Which ideas are circulating, and can these ideas be shaped by interests other than those that are profit-motivated and commercial?

The editors of this volume believe that the globalized political economy has both an ideological component and a material base. This volume examines not only its practices but also the way globalization is presented as an all-encompassing and irresistible idea. We do not believe that relying on the market to solve today's problems is the answer, and we assert that many of the globalization practices entering universities should be resisted. Globalization as an ideology has become, in Foucault's (1991) terms, a *regime of truth*, which tends to be all-encompassing or *totalizing* (Foucault, 1991). When most government agencies and politicians are speaking with one voice that suggests globalization practices are the only answer for all nations, it is difficult for other voices to be heard. When the supranational agencies, such as the World Bank, the International Monetary Fund (IMF), OECD, and governments, especially Anglo American governments, have all been stressing that economies need to be deregulated, social services privatized, and governments made smaller in both power and size, it is harder for individuals to think that the budget shouldn't be balanced, that workers shouldn't be made redundant, that we shouldn't pay for the services the state provides, and that taxes shouldn't be raised, not when such strong international voices are speaking in unison. These ideas have become almost like common sense and are not easily challenged. Why has there been this acquiescence to the notion of the supremacy of the market? The market is portrayed as neutral, as objective, as out there, and as free and ungovernable. This portrayal can surely be questioned.

ORGANIZATION OF THE BOOK

Part I of the book gives a theoretical overview of the globalization agenda. It subjects both the globalization agenda and its links with universities to critical and skeptical analysis. It shows how neo-liberal economic rationality of a globalizing capitalism has framed the restructuring of higher education, as a case study of more widespread changes. It also shows that there are limits to globalization forces and considerable scope for diversity. However, in the countries examined in this section—Australia, Canada, the United Kingdom, and the United States—there is a great deal of convergence toward accepting the rhetoric of globalization and moving to institutionalize its practices.

Part II gives three examples of national responses to the globalization agenda. The first two chapters contrast a country, Canada, that has taken up the economic imperative of reducing government debt, which translates into reduced funding for universities, with Norway, which is not in debt but still shows signs that the ideology of globalization is penetrating its universities. The third chapter in this section contrasts higher education reform in Australia and France and suggests that universities and nations are responding to the challenges of globalization differently. Although resistance has varied within these countries, academics are beginning to feel the implications of moving universities closer to the marketplace and to show a reluctance to simply "go along with" the globalization agenda.

Part III looks at universities to analyze the ways in which they have been shaped by particular globalization practices. Writers look first at how corporate managerialism is being institutionalized and is changing the way governance is structured within universities, and then look at the related movement toward greater accountability. Through examples drawn from Anglo American countries of Australia, Canada, and the United States, these chapters also examine the implications of corporate managerialism and the accountability movement for the autonomy of institutions and the academic staff. The next chapter explores the ways in which universities have been privatized and commercialized by focusing on the development of entrepreneurship in a university in the United States.

Part IV looks first at higher education institutions that cross national borders (such as distance education universities). It then describes how supranational agencies have attempted, with some success, to regulate universities. The two agencies that have been most active in these attempts have been the World Bank and OECD. The World Bank's (1994) proposals for reform are contained in its book *Higher Education: The Lessons of Experience*. Writers in this section examine the neo-liberal assumptions underlying the recommendations of such agencies. Another source of regulation of universities, the regional trade agreements, is also investigated. Here, one of the trade agreements, NAFTA, which unites the markets of Canada, the United States, and Mexico, is looked at from the point of view of Canadian and Mexican academics. The writers discover that certain standards are being imposed on universities and academics through agreements that prescribe the use of trilateral performance indicators. These have implications for the reorganization of the higher education environment, where changing practices are commensurate with government policies and the interventions of supranational bodies, which promote a particular brand of globalization.

The concluding chapter, "Repositioning the Local Through Alternative Responses to Globalisation," summarizes the main insights gained from the book and begins to look more holistically at alternatives to the globalization agenda that could be envisaged for universities. Drawing on the experiences of the writers who have contributed to this book and their lives as academics (which range from beginning academics to those with over 40 years of experience), it puts forward our vision of what universities could and should be like in the next century, including the values they should encapsulate.

NOTE

1. This interview came from Currie's study, Changing Nature of Academic Work, carried out in three Australian universities from 1994 to 1996.

REFERENCES

Adams, P. (1996, September 14-15). At your service. *The Weekend Australian*, p. 2.

Armitage, C. (1996, May 18-19). The threat to higher learning. *The Weekend Australian*, p. 1.

Buchbinder, H., & Rajagopal, P. (1996). Canadian universities: The impact of free trade and globalization. *Higher Education, 31*, 283-299.

Cox, E. (1995). *A truly civil society* (The 1995 Boyer Lectures). Sydney: Australian Broadcasting Corporation.

Currie, J. (1996, November). The effects of globalization on 1990s academics in greedy institutions: Overworked, stressed out, and demoralized. *Melbourne Studies in Education, 37*(2), 101-128.

Foucault, M. (1991). Governmentality. In G. Burchell, C. Gordon, & P. Miller (Eds.), *The Foucault effect: Studies in governmentality* (pp. 87-104). London: Harvester Wheatsheaf.

Guerrero, J. C. (1996, August). The NAFTA threat: Labor, academic, nonprofit activists discuss preserving public education. *Labor Notes*, p. 6.

Halsey, A. H. (1992). *The decline of donnish dominion*. Oxford, UK: Oxford University Press.

Hodges, L. (1994, July 27). World Bank pushes US tertiary model. *The Australian* (Higher Education Supplement), p. 24.

Kim, H.-M. (in press). *Voter ideology in Western democracies, 1946-1989.* Paper presented at the 1996 Annual Convention of the American Political Science Association and accepted for publication in the *European Journal of Political Research.*

Lingard, B. (1996). Educational policy making in a postmodern state: An essay review of Stephen J. Ball's *Educational Reform: A Critical and Post-Structural Approach. Australian Educational Researcher, 23*(1), 65-91.

Miller, H. (1995). States, economics, and the changing labour process of academics. In J. Smyth (Ed.), *Academic work* (pp. 40-59). Buckingham, UK: Open University Press.

Pannu, R. (1996). Neoliberal project of globalization: Prospects for democratization of education. *The Alberta Journal of Educational Research, 42*(2), 87-101.

Rees, S. (1995). The fraud and the fiction. In S. Rees & G. Rodley (Eds.), *The human costs of managerialism* (pp. 15-27). Leichardt, New South Wales: Pluto Press.

Richardson, J. (1995, December 13). Universities face radical reforms. *The Australian,* p. 1.

Robertson, R. (1992). *Globalization.* London: Sage.

Santamaria, D. A. (1996, June 15-16). Bankers' hegemony creditworthy? *The Weekend Australian,* p. 24.

Schmitz, G. J. (1995). Democratization and demystification: Deconstructing "governance" as development paradigm. In D. B. Booth & G. J. Schmitz (Eds.), *Debating development discourse: Institutional and popular perspectives* (pp. 54-90). New York: St. Martin's.

Waters, M. (1995). *Globalization.* London and New York: Routledge.

Wheelwright, T. (1995). The complicity of think tanks. In S. Rees & G. Rodley (Eds.), *The human costs of managerialism* (pp. 29-37). Leichardt, New South Wales: Pluto Press.

World Bank. (1994). *Higher education: The lessons of experience.* Washington, DC: Author.

PART I

GLOBALIZATION AS AN ANALYTICAL CONCEPT AND LOCAL POLICY RESPONSES

Jan Currie

Part I undertakes one of the main projects of this book: namely, to expose and critically analyze globalization as a discourse of neo-liberal capitalism. It distinguishes between globalization as process and globalization as ideology. It also differentiates between globalization and internationalization. For example, universities have always been international in their recruitment of staff and students and in their curriculum. The very fact that academics attend international conferences and exchange their ideas in international journals makes them international workers in their disciplines. However, the traditional sense in which universities have been viewed as truly global institutions differs from the globalization of university practices taking place today as part and parcel of their alignment with the marketplace.

The two chapters in this section analyze the ways in which different governments have responded to globalization. In the four countries examined in this section (Australia, Canada, Great Britain, and the United States), the responses have been similar—reduce the state to a minimalist state and increase the power of market forces. (This, at least, has been the rhetoric of the governments, although they have

15

maintained their power to intervene so that these governments in reality have not become the "night watchman" states that some politicians have desired.) These policy shifts have been achieved through changes in macro-economic policies and micro-economic reforms affecting both the private and public sectors. Universities have not been spared in this process.

Janice Dudley's chapter, "Globalization and Higher Education Policy in Australia," examines globalization in its various guises: social, political, and economic. She argues that economic globalization is a discursive construction that favors the market and free trade, unhampered by national regulations. It is not an objective and neutral concept as is often portrayed in the idea of the "invisible hand of the free market."

After describing the various dimensions of globalization and their principally Western focus, Dudley looks at two different responses to globalization: neo-Fordist (New Right, minimalist state) and post-Fordist (Left Modernizer, interventionist state). Drawing on the work of Brown and Lauder (1996), she analyzes the way past Australian Labor governments used both neo-Fordist and post-Fordist globalizing policies to respond to the unchallenged "reality" of globalization during the period of the 1980s and early 1990s. This period is put in its historical context by contrasting this policy strategy with the earlier history of the Australian Labor Party, which favored social protection over social amelioration. Over much of this century, the Australian Labor Party has been closely tied to the trade union movement, which wanted to protect its workers from outside competition and preferred high tariffs and a "living" wage. This was in contrast to countries that adopted social democratic models, where higher levels of taxation allowed for a greater distribution of social benefits and the development of a more extensive social welfare state, such as Germany and the Scandinavian countries.

Early in this century, Australia reached a compromise between capital and labor, termed the "Australian settlement," which protected businesses and workers from international competition. With globalizing processes invading the country at a faster rate toward the end of the century, Australia began to reassess its policies and the Australian settlement began to unravel. Even with Labor governments in power during the 1980s and 1990s and an "Accord" with the unions, the policies that were adopted signaled a move to the right economically. The language of economic rationalism (referring to making the economy more efficient and competitive through restructuring, downsizing, rightsizing, etc.), public choice theory, and "user pays" was prevalent on both the Labor and Liberal sides of politics. All sectors of the economy began to be deregulated and restructured to make the country competitive in international markets. Education, and particularly universities, became one of the tools of micro-economic reform, an important plank in developing the "clever country."

Dudley ends her chapter with a plea that "globalization talk" be contested so that it does not become a self-fulfilling prophecy. She opts for a social economy where community and human priorities take precedence over those of the market. She demands an alternative vision that would challenge the dehumanizing aspects of global markets.

Sheila Slaughter's chapter, "National Higher Education Policies in a Global Economy," concentrates on the United Kingdom and the United States, but it also shows how university policies in Australia and Canada are converging via strategies that will secure greater shares of global markets. This chapter demonstrates how these four countries have encouraged market-like activity on the part of academics and their institutions and moved decisively toward *academic capitalism*. This term recognizes the shift toward the market and the need for universities to secure private sector funding.

Slaughter analyzes theories of globalization and the transition to postindustrial economies to see who the winners and losers are. She identifies Japan and the newly industrializing countries (NICs) of Asia, Singapore, Malaysia, Hong Kong, Taiwan, and South Korea as making the greatest gains, while the United States and the United Kingdom are suffering the greatest losses. She describes the criticism offered by post-Keynesians, post-Marxists, and other political economists of globalization and the need they see for the state to be more involved in global strategies. In contrast to the approaches taken by the NICs, the countries she focuses on (Australia, Canada, the United Kingdom, and the United States) responded to the challenge of globalization forces with conservative political economic policies. They shifted public resources from social welfare to economic development and attempted to reduce the national debt. However, for the most part, the national debt increased, along with inequality of income, between the late 1970s and early 1990s. Nevertheless, these countries continued to pursue neo-liberal policies that suggested that the market knows best and minimalized interference by the government.

Slaughter then looks at the implications of globalization for higher education and identifies four: constriction of funding, growing importance of technoscience, growing relationship between multinationals and universities, and focus on intellectual property strategies. In Britain, Margaret Thatcher built an enterprise culture in universities. There was a call for higher education to develop more efficient managerial styles. Universities had to compete for students through bidding schemes. More places were created in science and technology, and research was targeted for commercial exploitation. Government policy began to focus on university-industry partnerships, which concentrated research resources in designated centers. The focus was on "wealth creation" through research.

In the United States, changes in a similar direction began in the 1970s but were not as systematic or as centrally controlled as in Britain. This was mainly due to the lack of federal control over higher education in the United States. Vehicles for policy in the United States were the Business–Higher Education Forum and the Government-University-Industry Research Roundtable, which crafted competition policies for universities. During the 1980s and 1990s, these were translated into laws that encouraged deregulation, privatization, and commercialization of university activities. In promoting this type of legislation, Ronald Reagan followed the lead of Thatcher.

Federal science and technology policy promoted science and engineering, which encouraged academic capitalism. This in turn affected undergraduate education, where funding for technosciences increased while that for the humanities and social sciences decreased.

Slaughter ends her chapter with a discussion of how the four countries converged in terms of academic capitalism. She also points out important ways in which they did not converge. Government support for students, for example, diverges, with the United States giving very little support, mainly through loans rather than grants, and the other three countries offering more generous government support, mainly through grants or, in the case of Australia, deferred payment of tax (which gives students the option of avoiding up-front fees and delaying payment until they are earning an income above the average wage, when their fees are taken out of their taxes). In all four countries, however, fees increased and government funding per student decreased. The fields of study that gained funding were those in technoscience and those closer to the market. Slaughter casts doubt on the gains these countries have made through these policies because it appears to be a jobless recovery. Moreover, for most academics in these countries, it has led to greater supervision of their work (see Part III on accountability), higher teaching loads, and, for some areas, job redundancies. Some academics have been the winners in this new regime and have been highly rewarded for accidentally being in the right field or for steering their research and teaching activities toward the market.

Both Dudley and Slaughter are skeptical about the gains that can be made by moving higher education closer to the market. Even those individuals outside of universities who have the most to gain from laissez-faire policies are beginning to question the social efficacy of ruling the global economy only by the exigencies of the free market. Writers on the left and right of politics are questioning the belief in the magic of the marketplace. Conservative politicians and business leaders are raising doubts about the societies we are creating, where there is an overabundance of competition and excessive individualism. The doubts that are emerging appear to be surfacing simultaneously in many Western countries.

George Soros (1997), a prominent American (and international) capitalist, writes,

> Although I have made a fortune in the financial markets, I now fear that the untrammeled intensification of laissez-faire capitalism and the spread of market values into all areas of life is endangering our open and democratic society. The main enemy of the open society, I believe, is no longer the communist but the capitalist threat. (p. 45)

He argues that by "declaring government intervention the ultimate evil, laissez-faire ideology has effectively banished income or wealth redistribution" (p. 52). He echoes a thought by Janet Holmes à Court (a prominent capitalist and the richest woman in Australia), when she delivered the March 19, 1997, graduation address for Murdoch University. She denounced the trend for people increasingly to rely on money as the criterion of value. Even the former prime minister of Australia under a Liberal (conservative) government, Malcolm Fraser (1997, p. 13), has called for a greater role for government in the process of change, giving the countries of Singapore, Malaysia, Taiwan, and South Korea as examples in which closer cooperation between government and industry has elicited positive economic growth embedded in societies that have strong community values.

Soros (1997) suggested that a belief in our fallibility may be a way to ensure an open society without relying on an ultimate truth, such as the absolutist belief in the free market. John Ralston Saul (1995), who delivered the 1995 Massey Lectures in Canada, identified a similar path to democracy: "Doubt is central to a citizen-based society; that is, to a democracy" (p. 41). In these lectures, Saul was particularly concerned about the power of marketplace ideology and the "passive acceptance of whatever form globalization happens to take" (p. 42). He accused universities of being too complacent:

> We are faced by a crisis of conformity brought on by our corporatist structures. While the universities ought to be centres of active independent public criticism, they tend instead to sit prudently under the protective veils of their own corporations. . . . The universities, which ought to embody humanism, are instead obsessed by aligning themselves with specific market forces. (Saul, 1995, p. 70)

This book is asking universities and academics to become more active in debating the ideology of the unencumbered (or laissez-faire) marketplace. It is casting doubt on the path that many countries are following, a path with one belief—a belief in the free market. Obviously there are alternatives that can be explored.

REFERENCES

Brown, P., & Lauder, H. (1996). Education, globalization, and economic development. *Journal of Education Policy, 11*(1), 1-26.

Fraser, M. (1997, March 26). Governments are still in control. *The Australian*, p. 13.

Saul, J. R. (1995). *The unconscious civilization* (CBC Massey Lectures Series). Concord, Ontario: Anansi Press.

Soros, G. (1997, February). The capitalist threat. *The Atlantic Monthly*, pp. 45-58.

CHAPTER 2

Globalization and Education Policy in Australia

Janice Dudley

Globalization—the international integration of communications and economies—has become a recognized phenomenon; indeed a cliché. Nation-states are losing some traditional roles; control over flows of information and, perhaps, the definition of cultural values; many aspects of independent economic management; and the capacity significantly to shift the distribution of income and wealth.

These trends are, however, exaggerated especially among both free market and Marxist ideologues, for whom the creation of a truly global capitalist system represents the fulfilment of dreams or dire predictions. Reality is more complex.

—*Cable, 1996, The World Today, p. 133*

Australia's integration into the global economy was the principal rationale shaping Australia's education policies during the 1980s and early 1990s. The goal of "the clever country" was Labor's response to globalization,[1] understood predominantly in terms of a global capitalist economy. The restructuring of the Australian economy, together with micro-economic reform, was the metapolicy (Yeatman, 1990, p. 102) or master discourse (Marginson, 1993, p. xii) determining public policy in Australia. An economic rationality was the framework within which the substance of policy was determined, as well as the processes of policy making and implementation. Economic rationalism and corporate management became the norm for public policy. Education policy was no longer a separate domain with policy determined according to educational principles, because education was no longer acknowledged as a unique activity. According to the discourses of economic rationalism and human capital, education was but an element of the micro-economy, with the role of providing skilled workers for the economy. The assumption was that the productivity, efficiency, and work orientation of these skilled workers would enhance Australia's competitiveness in the international capitalist marketplace.

Globalization is a narrative of incorporation into a world system. The central premise of this narrative is the new world order of a truly global economy. The new global order is argued to be the culmination of a number of interdependent developments, which include the following:

- The aspirations of virtually all societies throughout the world toward Western materialist/consumer-based lifestyles
- The penetration and near hegemony throughout the world of Western popular culture, particularly American expressions of this mass culture
- The increasing dominance of Western, and particularly U.S., models of production and consumption
- The increasing integration of world economies into a single global international market
- Free trade and the new international division of labor

Late-twentieth-century communications technologies, together with the post-Cold War peace—what Fukuyama (1993) has called "the end of history"—both facilitate and provide a context for processes of globalization. Although globalization ostensibly has cultural, political, and economic dimensions, all of the above developments are structured by a rationality that is principally Western and principally economic. Although the global culture that our increasing communications capacities is shaping appears to be principally social, it is a culture of mass consumption. It is hence ineluctably articulated into Western capitalism and global markets.

In this chapter, economic globalization is argued to be a discursively constructed myth, or grand narrative, rather than a neutral imperative to which governments and public policy can only respond or react. The grand narrative of economic globalization is a form of economic fundamentalism, an absolutist closed discourse that valorizes "the market"—an international capitalist marketplace of free trade, unfettered by national regulation. It is this neutral global market that becomes the paramount organizing principle to which all societies must become subject. Hirst and Thompson (1996) describe globalization as

> an anti-political liberalism. [. . .] realiz[ing] the ideals of mid-nineteenth century free-trade liberals . . . that is, a demilitarized world in which business activity is primary and political power has no other tasks than the protection of the world free trading system. (p. 176)[2]

DIFFERING RESPONSES TO GLOBALIZATION: POST-FORDIST OR NEO-FORDIST

In response to the changing economic circumstances of globalization, the state may be actively interventionist—a strategic player attempting, through education and training, as well as labor market policies, to facilitate the development of a high-wage, high-skill post-Fordist economy. Accordingly, education and training become increasingly conceived of as instruments of economic policy. Alternatively, the state can adopt the laissez-faire, minimalist neo-Fordist strategy of leaving economic restructuring to market forces. In attempting to engineer the clever country, the Hawke and Keating governments adopted the active strategic route to economic prosperity. Policies included the rationalization and expansion of higher education (the so-called Dawkins reforms); increased levels of secondary school retention, along with enhanced and more equitable participation in formal education and training (directed toward maximizing Australia's productive human resources); a focus on training (for example, the Australian Traineeship Scheme); and union restructuring, retraining, and multiskilling. This supply-side focus was to deliver, through the education and training sector, increased numbers of qualified graduates and hence workers, who would act as catalysts to business and industry and stimulate the development in

Australia of a high-skill, high-wage economy of the kind envisaged by Robert Reich (1991) in his influential book *The Work of Nations*. However, these post-Fordist directions were framed within neo-liberal economic and social policies of deregulation and privatization, user pays, and reduced levels of taxation (especially on business) to "free up" investment that had been "crowded out" by government deficits and government spending. The imposition of tuition fees, albeit in the form of a deferred payment of tax (the Higher Education Contribution Scheme [HECS]), is the most visible demonstration of the user-pays principle in Australia's publicly funded higher education system. Recent moves toward institutions charging full fees for graduate programs are further evidence of this approach. Of particular concern to educators in higher education has been the rise of the orthodoxy of managerialism in public administration.

GLOBALIZATION

Global Culture

Global culture cannot be reduced to a mere Americanization, imposed by the United States or the West, a form of cultural and economic imperialism. Although it is true that globalism is Western in origin (and continues to favor the West), non-Western cultures and societies have not been passively incorporated into a Western hegemony but have actively engaged, through unique and particular local cultural, economic, and political contributions, in transforming and reshaping Western influences into a global culture. Culture is actively produced and hence the forms and expressions of global cultural practice are no longer under the control of the West.

> Rather than emphasizing the crystallized structure of the world system . . . [it is necessary to stress] the processes of globalization and the continuing contentiousness of the global order . . . varying responses to globalization influence that very process, so that its direction and outcome, and hence the shape of the global field itself, are still very much "up for grabs." (Robertson in Spybey, 1996, p. 20)[2]

Robertson is particularly concerned to emphasize the interactiveness and reflexivity of global and local practice, "the 'interpenetration' between global cultural flows and local cultural patterns" (in Spybey, 1996, p. 6).[2] At all times, therefore, the global is local and the local is global. In this interpenetration of the global and the local, globalization at the end of the twentieth century is qualitatively different from earlier patterns of economic interdependence. Such relations were *international* rather than *global* and most often reflected Western hegemony and/or imperialism. International interdependence in earlier centuries, such as colonial relationships, also differed in the ways in which the local or traditional was affected. Thus, economic interdependence alone does not equal globalization; rather, other elements, particularly the interpenetration of Western and local cultural and economic practices, are necessary to any notion of global culture or globalization. Similarly, a focus on the cultural or social alone is itself only partial. The interpenetration of the cultural or social and the economic is also a necessary element of globalization. In effect, globalization constitutes the domination of the world by a Western economic rationality, by the worldview of Western capitalism.

Economic Globalization

The late twentieth century is characterized by changing patterns both in economic and trading relations and in the organization of production. These newly emerging relationships are usually referred to as economic globalization or, more simply, globalization.

The claim of globalization is that national economies are being increasingly subsumed into a global economy and that the discipline of international markets and money markets, rather than national, social, and/or political priorities, should determine public policy. These policies, almost without exception, require states to reduce public spending, deregulate capital and labor markets, minimize welfare provision, and either eliminate or privatize as much as possible of the welfare state.

The period between 1945 and the early 1970s was a period of economic stability and prosperity for Western nations, including Australia. This Keynesian/Fordist settlement between capital and labor of mass production and mass consumption was reinforced and supported by welfare state provisions. However, over the decade or so between the early 1970s and the early 1980s, this Keynesian/Fordist compromise unraveled as a result of the collapse of the

Bretton Woods international monetary system; the Organization of Petroleum Exporting Countries (OPEC) oil crisis and the subsequent oil price rises; the internationalization of financial markets and the abolition of exchange rate controls; deindustrialization; the rise, particularly in Asia, of the newly industrialized countries (the NICs); pressures for free trade and market deregulation; and new post-Fordist models of flexible, nonstandardized production (Hirst & Thompson, 1996, p. 5).[2] These, together with the ensuing inflation and elevated levels of unemployment (particularly long-term unemployment) in Western industrialized countries, have resulted in new international economic and trading relations.

In addition, the late twentieth century is characterized by changing patterns of production. The nationally based mechanized assembly line manufacture of Fordist mass production is being challenged by post-Fordist models of more flexible production, niche marketing, and niche manufacturing. This is a model of tailoring production more closely to the demands of international competition, and it is based on developments in computer technologies, laser technologies, communications technologies, and the like. Moreover, production is increasingly global—components are manufactured and/or assembled in factories and plants located in different world locations. It is not surprising that the symbol of global production is the world car—the archetypal industrial representation of individualism, freedom, modernity, and "the American dream."

This newly globalized economy is claimed to be dominated by multinational companies (MNCs) and transnational companies (TNCs) whose investment decisions are influenced by principles of efficiency and productivity, rather than by national loyalties. Thus, this new context of globalization consists of "a global auction for investment, technology, and jobs" (Brown & Lauder, 1996, p. 2) where "the prosperity of workers will depend on an ability to trade their skills, knowledge, and entrepreneurial acumen in an unfettered global market place" (Brown & Lauder, 1996, p. 3).

The Role of the State

Internationalist capitalist market forces are constructed in the rhetoric of globalization as neutral, inevitable, and objective reality. Similarly, the Organization for Economic Cooperation and Development (OECD, 1989) treats "change" as neutral, objective, and inevitable. There is no sense of human agency in change. Rather, human agency is in responding or reacting to change. Countries have no alternative other than reacting or responding to the changing economic circumstance occasioned by globalization. Policies and programs that are not compatible with the ideologies of free trade, the free market, and a minimalist state are unviable.

The rationality of economic globalization is that global market forces cannot be controlled, so the logic of the market necessarily and inevitably must become the logic of all other domains: the political, the social, the educational, the environmental. The state is cast as increasingly irrelevant when confronted by the "reality" of ungovernable international/global market forces. Nation-states are essentially ineffective in the face of global market forces, so that the era of the powerful nation-state would appear effectively to be over. National economic management, and national political and social policies are becoming increasingly irrelevant. International markets and international capital markets operate outside the control of national governments, while MNCs and TNCs locate wherever business conditions are the most amenable.

The state is reduced to the role of the "night watchman" of classical liberalism—maintaining law and order, protecting the sanctity of contract, and providing only the level of welfare necessary to protect property and facilitate the free operation of capitalist markets. MNCs and TNCs are argued to transcend and hence escape the regulatory capacity of the state. Independent of particular nation-states and operating within the context of free trade and the new international division of labor, they operate within, and indeed constitute, a truly global capitalism.

Globalization:
An Economic Account or
a Political Prescription?

Hirst and Thompson (1996) challenge and deny the rhetoric of economic globalization. In their recent book, *Globalization in Question,* they demonstrate that

(1) The present highly internationalized economy is not unprecedented. . . .

(2) Genuine transnational companies (TNCs) appear to be relatively rare . . . no major tendency towards the growth of truly international companies.

(3) Capital mobility is not producing a massive shift of investment and employment from the advanced to the developing countries [. . .].

(4) . . . trade, investment, and financial flows are concentrated in the Triad of Europe, Japan, and North America, and this dominance seems set to continue.

(5) These major economic powers . . . have the capacity . . . to exert powerful governance pressures over financial markets and other economic tendencies. *Global markets are thus by no means beyond regulation and control* . . . [italics added]. (p. 3)[2]

Hirst and Thompson (1996) do not deny that the economic and trading relations at the end of the twentieth century have changed substantially or that this may constrain particular types of national economic strategies. However, they claim that the "economic changes . . . are more complex and equivocal than the extreme globalists argue" (Hirst & Thompson, 1996, p. 1) and that the ungovernable international market of globalization is a myth.[2] They present a strong case to support their position that the claims of "globalization talk" are not supported by the evidence. This would indicate therefore that globalization talk is not an account of changing economic circumstances; rather, it is a set of normative principles concerning the relationship between capital and the state, between capital and society. It is a *particular* prescription for social and political organization—in fact, the political doctrine of neo-classical liberalism revisited.

Capitalism is a form of social and economic organization that is inherently unequal. Competition is its normative ideal, and the competition of the free market its coordinating mechanism for society. Democracy, on the other hand, is a model of political organization that recognizes the equal moral worth of each citizen—this equality is the basis of universal suffrage. Democracy and capitalism have an uneasy relationship. Because of the principles of freedom inherent in democracy, it is difficult to conceive of a democratic society that is not capitalist (social democratic societies are capitalist). However, societies that are capitalist but not democratic have existed and do exist; examples might include fascist Spain, Pinochet's Chile, Hong Kong, and arguably Singapore. Globalization privileges economic rationality and capitalism over democratic and social principles. Rather than enhancing democracy and citizenship, the state's role is to facilitate capital. Thus, globalization is a discourse of economic rather than political modernity. As Hirst and Thompson (1996, p. 176) argue, it is an antipolitical ideology of free trade.

The economic doctrine of globalization bears remarkable parallels to the modernization theory of development. According to modernization theory, all societies should and would inevitably evolve into Western and particularly U.S. models of modern capitalist societies. There is a logic of "development" that is constituted by the twin logics of industrialism and capitalism. Development culminates in mass production and mass consumption, according to Western and particularly U.S. patterns. In essence, therefore, like modernization theory, globalization talk is also neo-classical economics and neo-liberal politics repackaged into language appropriate to the economic developments of the late twentieth century.

Globalization as a Regime of Truth

Globalization is an economic doctrine claiming to be neutral, natural, objective reality. Its claims to objectivity and truth constitute its power; it is thus a "regime of truth." Foucault (1980) describes a regime of truth as "the ensemble of rules according to which the true and the false are separated and special effects of power attached to the true" (p. 132).

It is knowledge of or access to truth that constitutes power. The will to know, the will to truth (Foucault, 1984, pp. 111-114; Foucault, 1991, p. 96), is both inseparable from, and an imperative of modernity, whereas Western knowledge is discursively constructed through regimes of truth (Foucault, 1984, p. 113). At the same time, the will to know—the will to truth—is the will to power. Through regime(s) of truth, the will to power constructs particular claims to rationality. These effectively exclude or silence alternative claims to rationality. A regime of truth, which is a particular form of rationality, effects closure so that what counts as rationality is restricted and limited: "Certain discourses, for example, econometric expressions of neo-classical economics, function to effect discursive closure, that is, to bracket out the legitimacy and even existence of alternative economic discourses" (Yeatman, 1994, p. 25).

The economic narrative of globalization is a neo-classical economic rationality. It is the rationality of the market as objective reality, of the neutrality of market forces as "truth." Through the positivist construction of truth—of the form of rationality called neo-classical or neo-liberal economics—alternative ways of shaping policy, alternative assumptions regarding the meaning(s) and role(s) of education in a society, are silenced.

Thus far, this chapter has argued that globalization is a discursively constructed master discourse of uncontrollable global market forces that valorizes the economic rationality of neo-classical economics and the minimalist politics of neo-liberalism. Globalization talk pretends to certainty and truth, and particularly truth and certainty regarding the complexities, contradictions, fragmentation, and seemingly irreconcilable dilemmas of late twentieth century capitalism. It establishes a frame of changing economic circumstances—the *change* of the OECD's (1989) *Education and the Changing Economy*—to which nations and governments can merely respond or react. Australia's public policy has been incorporated into this globalization discourse. The discursive construction of globalization as a neutral and objective reality has not been challenged; globalization has been accepted uncritically as a reality to which Australia must respond. Not only *must* Australian public policy respond to the challenge of globalization; agency is restricted to reaction, that is, determining the most appropriate and strategic response. In this, Australia's policy responses have not been unique but have tended to resemble those of other OECD countries.

AUSTRALIA'S RESPONSES TO GLOBALIZATION

Economic restructuring was the major concern of the Hawke and Keating Labor governments. Australia's economy has been particularly susceptible to the cyclic booms and recessions of the world economy because of its dependence—some would claim overdependence—on the export of primary products (both agricultural and mineral) and its protected non–export-oriented manufacturing industries (Emy, 1993, pp. 14-20; Harcourt, 1992, pp. 7-10; Kelly, 1992, p. 30). A principal objective of public policy during the 1980s and 1990s, therefore, was to enhance Australia's economic efficiency and international competitiveness by "opening" the Australian economy to the world and subjecting it to the "discipline" of international markets. The initial stages were concerned with the structural framework of the economy as a whole, the macro-economic focus. These included the deregulation of the financial sector and the floating of the Australian dollar in December 1983. This was followed by a focus on micro-economic reform, including reform of the education "industry."

Neo-Fordist and Post-Fordist Responses to Economic Globalization

Brown and Lauder (1996) posit two ideal-type economic responses to the new conditions of economic globalization: neo-Fordism (or the New Right) and post-Fordism (which Brown and Lauder term *Left Modernizer*). These loosely correspond to demand-side and supply-side approaches, respectively. Thus, neo-Fordism is characterized by emphases on markets, labor market flexibility (through lower labor costs), efficiency (enhancing productivity through minimizing production costs), deregulation, privatization, and managerialism, while post-Fordism is a high-skill/high-wage route to national prosperity and is characterized by high-skill, high value-added innovative production and market flexibility through multiskilling. Although both neo-Fordist and post-Fordist responses place a high priority on education, the neo-Fordist vision of education is the production of the particular skilled workers in demand by business and industry. The role of education in a post-Fordist economy is more strategic, with the availability of a highly skilled and flexible multiskilled workforce fostering and catalyzing innovation and market leadership (see Table 2.1).

The Hawke and Keating governments' attempts to engineer the clever country were a contradictory combination of post-Fordist and neo-Fordist policies. This chapter argues that, at least in part, the basis of this contradictory post-Fordist/neo-Fordist Australian model for economic restructuring may be found in the Australian Settlement,[3] which has characterized relations between capital and labor in Australia since the beginning of the century (Kelly, 1992, p. 1). Castles's (1988) analysis of Australia's distinctive patterns of public policy provides an economic, social, and historical context for understanding the culture of relations between business and industry and

TABLE 2.1 Post-Fordist Possibilities: Alternative Models of National Development

Fordism	Neo-Fordism	Post-Fordism
Protected national markets	Global competition through productivity gains, cost-cutting (overheads, wages)	Global competition through innovation, quality, value-added goods and services
	Inward investment attracted by market flexibility (reduce the social cost of labor, trade union power)	Inward investment attracted by highly skilled labor force engaged in value-added production/services
	Adversarial market orientation: remove impediments to market competition. Create "enterprise culture." Privatization of the welfare state	Consensus-based objectives: corporatist "industrial policy." Cooperation between government, employers, and trade unions
Mass production of standardized products/low skill, high wage	Mass production of standardized products/low skill, low wage flexible production and sweatshops	Flexible production systems/small batch/niche markets; shift to high-wage, high-skilled jobs
Bureaucratic hierarchical organizations	Leaner organizations with emphasis on numerical flexibility	Leaner organizations with emphasis on functional flexibility
Fragmented and standardized work tasks	Reduce trade union job demarcation	Flexible specialization/multi-skilled workers
Mass standardized (male) employment	Fragmentation/polarization of labor force. Professional core and flexible workforce (i.e., part-time, temps, contract, portfolio careers)	Maintain good conditions for all employees. Noncore workers receive training, fringe benefits, comparable wages, proper representation

TABLE 2.1 *Continued*

Fordism	Neo-Fordism	Post-Fordism
Divisions between managers and workers/low trust relations/collective bargaining	Emphasis on "managers' right to manage." Industrial relations based on low-trust relations	Industrial relations based on high trust, high discretion, collective participation
Little "on-the-job" training for most workers	Training "demand" led/little use of industrial training policies	Training as a national investment/state acts as strategic trainer

SOURCE: Brown & Lauder, 1996, p. 6. Reprinted with permission of Taylor & Francis Group Ltd., London.

labor in Australia. These cultural patterns of understandings, behaviors, and responses are deeply embedded and difficult to change. They provide business and industry, labor, and policymakers with a frame for understanding the present and hence models that pattern reactions to changing circumstances.

The 1890s in Australia were a period of economic boom and depression. Capital and labor engaged in a long and bitter struggle that neither party wished to repeat. A settlement was reached between capital and labor, which was expressed upon Federation in the compromise of the living wage and tariff protection. These were to be determined fairly by the institutions of the Commonwealth Arbitration Court and the Tariff Board. This "historic compromise" (Castles, 1988, pp. 110-132) was Australia's economic, industrial, and social response to the essentially inequitable nature of capitalism. Castles interprets this Australian Settlement as a distinctive response to "social protection," that is, compensation for or amelioration of the negative social outcomes of capitalism—a "strategy . . . based less on income redistribution through social transfers and social wage benefits and more on regulatory intervention in the areas of industrial policy and wage determination" (Castles, 1988, p. viii). The notion of a living wage, the fundamental basis of the historic compromise, was established by the Harvester judgment of 1907 and was a wage sufficient to provide a decent standard of living for a worker and *his* dependents.[4] The concept of a living wage incorporates the cost of social welfare (the social wage) into wages paid by employers to employees. Thus, the level of wages becomes critical to social protection. In Australia, the labor movement therefore focused principally on wages rather than the provision of welfare through and by the state. Australia's model of social welfare was "the working man's welfare state," where benefits were the result of employment, rather than a citizen's welfare state, where benefits were the result of social entitlement, and all citizens were members by right. Welfare provision by the Australian state was minimal and residual. The Australian Labor Party developed more as a laborist party than a social democratic party, while the focus of industrial relations was the level of wages. Thus, for almost 90 years, the relationship between labor and capital was one of conflict over wages: The goal of labor was to maintain and increase wage levels because of the link between wages and workers' standard of living, while capital (business and industry) was concerned to contain labor costs (that is, wages) in the interests of productivity and profitability.

In addition to and complementary to the living wage was tariff protection. Tariffs were essential to industry to maintain the Australian Settlement, so that profitability was maintained at levels allowing business and industry to pay labor the living wage. Australia's historic settlement was encapsulated in the phrase "protection all round" (Castles, 1988, p. 144).

Castles terms this strategy *domestic defense* (pp. 91-104). He argues that Australian public policy directed toward domestic defense—conciliation and arbitration based on the principle of the living wage, together with high levels of protection—resulted in domestically oriented industries protected and insulated from international competition. Policies of domestic defense are relatively inflexible and unable to respond rapidly or efficiently to changing conditions in international markets.

The alternative model of social amelioration is the social democratic model, for which Castles (1988) uses the term *social compensation* (pp. 84-91). Under a public policy regime oriented toward domestic compensation, citizens do not need to *purchase* social benefits such as education, health care, or other welfare services and hence are not wholly dependent upon employment for their standard of living. Through higher levels of taxation and policies of income redistribution, the social wage is delivered by the state, together with unemployment benefits at levels adequate to ensure that the loss of a breadwinner's wage does not equal either personal or family catastrophe. Castles argues that this strategy of social amelioration delivers a more flexible economy. When a particular job is not the citizen's only defense against poverty and destitution, when a citizen's job is not the only source of security, then the unemployment that results from market responses to changing economic circumstances is not socially catastrophic. Castles argues that the security provided by public policies of domestic compensation (that is, the social democratic model) enhances an economy's capacity to compete successfully in the global marketplace. Such economies are open and unprotected—their capacity to respond flexibly and efficiently to market conditions constitutes their protection.

Since the 1970s, policies of the Australian Labor Party in particular have attempted to reshape the Australian economy away from policies of domestic defense and toward policies of social compensation. Thus, under the Whitlam government (1972-1975), tariffs were reduced, and Australia's pattern of welfare distribution began to shift away from strategies of the living wage to strategies of the social wage. Noteworthy examples of the shift of emphasis of the Labor Party away from laborist policies toward a more social democratic model were the abolition of tertiary fees and the introduction of universal health insurance (Medibank). Under the first and second Hawke governments (1983-1987), the central feature of further attempts to institutionalize the social democratic model of social compensation was the Accord. The Accord was a formal partnership between the trade union movement and the Australian Labor Party in government; it was an agreement that the union movement would participate in all policy making (Kelly, 1992, p. 62; Matthews, 1997, pp. 286-288). Under the original Accord agreements, the provision of an enhanced social wage, particularly in education and health care (for example, the reestablishment of universal health insurance through Medicare), was the trade-off for further reductions in tariff protection for industry and the muting of wage demands. Although Hawke's consensus style of policy making has been characterized as corporatist or neo-corporatist (Emy & Hughes, 1991, pp. 559-561; Gerritsen, 1986; Kelly, 1992, p. 62; Stewart, 1984), there was a loose connection only of business and industry to the corporatist framework. Only two of the three members of the classic corporatist triangle of state, capital (business and industry), and labor entered into the formal Accord agreement—in this case, only the government (or state) and labor. Although there was some cooperation from business and industry with the principles of the Accord, during the 1980s and early 1990s, workers' real incomes declined while executive and managerial salaries increased substantially.

Education as a Tool of Micro-Economic Reform

An economic rationality (particularly the rationality of the competitive marketplace) has dominated all Australian policy making since the late 1980s. Education policy was a particular focus of this economic rationality, because of education's perceived role in the restructuring of the Australian economy in the interests of efficiency, productivity, and global competitiveness. Prior to 1987, the Whitlam and Hawke governments were concerned to shift the Australian economy from one based on domestic defense, laborism, and the Australian Settlement to one based more on domestic compensation and a new economic-industrial-social compromise or settlement between capital and labor. The focus of reform was principally macro-economic. However, after the 1987 election, the Hawke and Keating governments respectively became concerned with micro-economic reform. The strategic role of education in contributing to the post-Fordist high-skill/high-wage economy of Labor's clever country necessitated an explicit focus on education as a tool of micro-economic reform.

After 1987, economic rationalism and human capital theories became the orthodoxy of education policy. Two policy strands were evident: first, the post-Fordist micro-economic reform of the economy via the strategy of "investing" in the education of students, who therefore would become the clever workers of the clever country; and second, the micro-economic reform of the education industry itself. The initial foci of reform were the structures and administration of education, in the interests of integrating education more closely with its "clients" (business and industry). Higher education, postcompulsory education and training, and compulsory schooling have each become in turn the focus of Commonwealth reform.

Australia Reconstructed?

In 1986, an Australian Council of Trade Unions (ACTU) study mission visited Sweden, Norway, Germany, Austria, and the United Kingdom to investigate their public policy responses to the changing of the world economy. Their report, *Australia Reconstructed: ACTU TDC Mission to Western Europe Report* (ACTU, 1987), was a highly influential document in shaping public policy, including education. *Australia Reconstructed* advocated the post-Fordist route to economic competitiveness and a social democratic settlement between capital and labor comparable to the one in Scandinavia and Germany. The report was concerned with industry restructuring, an active rather than reactive trade and industry policy on the part of government, and investment in industry and product innovation, together with emphases on training and union modernization.

Although the *Australia Reconstructed* agenda did not become the blueprint for the post-1987 Hawke and Keating Labor governments, the concerns of *Australia Reconstructed*—to advance strategic union-ism and enhance worker employability through multiskilling and formal training—are recognizable elements in the micro-economic reform policies of Labor after 1987. The existing Accord framework was used to advance this agenda, particularly multiskilling and trade union reform and restructuring (in particular, union amalgamations and enterprise bargaining). It is not insignificant that John Dawkins, the minister for trade at the time of *Australia Reconstructed,* became minister for employment, education, and training in July 1987 and initiated wide and sweeping reforms of all sectors of Australian education (most particularly higher education), as part of the gov-ernment's micro-economic reform agenda. There appeared to be substantial commitment to the cooperative implementation of this post-Fordist route to international economic competitiveness:

> The task of restructuring Australia is not simply a task for Govern-
> ment. We must all have a strong commitment towards fostering the
> highest possible economic growth and its equitable distribution, and
> to achieving the lowest possible levels of inflation and unemployment.
> Structural change and the promotion of a productive culture are
> necessary to enhance our international competitiveness, while em-
> ployers need to accept that structural change and new work organisa-
> tion are not simply opportunities to shed labour, and that workers

need to be a party to any change. Similarly, employers and unions need to recognise their obligation to tackle the problems of skill formation. (Bill Kelty, ACTU Secretary, in *Australia Reconstructed*, 1987, p. v)

However, a culture of industrial conflict and confrontation rather than corporatist cooperation is deeply embedded in both the labor movement and the business community in Australia. Trust and any sense of a common interest are only weakly developed. Castles's (1988) analysis, described earlier in this chapter, demonstrates how the historic compromise of the Australian Settlement entrenched a culture of adversarial relations and suspicion between business/ industry and labor (particularly the union movement). In particular, the historic compromise patterned reactions to industry policy, labor market policy, and industrial relations. In addition, understanding of and commitment to post-Fordist goals and a social democratic settlement are only weakly embedded in Australian society—if at all—so that vast cultural change would have been necessary to achieve such goals. Finally, there is a strong commitment within sections of the business community and the economics profession to New Right, neo-liberal economic, political, and social models.

The neo-Fordist, New Right route has been advocated by neo-classical and neo-liberal economists within the Commonwealth Departments of Treasury and Finance (Pusey, 1991) and the influential financial media (for example, Alan Woods, the financial editor of *The Australian* newspaper). The reduction of government spending is a high priority, along with productivity, efficiency, business profitability, managerialism, and labor market flexibility (principally lower wages).

Hence, within sections of both the business community and the union movement, there is a predilection toward neo-Fordist responses to the challenges of the changing international economy. In addition, comparable traditions within Australian education, particularly the hierarchical head/hand status dualism of our Anglo heritage, predispose Australian business and industrial culture toward neo-Fordist managerialist models of administration.

Thus, although the Labor government and the ACTU were pursuing education and training policies directed toward the development of a post-Fordist economy, fiscal and management policies were neo-Fordist. Thus, the policy framework of Labor's response to globalization was a contradictory combination of post-Fordism and neo-Fordism.

The Howard Liberal-National Party coalition government elected to power in March 1996, on the other hand, has eschewed post-Fordist strategies and is determinedly applying neo-Fordist models. Examples include either severe cuts to labor market programs or their complete abolition, substantial and continuing cuts in funding to higher education, and differential HECS fees determined according to both the cost of provision of a course and its expected market benefit.[5]

REALITY IS MORE COMPLEX

Constructed principally in econometric terms as an increasingly integrated world economy, globalization is discursively constituted as a regime of truth, inevitable, imperative, desirable. Under Labor, Australia responded to this imperative of economic globalization with policies to enhance the country's competitiveness in the international marketplace by opening up the Australian economy to the competitive pressures of the global economy.

The dilemma of globalization for social democrats (and perhaps the Labor Party was once a social democratic party) is that the imperative of globalization and its economic, political, and social policy prescriptions of small government, a minimalist state, and deregulated capital and labor markets undercut their traditional policies of social amelioration. The ineluctability of globalization renders their traditional statist policies unviable because globalization is seen as a truth, a neutral objective reality. The market forces of international capitalism are real, invincible, and unchallengeable. The response of social democrats, then, is the Left Modernizer route (Brown & Lauder, 1996), attempting to secure, through post-Fordist policies, a participation in the competitive international economy that minimizes the negative social impacts of global competition and economic restructuring.

The Hawke and Keating governments attempted to establish a new Australian settlement, a post-Fordist settlement of a high-wage, high-skill economy competing successfully in the increasingly integrated global capitalist marketplace. It was no less than an attempt to *reconstruct* Australia through the attempt to *construct* a new post-Fordist historic compromise of corporatist cooperation between capital and labor. Education was in a unique policy position because in addition to its social and political dimensions (socialization and citizenship), education makes a major contribution to a society's economy and economic competitiveness. However, Labor's policies were an unstable combination of post-Fordist and neo-Fordist strategies. Through the contradictory practice of imposing managerialism (which is neo-Fordist), Labor attempted to engineer post-Fordist reforms to education.

The Hawke and Keating governments were "irrevocably mesmerized" (Mahlab, 1996) by globalization talk. However, the assumption that globalization is inevitable and that all that nation-states can do is react or respond is problematic and open to criticism. Globalization, as an antipolitical myth of ungovernable global market forces, benefits the

> well off and privileged. . . . Those with professional qualifications and technical skills [who] . . . have greater room for manoeuvre. . . . The "club class" with managerial expertise, though relatively few in number, are the most obvious manifestation of this inequity. (Hirst & Thompson, 1996, p. 31)[2]

Furthermore, globalization is a discourse of unlimited growth, unlimited industrialization, and unlimited exploitation of the planet. It is therefore humanly, socially, and ecologically unsustainable.

CONCLUSION

There *have* been substantial changes in international economic relations since the early 1970s. TNCs and MNCs exist and are powerful. However, in spite of these demonstrable developments, reality is more complex, and there are alternative visions of the future. However, if globalization talk remains uncontested, if states accept that the global market is ungovernable, and withdraw, then in fact the market will be ungoverned, and societies and people and the planet will be increasingly at the mercy of global industrialism and capitalism. Globalization talk may thus become a self-fulfilling narrative. A post-Fordist response may perhaps balance the imperative of globalization with a commitment to social welfare and a continuing role for the state; however, it challenges neither the inevitability of globalization, nor the ungovernability of the market.

To contest the economistic discourse that is globalization—the primacy of international markets—is not to deny the reality of global concerns, not least those generated by the interconnectedness of life on this watery planet. Ecological degradation and human concern for our planet's reparation, and increasingly an international civil society of nongovernment organizations, are also global phenomena. The choices we face are not limited to the market or the state. There are alternative visions of a social rather than a market economy, where capital is social, rather than solely financial or economic, and where community and human priorities take precedence over those of the market. Meanwhile, John Dryzek (1992, 1995, 1996) and other Green political theorists are developing notions of environmental democracy and ecological citizenship. These ideas may be global, but they are concerned with human, social, and ecological sustainability, rather than competitive international capitalism.

The global interpenetration of community and ecological sustainability is a globalization we need not fear; rather, it may be a vision to sustain challenges to the inhuman, dehumanizing global market.

NOTES

1. The term *globalization* is used in this chapter principally to describe an economistic discourse of free trade and market primacy. However, the term may also be used descriptively.

2. Quotations from Hirst and Thompson (1996) and Spybey (1996) are used by permission of Polity Press.

3. "A settlement is a truce or compromise which establishes a framework for policy and practice. Within this framework disagreements and conflicts occur, but there is agreement over what to disagree about, over the mechanisms for resolving that conflict and over the range of what might be acceptable resolutions. Contesting and reconstructing the framework is not a major agenda item. A settlement persists over a period of time but ultimately the truce breaks down and the framework for policy and practice fractures. Then follows a period of intense politics. . . . The reconstruction of a framework for policy and practice is the agenda, and different social forces work to dominate that process. A new settlement emerges when there is agreement over the basic principles" Seddon, T. (1989, November 18-19), Which Way for Schooling?, *The Australian Teacher*, pp. 18-29; used by permission of the Australian Education Union.

4. The Harvester judgment of the Commonwealth Conciliation Arbitration Commission (together with later wage cases) maintained and reinforced the patriarchal assumptions and structures of society: The minimum wage for women (set in a later case in 1919) was 54% of that of males, because it was assumed that males were breadwinners and so, to maintain their dependents, needed a higher wage than women. That women were also breadwinners was a convenient oversight.

5. Law, for example, while a relatively inexpensive course to teach, is included in the highest rate band because of the higher-than-average incomes of legal practitioners.

REFERENCES

Australian Council of Trade Unions (ACTU). (1987). *Australia reconstructed* (Report of ACTU/TDC Mission to Western Europe). Melbourne: Australian Government Publishing Service. (Commonwealth of Australia copyright; reproduced by permission.)

Brown, P., & Lauder, H. (1996). Education, globalization, and economic development. *Journal of Education Policy, 11*(1), 1-26.

Cable, V. (1996, May). Globalisation: Can the state strike back? *The World Today,* pp. 133-137.

Castles, F. (1988). *Australian public policy and economic vulnerability.* St. Leonards, NSW: Allen & Unwin.

Dryzek, J. (1992, June). Ecology and discursive democracy: Beyond liberal capitalism and the administrative state. *Capitalism, Nature, Socialism, 3*(2), 18-42.

Dryzek, J. (1995, Winter). Political and ecological communication. *Environmental Politics, 4*(4), 13-30.

Dryzek, J. (1996, March). Foundations for environmental political economy: The search for homo ecologicus? *New Political Economy, 1*(1), 27-40.

Emy, H. V. (1993). *Remaking Australia: The state, the market, and Australia's future.* St. Leonards, NSW: Allen & Unwin.

Emy, H. V., & Hughes, O. E. (1991). *Australian politics: Realities in conflict* (2nd ed.). South Melbourne: Macmillan.

Foucault, M. (1980). Truth and power. In C. Gordon (Ed.), *Power/knowledge* (pp. 109-133). New York: Pantheon.

Foucault, M. (1984). The order of discourse. In M. J. Shapiro (Ed.), *Language and politics* (pp. 108-138). Oxford, UK: Basil Blackwell.

Foucault, M. (1991). What is enlightenment? In P. Rabinow (Ed.), *The Foucault reader.* Middlesex, UK: Penguin.

Fukuyama, F. (1993). *The end of history and the last man.* New York: Avon.

Gerritsen, R. (1986). The necessity of "corporatism": The case of the Hawke Labor government. *Politics, 21*(1), 45-54.

Harcourt, G. C. (1992). *Markets, madness, and a middle way* (The second Donald Horne Lecture, Ideas for Australia Program, National Centre for Australian Studies). Victoria: Monash University.

Hirst, P., & Thompson, G. (1996). *Globalization in question.* Cambridge, UK: Polity Press.

Kelly, P. (1992). *The end of certainty.* St. Leonard's, NSW: Allen & Unwin.

Mahlab, E. (1996, June 28). *Women in public life.* Keynote address, Women in Public Life—Celebrating Edith Cowan Conference, Perth, West Australia.

Marginson, S. (1993). *Education and public policy in Australia.* Melbourne: Cambridge University Press.

Matthews, T. (1997). Interest groups. In R. Smith (Ed.), *Politics in Australia* (3rd ed.). St. Leonard's, NSW: Allen & Unwin.

Organization of Economic Cooperation and Development (OECD). (1989). *Education and the changing economy.* Paris: Author.

Pusey, M. (1991). *Economic rationalism in Canberra.* Melbourne: Cambridge University Press.

Reich, R. (1991). *The work of nations: Preparing ourselves for 21st-century capitalism.* New York: Knopf.

Seddon, T. (1989, November 18-19). Which way for schooling? *The Australian Teacher,* p. 24.

Spybey, T. (1996). *Globalization and world society.* Cambridge, UK: Polity Press.

Stewart, R. G. (1984). The politics of the accord: Does corporatism explain it? *Politics,* 20(2), 26-35.

Yeatman, A. (1990). *Bureaucrats, technocrats, femocrats.* Sydney: Allen & Unwin.

Yeatman, A. (1994). *Postmodern revisionings of the political.* London: Routledge.

CHAPTER 3

National Higher Education Policies in a Global Economy

Sheila Slaughter

This chapter examines structural changes in the global economy and the restructuring of national higher education policies. It begins by exploring the differences between industrial and postindustrial political economies and then looks at some countries that are winners and losers in the global marketplace. I focus on Australia, Canada, the United Kingdom, and the United States, giving greatest attention to the United Kingdom and the United States. I review briefly theories of globalization that purport to explain why particular nations are successful in the global economy. I link changes in the global economy to higher education by outlining the ways in which globalization theory explains the increased centrality of higher education systems to national strategies for securing shares of global markets. Finally, I examine changes in national higher education policies in the 1980s and 1990s and the ways in which they deal with access to higher education, curricula, research, and autonomy.

I identified these changes through numerous secondary sources and by a comparative analysis of policy documents (white papers, legislation, and policy directives from administrative agencies)

AUTHOR'S NOTE: I would like to thank Philip Altbach, Robert Berdahl, Jan Currie, Ross Harrold, John Levin, Gary Rhoades, and Michael Skolnik for their careful reading and helpful comments on this chapter.

45

concerned with higher education. My investigation focused on two research questions:

1. What forces were driving the restructuring of higher education and research in the 1980s and 1990s?
2. How were these forces manifested in national policy in these countries?

Generally, I found that all four countries instituted policies that encouraged commercial research and development and business/ vocational curricula, emphasizing the value of higher education to national economic activity and displaying a preference for market and market-like activity on the part of faculty and institutions. With regard to access, higher education policies encouraged greater student enrollment, but at a lower national cost. Rather than financing students, all countries raised tuition fees and switched from heavy reliance on grants to greater use of loans. In terms of curricula, national policies exhibited a strong preference for departments and colleges with relevance to the market. The four countries moved away from basic research toward applied or entrepreneurial research. All began integrating higher education into broad government planning processes, processes that focus primarily on economic development. In short, national policies in all four countries moved decisively toward academic capitalism, which refers to the movement by universities toward the market to secure external funds. This shift is most noticeably seen in large research universities that have developed commercial arms and links with industries to exploit intellectual capital to generate funds for universities.

Although I make the case that national higher education policies are converging in some very important areas, I do *not* see Australia, Canada, the United Kingdom, and the United States as necessarily responding to globalization in the same ways. They take divergent paths to policies that support and strengthen entrepreneurial activities. For example, higher education policies that promoted closer relations between postsecondary institutions and various markets were initiated under conservative governments in the United Kingdom and the United States but under a Labor (liberal) government in Australia. In the United States and Canada, the several states and provinces often pioneered partnerships that involved universities in academic capitalism, whereas in the United Kingdom and Australia, centralized higher education ministries guided these processes. In contrast, in the United States, at the national level, Congress rather than the executive branch actively developed legislation that fostered academic capitalism.[1] In other words, globalization is a universal force to which countries, states, and provinces develop unique responses, but the system effects are so powerful that higher education policies in some areas—access, curricula, research, autonomy for faculty and institutions—converge.

INDUSTRIAL AND POSTINDUSTRIAL ECONOMIES

In this section, I outline the scope of economic change that characterizes the last quarter of the twentieth century. I make the case that the four countries considered here are moving from industrial to postindustrial societies. Higher education is more important to postindustrial than industrial societies because there is a greater dependence on higher education for training and research and greater development than in industrial societies. Postindustrial economies require fewer workers, regardless of level of education, than industrial societies, and postindustrial society may not need these workers' skills for a lifetime, rendering obsolete traditional understandings of the relation of higher education to careers.

Researchers address these differences through a variety of competing dichotomies: industrial versus postindustrial (Bell, 1973); Fordist versus post-Fordist (Jessop, 1993); mass production versus flexible production (Cohen, 1993); manufacturing versus service industries (Sassen, 1991; Thrift, 1987); low technology versus high technology (Reich, 1991; Tyson, 1992); industrial versus informational economies (Castells, 1993). Within each of these dichotomies, there is intense controversy (e.g., Bonefeld, 1993, versus Jessop, 1993; Reich, 1991, versus Tyson, 1992; World Bank, 1993, versus Sakakibara, 1993).

The technological revolution that is sweeping the world today is powered by advances in applied science and engineering, particularly in areas that deal with information generation, processing, and storage (Castells, 1993). Among these new technologies are "advanced materials, advanced semi-conductor devices and processes, digital imaging technology, high-density data storage and opto-electronics . . . artificial intelligence, biotechnology, flexible computer-integrated manufacturing, medical . . . diagnostics and sensor technology" (Cohen, 1993, p. 135).

As important as the products derived from these processes are the services—telecommunications packages, financial instruments, and legal tools that are as much product as service in that they can be sold and traded rather than immediately consumed. These make possible global trade and marketing of high technology goods and services (Sassen, 1991; Thrift, 1987).

As many of the inventions of the Industrial Revolution were made by nonschooled amateurs and inventors as by trained scientists (Ben-David, 1965; Noble, 1976); most of the discoveries of the current technological revolution were made by people with at least some college education. Universities provide the training necessary for the increasing numbers of professionals employed by corporations to invent, maintain, and innovate with regard to sophisticated technologies and products. In an increasing number of cases, the university is the site where new technologies and products are developed, often in partnerships with business, through funding supplied in part by the state.

In the early part of this century, Henry Ford developed production with assembly lines, and this mode of production has been termed *Fordism* by some academics. As the term *Fordism* suggests, mass production was characterized by highly standardized procedures, typified by the assembly line, and by Taylorism (scientific management, exemplified by supervisory control over the workers' most minute movements on the assembly line), and usually occurred in vertically integrated, large-scale organizations. The system was fairly inflexible; products were not easily altered. It depended on massive accumulations of capital, top-down planning, and very long production runs. Tasks were closely supervised and repetitious. In contrast, organization of production in the dawning postindustrial era, exemplified by the organization of Japanese industry, is *flexible-volume production*, which uses fewer workers, uses less space, and takes

> half the investment in tools and machinery, half the engineering hours to develop a new product, and half the time to develop a new product. It also requires less than half the needed inventory on site, turns out products with far fewer defects, and yields a greater and growing variety of products. (Cohen, 1993, p. 106)

Flexible-volume production is a complex organizational strategy and is not a technological solution that can be easily imposed on manufacturing problems. Although the strategy can be learned, it is alien to Fordist organization of production and is correspondingly difficult for Fordist corporations to assimilate. Although a number of Fordist corporations have attempted Japanese-style management aimed at incorporating production workers into organizational decision making with regard to manufacturing, these efforts, often labeled total quality management,[2] are not notably successful, in large part because Fordist management and workers seem unable to abandon their historic adversarial relationships.

Globally successful systems of flexible production are usually employed by multinational corporations. As the trust was to the national economies of the late nineteenth century, so the multinational conglomerate will be to the emerging global economy of the twenty-first century (Fligstein, 1990). Multinational corporations are at the cutting edge of the market in most industrialized countries. From 1975 to 1990, U.S. multinationals' annual sales grew substantially faster than the U.S. economy as a whole: "The sales of the fifty largest industrial multinationals were 28% of U.S. GNP in 1975 and 39% of U.S. GNP in 1989" (Carnoy, 1993, p. 49). Multinational services, particularly financial services, grew rapidly. The world's fifty largest banks more than doubled their assets between 1980 and 1990 (Carnoy, 1993, Figure 3.2, p. 51; see also Cohen, 1993; Sassen, 1991).

The significance of multinational corporations to the world economy was enhanced in the 1980s when computers, harnessed to new telecommunications infrastructures, created a global market. For industrial corporations, this meant managers were able to supervise far-flung business empires electronically,

> so that the national economy now works as a unit at the world level in real time. In this sense, we are not only seeing a process of the internationalization of the economy, but a process of globalization—that is, the interpenetration of economic activities and national economies at a global level. (Castells, 1993, p. 19)

With regard to financial services, advances in telecommunications in the 1980s made possible for the first time global trade in equities, bonds, and currency as well as more speculative financial instruments (Sassen, 1991). Multinationals, then, were key organizational vehicles of globalization.[3] The infrastructure of the global economy—computers, telecommunications, producer services—depends on highly trained personnel for continued innovation and for maintenance.

Under the postindustrial organization of production, labor looks very different from the industrial era, especially in Japan and the newly industrializing countries. Flexible-volume production does away with the assembly line, instead taking a team approach. The distance between supervisor and worker is somewhat ambiguous, given that all employees are team members. Moreover, the team approach requires all workers to have a substantial grasp of design, engineering, and production processes. Sometimes, production workers are even encouraged to participate in discussions about the organization of work and to introduce product and process changes. Workers who engage in the new organization of production—particularly in Japan, Sweden, and Germany—are well paid and receive a substantial array of benefits.

However, much of the work in established industrial countries has not shifted to flexible-volume production or has adopted some features of the new organization of production and not others. Generally, redesign of work in traditional industries in established industrial countries means that labor costs are reduced by forcing down wages while at the same time reducing expenditures on working conditions and social benefits, so that, all else being equal, profit ratios increase proportionately (Henderson & Castells, 1987). Productivity and profitability are also increased by elimination of redundant workers, reductions of work time, technical innovations, and speed-up (Harrison & Bluestone, 1990). In their home countries, multinationals in traditional industries employ declining numbers of workers who labor longer hours for less pay and substantially reduced benefits. As part of the process of making production "lean," automation increases and jobs are relocated to less costly production sites, the use of part-time labor grows, and unemployment increases.

Although I posit a set of neat dichotomies to mark the differences between industrial and postindustrial political economies, reality is less tidy. Neither corporations nor countries adopt technologies and strategies for organization of production in a uniform manner. This unevenness is perhaps clearest with regard to the labor force. In established industrial countries, some workers who are involved in flexible-volume production have interesting and responsible, well-paid jobs with high benefits. But other workers, particularly in manufacturing jobs, work longer hours for less pay at repetitious jobs that have fewer and fewer benefits (Harrison & Bluestone, 1990; Phillips, 1993).

WINNERS AND LOSERS: THEORIES OF GLOBALIZATION

As the world makes the transition to postindustrial political economies, some countries do better than others. Overall, the rise of Japan and of a number of newly industrializing countries in Asia—Singapore, Hong Kong, Taiwan, South Korea, Malaysia—as well as China, and now Vietnam, has destabilized the bipolar trade relations that dominated world trade for most of this century. For most of the twentieth century, trade was dominated first by Great Britain, and, after World War II, by the United States. Trade relations were bipolar in that most world trade flowed between the United States and Europe. In the 1970s, as established industrialized countries lost some of the advantages conferred by early industrialization, empire, and neo-colonial trade relationships, world trade became more diverse (Carnoy, 1993; Cohen, 1993). Indeed, some argue that the center of growth of the global economy has moved to the Pacific Rim (Castells, 1993).

Examination of national shares of world output shows that Japan increased its share from 5.8% in 1967 to 7.7% in 1986, and the developing Asian countries increased theirs from 10.8% to 17.4% during the same period. Japan and China raised output more rapidly than any other countries in the world, and the developing Asian countries in general far outdistanced any others. The United States and the United Kingdom lost shares, Australia and New Zealand held steady, and Canada made a very slight gain. The United States declined from 25.8% in 1967 to 21.4% in 1986; the United Kingdom declined from 4.8% to 3.5%. Australia and New Zealand held steady a 1.2% share, whereas Canada grew from 2.1% to 2.2% (Castells, 1993, Table 2.1, p. 25). If only gains and losses in manufactured exports (the sector of national economies usually seen as most important to global competition) are examined, the shift with regard to winners and losers is even more dramatic. Again, Japan and the newly industrializing countries of Asia made the greatest gains, whereas the United States and the United Kingdom suffered the greatest losses.

As world output was redistributed, several of these countries increased their national debt. The United States' net government debt as a percentage of GNP/GDP increased from 19.2% in 1979 to 25.3% in 1984, to 31.2% in 1990. Canada increased from 12.0% in 1979 to 26.1% in 1984 and to 40.3% in 1990. The United Kingdom's debt decreased from 47.9% in 1979 to 47.4% in 1984 and to 28.9% in 1990. Only Australia brought its debt level close to that of Japan. Australia's debt was 27.7% in 1979, 25.1% in 1984, and 13.2% in 1990. Japan's net government debt was 14.9% in 1979, 27.0% in 1984, and 10.9% in 1990 (Oxley & Martin, 1991, Table 1, p. 148).

At the same time, Australia, the United Kingdom, and the United States increased inequality of income between the late 1970s and mid-1980s. "There was virtually no change in Canada. . . . Changes of around 1 percentage point in the Gini coefficient were observed in . . . Australia. . . . in the United Kingdom and the United States there was more than a 3 percentage point increase" (Atkinson, Rainwater, & Smeeding, 1995, p. 49, Table 4.8).

The neo-liberal or Chicago school of economics explains these changes by deemphasizing the polity, instead stressing the role of the market in national economic success. The neo-liberal school sees market forces as impersonal, disembodied, and inexorable, as supplanting national economies with a global market. To compete successfully in the new global market, nations have to cut back, reducing social welfare and entitlement programs, freeing capital and corporations from taxation and regulation and allowing them to operate unfettered (Friedman, 1981, 1991; Friedman & Leub, 1987). In the neo-liberal model, the only acceptable role of the state is that of global police officer and judge, patrolling the edges of the playing field to make sure it remains level and adjudicating trading infractions and transgressions. In this model, the private sector is privileged as the engine of competition, and the state is no more than a drag on economic growth. A major problem for this explanation of losers and winners in global competition is that the most successful countries in the past twenty years are Japan and the newly industrializing Asian countries, all of which have well-developed industrial policies that rely heavily on the state to coordinate their multinationals' global strategies. (For a dramatic instance of conflict over the Chicago model, see the Japanese objection to the World Bank, 1993, report; for further elaboration, see Sakakibara, 1993.) Indeed, the Asian countries seem not to employ the same rigid distinctions as do Western countries with regard to private and public or, to speak somewhat more broadly, between civil society and the state, and instead see public and private as permeable and complementary.

Keynesian economic policies were built at the level of the nation-state, and control of money supply was used to stimulate or slow national economies, thereby avoiding depression. As global markets emerged and national controls on international flows of capital were eased to take advantage of expanded opportunities, capital mobility increased. Greater international capital mobility made manipulation of the economy at the national level more difficult. At the same time, the warfare-welfare approach to the political economy characteristic of the United States and the United Kingdom became more difficult to sustain. The end of the Cold War, together with the growing critique of defense research and development (R&D) as a tool for technology innovation, made stimulation of the economy through military expenditures problematic. Simultaneously, increased global competition made political and economic justification of the social wage or social safety net more difficult (Melman, 1982; Thurow, 1980). In other words, the growth of a global economy, the increase in capital mobility, the end of the Cold War, and the erosion of the social wage made Keynesianism inadequate in the postindustrial era.

Liberals or post-Keynesians have tried to devise industrial policies that enable established industrial nations to compete more success-fully in traditional "smokestack" industries and that stimulate new high-technology industries, largely through increasing R&D and productivity (Porter, 1990; Reich, 1991; Tyson, 1992). In this view, the nation-state plays a role in stimulating high-technology innovation, in building human capital to exploit high technology in multina-tional corporations, and in creating a climate favorable to investment at home (Carnoy, Castells, Cohen, & Cardoso, 1993).

Although post-Keynesian political economists emphasize the stimulating and supportive role the state plays with regard to the economy, they simultaneously embrace free trade. For the most part, they eschew direct mechanisms for planning, relying instead on a bottom-up approach, in which industry, by taking advantage of government-subsidized opportunities for R&D stimulation—for ex-ample, the Advanced Technology Program in the United States—targets areas for state support in developing products for the global market (Etzkowitz, 1994). A major problem for proponents of this type of post-Keynesian approach to the political economy is that the United States and the United Kingdom had substantial increases in productivity in the late 1980s and early 1990s, but these did not translate into increases in wages and standards of living.

Post-Marxists continue to develop an important critique of global capitalism, even as they recognize that highly centralized state socialism is no longer a viable political/economic alternative (Bowles, 1992). Post-Marxists see the private sector as working through nation-state mechanisms and through various international trade organizations and tribunals to level the playing field so that multinational corporations can dominate the global economy, establishing a new international division of labor. In this new international division of labor, multinational conglomerates move production facilities to those parts of the world that provide the most profitable combination of capital and labor—disproportionately to the lowest-wage states that offer the greatest incentives to multinationals (Chomsky, 1994; Frobel, Heinrichs, & Kreye, 1980). Multinational chief executive officers (CEOs) are able to manage far-flung global production through the information superhighway and telecommunications. In this model, owners and managers of multinationals, as well as owners and managers of the many ancillary businesses that serve them, are winners, and workers, whether high-tech or low, and the unemployed, trapped in technologically advanced nation-states, are losers.

The major problem for this explanation, as other post-Marxists as well as post-Keynesians have noted, is that there is little relationship between labor costs and international competitiveness. Much more important than labor costs in predicting an economy's productivity is the technological level of the industrial sector (Castells, 1993; Castells & Tyson, 1988). In other words, when multinationals relocate plants, they choose industrializing countries with relatively high levels of technological development, avoiding the lowest-cost, least-developed countries, especially in Africa and in parts of South America, which some economic geographers now refer to as the Fourth World (Castells, 1993).

Political economists who are neither post-Keynesians nor post-Marxists, but perhaps fall somewhere in between the two camps, argue that established industrial countries should model themselves more closely on Japan and newly industrializing Asian countries, developing state planning capacities as well as mechanisms for capturing and redistributing more equitably the profits from multinational enterprises. They argue that national policies strongly influence competitiveness, especially policies on labor availability and technological infrastructure, R&D, high technology and management training, and protection from foreign competition and concessions from foreign multinationals (Barnet & Cavanagh, 1994; Carnoy et al., 1993; Harrison & Bluestone, 1990). However, they do not deal with the political strategies and governmental mechanisms that would make such policies viable, particularly in countries such as the United States and the United Kingdom, which have traditionally tried to minimize the role of government in economic planning.

GLOBALIZATION AND HIGHER EDUCATION

Globalization has at least four far-reaching implications for higher education. First is the constriction of monies available for discretionary activities, such as postsecondary education. Second is the growing importance of technoscience and fields closely involved with markets, particularly international markets. Third is the tightening relationship between multinational corporations and state agencies concerned with product development and innovation. Fourth is the increased focus of multinationals and established industrial countries on global intellectual property strategies.

Despite the lack of a coherent understanding of why some countries are winners and others losers, the four established industrial nations that I studied responded to increased global competition with conservative political economic policies. The policies are conservative in that they are aimed at regaining the nation's past position: in the case of the United States and the United Kingdom, positions of global preeminence; in the case of Australia and Canada, positions that retain prosperity rooted in material abundance based on agricultural and extractive industries. In the 1980s and 1990s, the four nations, regardless of the political party in power, pursued supply-side economic policies, shifting public resources from social welfare programs to economic development efforts, primarily through tax cuts for the business sector, but also through programs that stimulated technology innovation, whether through military or civilian R&D (Jessop, 1993; Mowery, 1994). At the same time, all four countries attempted to reduce government expenditures that contributed to their national debt. As supply-side economic and debt reduction policies were instituted, entitlement programs, particularly social security, medicare, and primary and secondary education, expanded enormously, largely in response to demographic changes (Slaughter, 1998).

This combination of policies—supply-side economics, debt reduction, and increased entitlements—had powerful consequences for postsecondary education. Although postsecondary participation rates vary greatly among the four countries, none of the nations treat higher education as an entitlement program. Given the fiscal constraints imposed by conservative supply-side economic and debt reduction policies, together with the growth of entitlement programs, less public money was available for postsecondary education, and what new money was available was concentrated in technoscience and market-related fields in what amounted to a higher education version of supply-side economics. In the words of a recent British White Paper, postsecondary education in all four countries was directed toward national "wealth creation," and away from its traditional concern with the liberal education of undergraduates (Great Britain White Paper, 1993).

Technoscience makes impossible the separation of science and technology, basic and applied research, discovery and innovation (Aronowitz & Di Fazio, 1994; Lyotard, 1984). Technoscience is at once science and product. It collapses the distinction between knowledge and commodity: Knowledge becomes commodity. Telecommunications and biotechnology exemplify technoscience (Kevles & Hood, 1992; Sassen, 1991).

As movement from bipolar to regional world trade patterns heightens global competition, corporations and state agencies often work together to stimulate technoscience. Business leaders want increased civilian R&D to develop technoscience products competitive in global markets (Etzkowitz, 1994; Mowery, 1994; Slaughter & Rhoades, 1996). Political leaders seek to stimulate technoscience as a way out of the impasse created by the failure of the Keynesian nation-state. National leaders, corporations, and universities hope that the subsidy of technoscience will re-create the prosperity of the post-World War II period (1945-1970). Specifically, they see technoscience as generating numerous high-paying jobs that will replace the well-paid blue-collar manufacturing jobs characteristic of Fordism. In the four countries, state and business leaders have joined in programs to stimulate innovation, usually through building industry-government-academic partnerships led by industry, held together by government, and serviced by universities on the technoscience side (Buchbinder & Newson, 1990; Business-Higher Education Forum, 1983; Council for Industry and Higher Education, 1987).

Because multinationals and nation-states are pursuing technoscience as the way to increase shares of world markets, they are simultaneously pursuing intellectual property protection strategies. To reduce competition, especially from states with low labor costs and rising educational attainment, established industrial countries have assiduously worked to establish protection of the intellectual property embodied in technoscience. The European Community (EC), General Agreement of Tariffs and Trade (GATT), and North American Free Trade Agreement (NAFTA) all recognize copyright and patents and attendant royalty and licensing agreements and have strong sanctions for violation.[4] Universities are a source that corporations and governments look to for discovery that will yield intellectual property. (To some degree, universities, at least in the United States, also compete with corporations, given that many universities have established technology licensing programs to increase institutional revenues; Slaughter & Rhoades, 1993.) Leaders of corporations, governments, and tertiary institutions increasingly see faculty work as possible intellectual property, more valuable in global markets as product or commodity than as a free contribution to an international community of scholars.

Globalization theories underline the importance of higher education to technoscience, to industrial policy, and to intellectual property strategies. Universities are the central producers of technoscience, the primary product of postindustrial economies. At the R&D level, faculty and graduate students participate in innovation, increasingly working with industry on government-sponsored technoscience initiatives. Advances in R&D create new fields of knowledge—materials science, optical science, electronic communications, biotechnology—that reshape undergraduate education. Universities provide the high level of training, at the undergraduate and graduate level, essential to technoscience. Increasingly, the service component of universities is being reinterpreted as contributing to national "wealth creation"

(Great Britain White Paper, 1993). As Guy Neave (1988), writing about European countries, puts it, "education is less part of social policy but is increasingly viewed as a subsector of economic policy" (p. 274).

NATIONAL HIGHER EDUCATION POLICIES

To understand more fully the impact that globalization has had on higher education policy from 1980 onward, I review both science and technology policy (research and graduate level education) and access, curricula, and financial aid policies (undergraduate level education). Graduate and undergraduate policies cannot be understood separately, given the degree to which graduate education drives undergraduate education. I also look closely at the way changes in higher education policy at the national level shape institutional and faculty autonomy. In particular, I examine the degree to which national policies encourage profit-driven university R&D. I concentrate here on the policies in two countries, the United Kingdom and the United States, because Canada and Australia are covered in Chapter 2 (Dudley), Chapter 4 (Fisher & Rubenson), and Chapter 6 (DeAngelis). (For my analysis of Australia and Canada on the points raised in this chapter, see Slaughter & Leslie, 1997, Chapter 2.)

The United Kingdom

The United Kingdom dramatically demonstrates the pattern of change that has taken place in tertiary education in the four countries in response to global competition. With regard to access, in a twenty-year period, it moved from an elitist binary system, with the greatest numbers of students in the lower tier, to a unitary system that was expanded at the expense of the higher tier. In terms of career training and curricula, national policies favored science and technology in both research and numbers of student places. National research policies moved away from basic or "pure" research to research more tightly tied to state initiatives aimed at increasing industrial competitiveness. Overall, the system lost autonomy due to major changes in governance structures, and professors lost many of their prerogatives with regard to control over their work.

Like many others, the British higher education system expanded greatly in the post-World War II period, nearly quadrupling in size between 1945 and 1970, doubling from 7% in 1964 to 13% of the age cohort in 1971 (Kogan & Kogan, 1983; McFarland, 1993). The high point of expansion was probably reached with the Robbins Committee in 1963, which articulated the principle that all those who qualified for entry and wanted a place should be able to attend a college or university. Universities were characterized by a powerful professional culture that explicitly rejected entrepreneurial initiatives and business goals (Robins & Webster, 1985). Universities enjoyed a great deal of autonomy (Berdahl, 1959). The University Grants Committee (UGC) acted as a buffer between the state and the institutions and had the authority to make decisions on institutional requests for research resources, drawing funds directly from the Treasury after making decisions about research funding on the basis of national needs in particular areas and on academic criteria for excellence in research (Shattock & Berdahl, 1984).

Although tertiary education was not favored in terms of resources in the 1970s, higher education policy did not change dramatically in the United Kingdom until the 1980s. Thatcherism was the driving force behind the change (Gamble, 1989). According to Michael Shattock,

> Within three days of Mrs. Thatcher's taking office in 1979, 100 million pounds were cut overnight from the universities' budgets, and, between 1980 and 1984, 17% was removed from the grants made by government to the UGC (University Grants Council, which, at that point provided about 90% of the operating costs of British universities). . . . Four thousand academic posts were lost, mostly through government-funded early retirement. And, from 1985 onwards, the universities have lost a further 2% per annum from their budgets. (Shattock, 1989, p. 34)

In the mid-1980s, British business leaders worked with the Thatcher government to build an "enterprise" culture in tertiary education. The push was articulated forcefully by the Jarrett Committee in 1985, chaired by a leading industrialist, which called for higher education to adopt more efficient managerial styles and structures. Business leaders organized the Council for Industry and Higher Education, an independent body supported by corporations. The Council was composed of thirty-two heads of large companies and twelve heads of tertiary institutions. "Its aim was to encourage industry and higher education to work together, and its policy paper, *Towards Partnership* (Council, 1987), argued for greater access to and more variety in higher education, as well as a shift toward science and technology provision" (Pratt, 1992, p. 38). This group success-fully sought to increase places in science and technology, particularly in the less costly polytechnic sector, and to increase civilian R&D, integrating it with economic development. The work of politicians, industrialists, and higher education managers bore fruit in the 1988 Education Act. A White Paper prior to this act called for higher education to serve the economy more effectively, have closer links with industry and commerce, and promote enterprise; it wanted research to target prospects for commercial exploitation.

The 1988 Education Act began to make these intentions law. It lessened differences between universities and polytechnics and abol-ished the UGC, along with the polytechnic board, replacing them with smaller boards dominated by business leaders (Fulton, 1991). This was a powerful attack on the autonomy of academics, symbolic of the end of an era of independent academic culture (Shattock, 1994). Along with the demise of the UGC, the government directed that "state expenditures on higher education should be regarded as pay-ments for services provided rather than as block grants to institu-tions" (Johnes, 1992, p. 173). Universities and polytechnics were forced to develop competitive "bidding schemes" for students to increase institutional cost-effectiveness.

In 1992, the binary system was abolished by the Department of Education and Science (DES). Teaching and research, once consid-ered a single function in university funding, were differentiated and each allocated to institutions on a separate bidding system. Teaching monies depended on numbers of undergraduate students and qual-ity assessments, which looked at quantifiable outcomes and which were performed by agencies outside the institutions (Peters, 1992). The research allocations previously incorporated in large institu-tional grants given automatically to universities were taken away, and competition for research was opened up to the system as a whole (Scott, 1993).

According to Martin Trow (1992), Sir Peter Swinnerton-Dyer, head of the Universities Funding Council, which oversees the new unitary system, takes the following position:

Public policy for higher education in this country has as its main goals to get more teaching and research for less public money, at less per unit of teaching and research. On the whole this is to be seen as an improvement in the efficiency of your institutions. (p. 214)

In other words, abolishing the binary divide was a way of reducing the very high costs of universities by allowing less prestigious polytechnics and colleges to compete openly with them. By competing among themselves, institutions in the postsecondary sector would provide the finances for expansion of the system to meet rising enrollment demands by leveling down, not up, undercutting the rich resource base of the universities, yet not providing the polytechnics with the same resources as universities.

The demise of the binary system and the institution of competition for research funds formalized the steady erosion of the research component of general university funds (GUF) throughout the 1980s. Between 1980 and 1987, GUF funding in Great Britain grew by 10%, whereas separately budgeted funding increased by 32% (Martin, Irvine, & Isard, 1990). Rather than automatically receiving institutional funds for research, professors increasingly had to compete for funds targeted to strategic goals in technoscience areas. Government science and technology policy began to focus on "university-industry relations and upon the development of 'strategic' research to underpin new fields of technology, often across the boundaries of established disciplines," with special attention to "exploitable areas of science" (Gummett, 1991, p. 35; see also Leydesdorff, 1994). These policies led to concentration of research resources in Interdisciplinary Research Centres won through competitive bidding and to development of patent exploitation and technology licensing programs (Gering & Schmied, 1993; Williams, 1992).

The United States

Although Margaret Thatcher and Ronald Reagan had similar political philosophies and were heads of state at approximately the same time, their specific policies for higher education were quite different, due at least in part to the different state structures, political economies, and academic cultures. In the United Kingdom, change began in the 1980s and was rapid and systematic, initiated by the government through DES, and encompassing undergraduate as well as graduate education and research. In contrast, change in the United States at the federal level occurred over a long period of time and through a variety of government bodies and agencies. Change began in the 1970s, with congressional legislation on financial aid for undergraduate education. Change in the 1980s focused on research policy and was piecemeal, emanating as much from Congress as from the executive branch. Corporate and political leaders worked with heads of universities to shift research away from basic and military fields to civilian technoscience research that met postindustrial needs (Etzkowitz, 1994; Slaughter & Rhoades, 1996).

In the early 1970s, the Nixon administration, working with national policy groups such as the Committee for Economic Development, foundations such as the Carnegie Foundation for the Advancement of Teaching, and private and public higher education institutions, introduced the idea of market forces in higher education (Committee for Economic Development, 1993). Together, they developed higher tuition fees combined with higher aid to students through which government gave aid to students rather than institutions, thus making students "consumers" of tertiary education. Institutions competed with each other to attract students and their grants (McPherson & Schapiro, 1993). The policy worked, so long as grants matched costs and were equally available to all students in various sectors of higher education (Kimberling, 1995).[5] By the mid-1980s, student assistance funds stagnated, while tuition fees rose dramatically, undercutting the high tuition/high aid policy.

With regard to access, the number of students overall increased somewhat, but this varied greatly by sector. The greatest growth in the tertiary sector was in the lowest tier, the community college sector (National Center for Educational Statistics, 1995). Paradoxically, low-cost community colleges received the least of all postsecondary institutions in terms of aid because of eligibility rules that penalized part-time students (Hearn & Longanecker, 1993). High tuition/high aid policies did not cover the full costs of most students, as the price of higher education rose dramatically, especially in four-year institutions, and the proportion of the costs borne by students increased concomitantly. As costs increased, federal legislation promoted loans as a way to bridge the growing gap between federal aid grants and college costs (Breneman, 1993).

As in the United Kingdom, research policy in the United States was shaped by leaders of large corporations, heads of universities, and political leaders. In the United States, vehicles for policy development were organizations such as the Business–Higher Education Forum (1983, 1986) and the Government-University-Industry Research Roundtable (1992). These groups crafted a policy of competitiveness that emphasized the role high-technology research played in national economic development. At the same time, a strong coalition emerged in Congress, ready to translate competitiveness policies into law (Slaughter & Rhoades, 1996). Generally, these laws allowed universities to participate in profit-taking, permitted corporations exclusive access to government-funded research performed in universities and federal laboratories, and promoted joint ventures between universities and corporations, breaking down the relatively rigid organizational boundaries that had previously guarded universities' autonomy.

The Bayh-Dole Act of 1980 signaled the inclusion of universities in profit making. It permitted universities and small businesses to retain title to inventions developed with federal research and development monies. In the words of Congress, "It is the policy and objective of the Congress . . . to promote collaboration between commercial concerns and nonprofit organizations, *including universities* [italics added]" (Bayh-Dole Act, 1980). Prior to the Bayh-Dole Act, universities were able to secure patents on federally funded research only when the federal government, through a long and cumbersome application process, granted special approval. In a very real sense, the Bayh-Dole Act encouraged academic capitalism. Many other laws in the 1980s promoted competitiveness and encouraged deregulation, privatization, and commercialization of university activities and services.

In terms of university curricula and training, there was little formal policy discussion at the national level in the 1980s and 1990s, in large part because higher education was the province of the several states, and curricula were set by faculty at the institutional level. However, federal grant and contract monies for technoscience increased somewhat, whereas monies for the humanities and social sciences decreased dramatically. Given that the number of places for graduate students was strongly, albeit indirectly, influenced by grant and contract monies, the R&D function of universities concentrated increasingly on the sciences and engineering. In the period 1983-1993, federal R&D in the science and engineering fields became more applied. Universities' share of basic research remained the same, but applied research increased by 6% and development by 4% (National Science Foundation, 1993).[6]

Overall, in the 1980s and 1990s, U.S. policy at the federal level shifted so that colleges and universities were able to engage in academic capitalism. Professors were discouraged from pursuing pure research and encouraged to engage in more practical matters (Etzkowitz; 1994, Etzkowitz & Leydesdorff, 1996). In contrast to the other three countries, the U.S. government did not institute anything like quality assessments at the national level; however, a number of states established the equivalent of quality assessments—rising junior exams, junior writing exams, value-added assessments, more standardized teaching evaluations, and performance-based budgeting—which more closely regulated the faculty's instructional work (Guthrie & Pierce, 1990). Although occurring in piecemeal fashion, policy changes in the United States were not dissimilar to those that took place in the United Kingdom.

CONCLUSION

In the 1980s and 1990s, the higher education policies of Australia, Canada, Great Britain, and the United States began to converge. The areas of convergence were science and technology policy, curriculum, access and finance, and degree of autonomy. For the most part, these policies are concerned with economic competitiveness: fostering product and process innovation, channeling students and resources into curricula that meet the needs of a global marketplace, preparing more students for the postindustrial workplace at lower costs, and managing faculty and institutional work more effectively and efficiently. Each of the countries developed a number of policies outside these parameters that did not converge. Even in the areas of convergence, the four countries arrived at similar policies by very different paths. Australia and the United Kingdom used their ministries of education, the former led by a Labor government, the latter by a Conservative government. In Canada and the United States, the provinces and the several states, as would be expected in relatively decentralized systems, often developed their own initiatives to promote profit-driven R&D. In the United States, Congress was more aggressive than the executive branch in creating an infrastructure for profit-driven R&D. Despite the very real differences in their political cultures, the four countries developed similar policies at those points where higher education intersected with globalization of the postindustrial political economy. Tertiary education policies in all countries moved toward increased student access at lower government cost per student and toward organizational policies that undercut the autonomy of academic institutions and faculty.

Although these countries promoted profit-driven R&D as a means of stimulating national growth, the success of these policies to date is mixed. Productivity and GDP increased somewhat in the 1990s, but income inequality increased in three of the four countries (Australia, the United Kingdom, and the United States, with the increases being greatest in the latter two; Atkinson, Rainwater, & Smeeding, 1995). National wealth creation, as a policy, may be succeeding in terms of productivity and profitability, but recovery is not generating highly paid jobs. Indeed, relatively high levels of unemployment, combined with the growth of poorly paid full-time jobs and an increasing number of part-time jobs, have given rise to the concept of "jobless recovery" (Rifkin, 1995). The duration of these trends and what they will mean in terms of popular support for higher education is not yet clear.

NOTES

1. Despite the recently created Department of Education, the United States does not have a national ministry of education equivalent to those of Australia and the United Kingdom. As in Canada, higher education in the United States is decentralized. Nonetheless, the United States makes national higher education policy through federal student aid policies and through a wide array of R&D agencies, ranging from mission agencies to the National Science Foundation to, most recently, the Department of Commerce. Policy directions established at the national level are often complemented by the several states, as with supplemental educational opportunity grants and university-industry-state government commercial development projects.

2. Total quality management (TQM) focuses on the customer and the point of production rather than on management. Customer feedback is as important as worker input. Workers committed to the corporation should be able to constructively criticize and improve the production process, creating more satisfied customers. TQM depends

on shared commitment by management and workers to company goals and on a commitment by management to workers, and vice versa (Peters & Peters, 1991). A TQM management would be unlikely to fire large numbers of workers during restructuring, because that would create distrust and resistance, undermining efforts to increase productivity. Given the adversarial relationships that often characterize Fordist manufacturing, the requisite level of trust is difficult to achieve, especially during periods in which downsizing takes place.

3. As a number of scholars note, the nationality of a corporation is sometimes very difficult to determine. For example, joint ventures allow U.S. automakers to market, under their company names, popular Japanese cars, as in the case of Mazda Navajo, which is Ford Explorer made in Kentucky, and Geo Prism, which is a Toyota Corolla made in California. Conversely, Jaguars are made in England by a wholly owned Ford subsidiary. Increasingly, multinationals, regardless of country of origin, use their "overseas subsidiaries, joint ventures, licensing agreements, and strategic alliances to assume foreign identities when it suits their purposes" (Barnet & Cavanagh, 1994, pp. 279, 280).

4. Copyrights and patents in the United States are monopolies, protecting their holders from competition for various periods of time. Patents provide a seventeen-year period, with possible renewal at the end of that time. The Copyright Act of 1976 provides for copyright for the lifetime of the author, plus an additional fifty years. During the period in which the patent or copyright is held, it is possible for the owner to gain control of markets and eliminate competition. The counterargument is that authors and inventors would not create intellectual property without the possibility of being rewarded through royalties and licenses derived from copyright and licensing, nor would businesses invest in new products unless they were able to reduce risk somewhat through purchase of copyrights and patents.

5. After legislation shifted federal financial aid from grants to institutions to grants to students in 1972, financial aid was initially concentrated on lower-income students. However, the Middle Income Assistance Act was passed in 1980. It provided federal grants to students whose parents had quite high income levels. After its peak in the mid-1980s, the Middle Income Assistance Act was gradually constrained. Although middle-income students were still able to receive grants, the caps on parental income were lowered.

6. For an analysis of the gender implications of the restructuring precipitated in part by competitiveness R&D, see Slaughter (1993).

REFERENCES

Aronowitz, S., & Di Fazio, W. (1994). *The jobless future: Sci-tech and the dogma of work.* Minneapolis: University of Minnesota Press.

Atkinson, A., Rainwater, L., & Smeeding, T. M. (1995). *Income distribution in OECD countries: Evidence from the Luxembourg Income Study.* Paris: Organisation for Economic Co-operation and Development.

Barnet, R., & Cavanagh, J. (1994). *Global dreams: Imperial corporations and the new world order.* New York: Simon & Schuster.

Bell, D. (1973). *The coming of post-industrial society.* New York: Basic Books.

Ben-David, J. (1965, Autumn). The scientific role: The conditions of its establishment in Europe. *Minerva, 4,* 15-54.

Berdahl, R. O. (1959). *British universities and the state.* Berkeley: University of California Press.

Bonefeld, W. (1993, Summer). Crisis of theory: Bob Jessop's theory of capitalist reproduction. *Capital and Class, 50,* 25-47.

Bowles, S. (1992). Post-Marxian economics: Labour, learning, and history. In U. Himmelstrand (Ed.), *Interfaces in economic and social analysis* (pp. 95-111). London & New York: Routledge.

Breneman, D. W. (1993). Guaranteed student loans: Great success or dismal failure? In D. W. Breneman, L. L. Leslie, & R. Anderson (Eds.), *ASHE reader on finance in higher education* (pp. 377-387). Needham Heights, MA: Ginn.

Buchbinder, H., & Newson, J. (1990). Corporate-university linkages in Canada: Transforming a public institution. *Higher Education, 20,* 355-379.

Business–Higher Education Forum. (1983, April). *American competitive challenge: The need for a national response.* Washington, DC: Author.

Business–Higher Education Forum. (1986, January). *Export controls: The need to balance national objectives.* Washington, DC: Author.

Carnoy, M. (1993). Multinationals in a changing world economy: Whither the nation state? In M. Carnoy, M. Castells, S. S. Cohen, & F. H. Cardoso (Eds.), *The new global economy in the information age: Reflections on our changing world* (pp. 45-96). University Park: The Pennsylvania State University Press.

Carnoy, M., Castells, M., Cohen, S. S., & Cardoso, F. H. (Eds.). (1993). *The new global economy in the information age: Reflections on our changing world.* University Park: The Pennsylvania State University Press.

Castells, M. (1993). The informational economy and the new international division of labor. In M. Carnoy, M. Castells, S. S. Cohen, & F. H. Cardoso (Eds.), *The new global economy in the information age: Reflections on our changing world* (pp. 15-44). University Park: The Pennsylvania State University Press.

Castells, M., & Tyson, L. D'A. (1988). High technology choices ahead: Restructuring interdependence. In J. Sewell & S. Tucker (Eds.), *Growth, exports, and jobs in a changing world economy.* Washington, DC: Transaction Books.

Chomsky, N. (1994). *World orders old and new.* New York: Columbia University Press.

Cohen, S. S. (1993). Geo-economics: Lessons from America's mistakes. In M. Carnoy, M. Castells, S. S. Cohen, & F. H. Cardoso (Eds.), *The new global economy in the information age: Reflections on our changing world* (pp. 97-148). University Park: The Pennsylvania State University Press.

Committee for Economic Development. (1993). A strategy for better-targeted and increased financial support. In D. W. Breneman, L. L. Leslie, & R. Anderson (Eds.), *ASHE reader on finance in higher education* (pp. 61-68). Needham Heights, MA: Ginn.

Council for Industry and Higher Education. (1987). *Towards partnership.* Washington, DC: Author.

Etzkowitz, H. (1994). Academic-industry relations: A sociological paradigm for economic development. In L. Leydersdorff & P. Van den Besselaar (Eds.), *Evolutionary economics and chaos theory: New directions in technology studies?* (pp. 139-151). London: Pinter.

Etzkowitz, H., & Leydesdorff, L. (1996, April). *The triple helix: University-industry-government relations. A laboratory for knowledge-based economic development.* Theme paper for Triple Helix Conference, Amsterdam.

Fligstein, N. (1990). *The transformation of corporate control.* Cambridge, MA.: Harvard University Press.

Friedman, M. (1981). *The invisible hand in economics and politics.* Pasir Panjang, Singapore: Institute of Southeast Asian Studies.

Friedman, M. (1991). *Monetarist economics.* Oxford, UK: Blackwell.

Friedman, M., & Leub, K. R. (1987). *Essence of Friedman.* Stanford, CA.: Hoover Institution Press.

Frobel, F., Heinrichs, J., & Kreye, O. (1980). *The new international division of labor.* Cambridge, UK: Cambridge University Press.

Fulton, O. (1991). Slouching towards a mass system: Society, government, and institutions in the United Kingdom. *Higher Education, 21,* 589-605.

Gamble, A. (1989). Privatization, Thatcherism, and the British state. *Journal of Law and Society, 16*(1), 1-20.

Gering, T., & Schmied, H. (1993, March). Intellectual property issues: Technology licensing—costs versus benefits. *Higher Education Management, 5*(1), 100-110.

Government-University-Industry Research Roundtable. (1992). *Fateful choices: The future of the U.S. academic research enterprise.* Washington, DC: National Academy Press.

Great Britain White Paper. (1993). *Realizing our potential: Strategy for science, engineering and technology.* London: Her Majesty's Stationery Office.

Gummett, P. (1991). The evolution of science and technology policy: A UK perspective. *Science and Public Policy, 18*(1), 31-37.

Guthrie, J. W., & Pierce, L. C. (1990). The international economy and national education reform: A comparison of educational reforms in the United States and Great Britain. *Oxford Review of Education, 16,* 179-205.

Harrison, B., & Bluestone, B. (1990). *The great U-turn: Corporate restructuring and the polarizing of America.* New York: Basic Books.

Hearn, J. C., & Longanecker, D. (1993). Enrollment effects of postsecondary pricing policies. In D. W. Breneman, L. L. Leslie, & R. Anderson (Eds.), *ASHE reader on finance in higher education* (pp. 275-290). Needham Heights, MA: Ginn.

Henderson, J., & Castells, M. (1987). *Global restructuring and territorial development.* London: Sage.

Jessop, B. (1993, Spring). Towards a Schumpeterian workfare state? Preliminary remarks on post-Fordist political economy. *Studies in Political Economy, 40,* 7-39.

Johnes, G. (1992). Bidding for students in Britain—why the UFC auction "failed." *Higher Education, 23,* 173-182.

Kevles, D. J., & Hood, L. (Eds.). (1992). *The code of codes: Scientific and social issues in the human genome project.* Cambridge, MA: Harvard University Press.

Kimberling, C. R. (1995). Federal student aid: A history and critical analysis. In J. W. Sommer (Ed.), *The academy in crisis: The political economy of higher education* (pp. 69-93). New Brunswick, NJ: Transaction.

Kogan, M., & Kogan, D. (1983). *The attack on higher education.* London: Kogan Page.

Leydesdorff, L. (1994). New models of technological change: New theories for technology studies? In L. Leydesdorff & P. Van den Besselaar (Eds.), *Evolutionary economics and chaos theory: New directions in technology studies?* (pp. 180-192). London: Pinter.

Lyotard, J.-F. (1984). *The postmodern condition: A report on knowledge* (G. Bennington & B. Massumi, Trans.). Minneapolis: University of Minnesota Press.

Martin, B. R., Irvine, J., & Isard, P. A. (1990, February). Input measures: Trends in UK government spending on academic and related research: A comparison with F R Germany, France, Japan, the Netherlands and USA. *Science and Public Policy, 17*(1), 3-13.

McFarland, L. (1993). Top-up student loans: American models of student aid and British public policy. *Oxford Studies in Comparative Education, 3*(1), 49-67.

McPherson, M. S., & Schapiro, M. O. (1993). Changing patterns of college finance and enrollment. In D. W. Breneman, L. L. Leslie, & R. Anderson (Eds.), *ASHE reader on finance in higher education* (pp. 163-179). Needham Heights, MA: Ginn.

Melman, S. (1982). *Profits without production.* New York: Knopf.

Mowery, D. C. (1994). *Science and technology policy in interdependent economies.* Dordrecht: Kluwer Academic.

National Center for Educational Statistics. (1995). *The condition of education.* Washington, DC: U.S. Department of Education.

National Science Foundation. (1993). *Federal funds for research and development: Federal obligations for research by agency and detailed field of science and engineering: Fiscal years 1071-1993* (Prepared by Quantum Research Corporation). Washington, DC: Author.

Neave, G. (1988). Education and social policy: Demise of an ethic or change of values? *Oxford Review of Education, 14*(3), 273-283.

Noble, D. (1976). *America by design: Science, technology, and the rise of corporate capitalism.* New York: Knopf.

Oxley, H., & Martin, J. P. (1991, Autumn). Controlling government spending and deficits: Trends in the 1980s and prospects for the 1990s. *OECD Economic Studies, 17*, 145-201.

Peters, B. H., & Peters, J. L. (1991). *Total quality management.* New York: New York Conference Board.

Peters, M. (1992). Performance and accountability in "post-industrial society": The crisis of British universities. *Studies in Higher Education, 17*(2), 123-139.

Phillips, K. (1993). *Boiling point: Democrats, Republicans, and the decline of middle-class prosperity.* New York: Random House.

Porter, M. (1990). *The comparative advantage of nations.* New York: Free Press.

Pratt, J. (1992). Unification of higher education in the United Kingdom. *European Journal of Education, 27*(1/2), 29-43.

Reich, R. (1991). *The work of nations: Preparing ourselves for 21st century capitalism.* New York: Knopf.

Rifkin, J. (1995). *The end of work: The decline of the global labor force and the dawn of the post-market era.* New York: G. P. Putnam's.

Robins, K., & Webster, F. (1985, November). Higher education, high tech, high rhetoric. *Radical Science Journal, 18*, 36-57.

Sakakibara, E. (1993). *Beyond capitalism: The Japanese model of market economics.* Lanham, MD: University Press of America.

Sassen, S. (1991). *The global city: New York, London, Tokyo.* Princeton, NJ: Princeton University Press.

Scott, P. (1993). The idea of the university in the 21st century: A British perspective. *British Journal of Educational Studies, 41*(1), 4-25.

Shattock, M. (1989, September/October). Thatcherism and British higher education: Universities and the enterprise culture. *Change, 21*(5), 31-39.

Shattock, M. (1994). *The UGC and the management of British universities.* London: The Society for Research into Higher Education & Open University Press.

Shattock, M., & Berdahl, R. O. (1984). The British University Grants Committee 1919-83: Changing relationships with government and universities. *Higher Education, 13*(5), 471-499.

Slaughter, S. (1993). Retrenchment in the 1980s: The politics of prestige and gender. *Journal of Higher Education, 64,* 250-281.

Slaughter, S. (1998, Spring). Supply-side economics, national higher education policy, and institutional resource allocation policy: ASHE Presidential address. *The Review of Higher Education 21*(3), 209-244.

Slaughter, S., & Leslie, L. (1997). *Academic capitalism: Politics, policies and the entrepreneurial university.* Baltimore, MD: Johns Hopkins University Press.

Slaughter, S., & Rhoades, G. (1993). Changes in intellectual property statutes and policies at a public university: Revising the terms of professional labor. *Higher Education, 26,* 287-312.

Slaughter, S., & Rhoades, G. (1996, Summer). The emergence of a competitiveness research and development policy coalition and the commercialization of academic science and technology. *Science, Technology, and Human Values, 21*(3), 303-339.

Thrift, N. (1987). The fixers: The urban geography of international commercial capital. In J. Henderson & M. Castells (Eds.), *Global restructuring and territorial development.* London: Sage.

Thurow, L. (1980). *The zero-sum society: Distribution and the possibilities for economic change.* New York: Basic Books.

Trow, M. (1992, Summer). Thoughts on the White Paper of 1991. *Higher Education Quarterly, 46*(3), 213-226.

Tyson, L. D'A. (1992). *Who's bashing whom: Trade conflicts in high technology industries.* Washington, DC: Institute for International Economics.

Williams, B. (1992). The rise and fall of binary systems in two countries and the consequence for universities. *Studies in Higher Education, 17*(3), 281-293.

World Bank. (1993). *The East Asian miracle: Economic growth and public policy.* Washington, DC: Author.

PART II

NATIONAL RESPONSES
TO GLOBALIZATION

Janice Newson

The three chapters included in Part II focus on the higher education policy options that have been adopted as responses to globalization in different national and regional contexts. These chapters further complicate the analyses of globalization developed in Part I.

As argued in Part I, the term *globalization* identifies a package of coinciding and converging social, political, and economic changes that are increasingly exhibited in various industrially advanced Western societies. They include macroeconomic choices that prevailing governments have adopted in response to the globalization imperative and microeconomic reforms flowing from these choices that have been imposed on public and private sector institutions, including higher education systems and institutions. Part II offers a closer look at reforms in higher education systems in Canada, Norway, France, and Australia that display the complexity and variety of changes and provides analyses of the specific policy options that are being pursued.

The chapter by Donald Fisher and Kjell Rubenson examines the changing role of universities in Canadian society against the backdrop of "fundamental shifts in the relation between capital and labor and between public and private spheres." Using a political economy approach, they focus on the university in capitalist democracies as an institution engaged in "the exercise of mutual legitimation." The authors review the macroeconomic choices made by Canada's federal government over the past decade and a half in response to the package of economic, political, and social pressures that Dudley and Slaughter associate with globalization. Much like Australian governments (as Dudley describes their choices), successive federal governments in Canada—in spite of apparent differences in their political philosophies—have opted for the strategy of reducing the welfare state and "freeing the market." Fisher and Rubenson make the important point that, although neo-liberal discourse advocates a reduced role for government and thus promotes drastic reductions in public spending and increased reliance on the private sector, nevertheless the governments that promote these views are themselves very active. Indeed, they must be active in order to advance these policies.

Drastic reductions in spending at the federal level have imposed severe budget cuts on the provincially governed universities. Fisher and Rubenson show us that money is not the only issue, however. Universities have been harnessed with new responsibilities for manpower training to improve Canada's competitiveness in world markets. The combined effects of governments' fiscal policies and the merging of education with training have led toward differentiation and specialization within and among higher education institutions, as well as increasing vocationalism in university curricula. Associated with these institutional tendencies, university culture has become more commercial and entrepreneurial, and university organization has become more bureaucratic and corporate.

Arild Tjeldvoll's case study of a single university in Norway, the University of Oslo, extends and deepens the analysis provided by Fisher and Rubenson. On the one hand, Tjeldvoll appears less critical than other writers in this book of assumptions such as the "need" for universities to contribute to the economic competitiveness of society, the importance assigned to technoscience in the apparently inevitable advancement toward the knowledge society, and the requirement that universities become more efficient and cost-effective. Albeit with some caution about threats to the democratic functions of universities, he positively embraces the "service university movement"[1] as a means by which universities can become more relevant and useful to their local regions and society in general.

On the other hand, his carefully detailed analysis of whether and how the University of Oslo is moving toward the service university model shows how a single institution's response to the Norwegian government's new approach toward the financing of higher education and to "internationalizing pressures" is based on its own history and conception of its educational mission. Tjeldvoll's chapter thus underscores the idea introduced by Fisher and Rubenson that changes attributed to globalization are modified and fashioned by the particular circumstances and choices of local institutions.

The Norwegian case is especially interesting insofar as Norway's economy has performed more favorably than those of countries such as Australia, Canada, New Zealand, the United Kingdom, and the United States. Nevertheless, changes in higher education are being promoted by the Norwegian government that are similar to those advanced in societies that have been experiencing less favorable economic circumstances.

For example, Tjeldvoll identifies trends in Norway that are similar to those identified by Fisher and Rubenson, such as the trend toward institutional specialization and decentralization, as well as the expectation that universities should become more accountable and more attuned to servicing a market-centered economy. Through a detailed examination of policy documents of the University of Oslo, Tjeldvoll displays how this growing tendency toward differentiation and specialization at the level of institutions is related to the government's insistence that universities should become more autonomous by competing with each other for financial resources from clients that they serve, such as industrial clients and government ministries.

Tjeldvoll also shows how the recent creation of a National Research Council is designed to achieve greater integration of university-based research with government economic and political objectives, as Claire Polster's study (1994) of the role of the federal government in reorganizing the social relations of academic research in Canada has also demonstrated. Within the University of Oslo, the implications of this integration are reflected in the growing competition between teaching and research activities, as well as the blurring of distinctions between basic and applied research, between academically centered education and vocationally oriented job training, and between the university and the college systems within higher education.

Insofar as the policy directions that are being taken up in a Norwegian university are similar to those in Canadian and other societies' universities, Tjeldvoll's chapter suggests that the financial constraints created by economic pressures are not the major impetus of these directions. On the other hand, it also suggests that such constraints and pressures are critical to bringing them into effect. Tjeldvoll informs us that, notwithstanding the rhetoric of policy documents and university leaders, at the practical level, very little is happening at the University of Oslo in terms of these changes. Yet in Canada and Australia, where financial cutbacks to universities have occurred in the context of a gloomy economic picture, these policy directions have been translated into practical action and have already led to significant structural and programatic changes. It thus appears that "real" financial pressures act as a lever for bringing these policy directions into practice.

Richard DeAngelis's chapter is a fitting closure to this section because he punctuates a theme that is implicit in Fisher and Rubenson's and Tjeldvoll's chapters. Against the backdrop of a similar package of globalizing forces, Fisher and Rubenson display variations among the provincial systems and institutions of higher education in Canada, whereas Tjeldvoll exposes the possibilities for choice available to the University of Oslo. DeAngelis centers his chapter around this theme of diversity and choice in response to globalization. He explicitly challenges the representation, made by both advocates and critics, that globalizing forces are qualitatively new, inevitable, constraining, and homogenizing. He argues instead that there are "real limits" to these forces and, thus, there is considerable scope for responding to them.

DeAngelis's contribution is to systematize some of the important factors or variables that distinguish national systems, regions, and individual institutions from each other in terms of their response to globalization. He argues that local traditions; bureaucratic and policy networks; shared knowledge; interest group mobilization; public policy priorities such as social justice, equity, ethnic diversity, and public order; policy creativity or ineptitude—all of these play into various responses to globalizing forces. Moreover, DeAngelis argues that such factors not only shape the particular forms that globalization will take in specific nations, regions, and institutions but also provide the basis for resistance and countervailing tendencies. He illustrates his argument through a comparison of France and Australia, which constitute "polar opposites" in their political systems, politics, and higher education policy reform. He shows how they exemplify diversity and resistance to global uniformity and the elimination of the local.

NOTE

1. For a critique of the service university model and its underlying assumptions, see J. Newson, "Constructing the 'Post-Industrial University': The Institutional Shape of Budget-Based Rationalization and University-Corporate Linkages." In P. Altbach & B. Johnstone (Eds.), *International Perspectives on Funding of Higher Education*. New York: Garland, 1993.

CHAPTER 4

The Changing Political Economy

*The Private and Public Lives
of Canadian Universities*

*Donald Fisher
Kjell Rubenson*

The Canadian postsecondary system has developed
a distinctive and unique character since the Second World War. The
transition from an elite to a mass system has already taken place
(Scott, 1995). In 1994-1995, Canada spent $15.9 billion on postsecon-
dary education, which represents 2.09% of gross domestic product
(GDP). Canada has consistently been at the top of the range in the
Organization for Economic Cooperation and Development (OECD)
when expenditures are calculated as a proportion of the GDP. Governments are the primary source, providing 76% of direct funding.
The participation rates in 1994 among 18- to 21-year-olds and 22- to
25-year-olds was 40.3% and 22.8%, respectively. With these rates,
Canada was at the top of the OECD table for the 18- to 21-year-olds
and third for the 22-to 25-year-olds (Government of Canada, 1996,
p. 3; OECD, 1996, pp. 61, 131). The commitment to egalitarianism
rather than elitism is expressed in the relatively low fees charged to
students. Similarly, the level of institutional autonomy is probably
more pronounced in Canada than in any other OECD country. The
system can be characterized as soft federalism. Although the federal
government has, since the 1950s, shouldered a significant portion of

the bill for universities, the constitutional responsibility has remained with the provinces. In 1994-1995, federal support to postsecondary education represented 52% of the total cost of postsecondary education in that year (Government of Canada, 1996, p. 3). The public monopoly over the binary structure (colleges and universities) accounts for the limited competition and the perceived equivalence between credentials across the country. This state public system is relatively homogeneous and, as a vestige of its roots in the United Kingdom, is still committed to the ethos of liberal education rather than vocationalism. However, strong external and internal pressures are currently pushing universities in the latter direction.

The intent of this chapter is to lay the groundwork for understanding the changing role of universities in Canadian society during a time of fundamental shifts in the relation between capital and labor and between the public and private spheres. Like all modern institutions in capitalist democracies, universities are involved in an exercise of mutual legitimation, as academics attempt to balance elements of *bildung* against the structural force of commodification. When trying to understand the operation of social forces in and through a university system, it is useful to divide the life of the system into its external and internal components (Clark, 1983), or expressed differently, the division between demand (for education, specialist training, research services of various kinds) and response (by the university system and individual institutions). These divisions help to focus attention on changes in university culture and the contents of the intellectual field (Bourdieu, 1969; Ringer, 1992).

Four objectives are of concern in this chapter. First is to describe and interpret the political economic trends that form the backdrop to current changes in the vocational contours of university education in Canada. Against this background, a brief historical account is provided of the gradual withdrawal of the federal government from funding the system. Second is an analysis of the new discourse on vocationalism at both the federal and provincial levels of government. This discourse is shaped by three overlapping social forces: the fiscal crisis of the state, the ideological dominance of neo-liberalism, and the perceived need for human resource development. Third is a case study analyzing the changes in the vocational role performed by universities in British Columbia. The conclusion locates the above discussion in a broader theoretical framework and speculates on the future implications of current trends.

CHANGES IN CANADIAN
POLITICAL ECONOMY

The social demand that once directed the growth of the postsecondary education system is gradually giving way to a new, economically driven imperative that places importance on highly developed human capital, science, and technology to support Canada's needs for economic restructuring and greater international competitiveness. This economic imperative has been amplified by severe limitations on public expenditures and the emergence of the accountability movement, which is based on a general suspicion of public institutions and a belief in the greater efficiency of free market forces. In this section, we will look at the changing political landscape and the changing link between education and the economy.

During successive Conservative administrations between 1984 and 1993, the federal policy agenda was grounded on a neo-liberal ideology, with an emphasis on shrinking the Keynesian welfare state and freeing the market. The contradiction apparent in the United Kingdom is that whereas an activist and strong state is condemned in theory, in practice it is needed to carry out the policies. A privatization trend that cut across most OECD countries during this period meant the transfer of costs and responsibility from public or state control to private control. This involved selling off crown corporations to private investors and shifting from compulsory taxation to a voluntary, user-pay approach to public services (Stanbury, 1989, p. 274). According to the Conservatives, their approaches to social welfare and labor market policy can be justified on the grounds that the government has little or no choice. Not only does the nation-state lack the power to resist global economic forces, but the well-being of citizens is served if the country opens up to international market forces (Johnson, McBride, & Smith, 1994, p. 9).

Barlow and Cambell (1991) see the Canada–United States Free Trade Agreement (FTA) and the later North American Free Trade Agreement (NAFTA) as the cornerstones in the Conservative and corporate agenda to reshape Canada. The agreements prevent the reestablishment of an interventionist state and firmly establish a free market and entrepreneurial spirit in Canadian political culture. For the Conservative government, a free-trade solution was an alternative economic model to the Keynesian policy paradigm (McBride &

Shields, 1993, p. 134). As a means of achieving a level playing field, free trade provided the justification for the neo-conservative agenda to reduce business taxes and various forms of social benefits. Having achieved political dominance in the 1980s, the Mulroney government and its business supporters then sought to insulate their achievements from the democratic processes during the 1990s (McBride & Shields, 1993, p. 169).

The need for Canada to become more competitive became the basis for Conservative economic and social policy housed in the free trade agreements (Abele, 1992). Policy initiatives such as training the labor force, overhauling the unemployment insurance system, and reducing the deficit and inflation were all promoted as measures to improve Canada's competitiveness. Yet, adoption of a New Right ideology as a response to fiscal crises came late in Canada, and policies of monetarism, deregulation, privatization, and reduced social expenditure were not as draconian as in Thatcher's England or Reagan's United States (Mullay, 1994). The Conservative government's approach was incremental and favored greater selectivity, setting ceilings on program costs and in some instances, making them self-financing. Despite tough talk about bringing down the deficit, the Conservative government was only partially successful in shrinking the federal state. This was in large part due to the cost of servicing the debt. As McBride and Shields (1993) point out, if program expenditures are considered in isolation from debt-servicing costs, the statistics show a major reduction. Program expenditures shrunk from 19.4% of GDP in 1983-1984 to 16.0% in 1990-1991.

The Conservatives were replaced in 1993 by a Liberal government that had campaigned on job creation and debt and deficit reduction. In comparison with other major industrialized countries, Canada, it was stressed, had the second-largest deficit and debt relative to GDP and, by a large margin, the highest level of foreign debt relative to GDP. The Liberals quickly set out to do what the Conservatives only marginally had been able to do—cut the deficit. Without the ideological overtures of neo-liberalism that characterized the former governments' policy rhetoric, more severe spending cuts were put in place. The 1995 budget introduced measures that will gradually reduce the deficit to 3% of GDP in 1996-1997 (half of the 1993 figure) and 2% the year after. A major part of the savings are coming from a drastic reduction of financial transfers to the provinces for income assistance, health, and postsecondary education. The Established Programs Fund (EPF) entitlement, the major educational transfer from the federal government to the provinces, will be entirely paid for in the form of taxes forgone. This will be a loss to the provinces of $14 billion (Government of Canada, 1996). The EPF and the Canada Assistance Plan have been combined into one single mechanism, the Canadian Health and Social Transfer (CHST). By 1997-1998, the federal government will have cut $4.5 billion from the cash component of the CHST. As a result of these cuts, the province of New Brunswick in 1995-1996, for example, faced a 17% reduction in federal transfer payments for social programs, including postsecondary education, from the previous year (Department of Finance, New Brunswick, 1996). The result of these changes in transfers to the provinces will likely lead to a balkanization of social programs and an abdication of the federal government's responsibility to ensure that all have access to a high-quality medicare, postsecondary education, and adequate social assistance.

Universities face further cuts in their budgets because the federal government decided in 1995 to cut 14% over three years to the major federal research councils, the Social Sciences and Humanities Research Council of Canada (SSHRCC) and the Natural Sciences and Engineering Research Council of Canada (NSERCC).

During the past fifteen years, the postsecondary system has had to accommodate a very large increase in student numbers with moderate budget increases, resulting in substantial reduction in cost per student. The spending on postsecondary education per student has been reduced from $12,011 in 1975 to $9,190 by 1990 (Horry & Walker, 1994).

To make things worse, not only do the provinces have to accommodate large federal cuts, but they also have to cut their own debts and deficits. The combined impact of the fiscal crisis at both levels of the state has created enormous pressure to reduce public expenditures. In this climate, Ontario and Alberta have elected populist New Right governments that are not satisfied with scaling back the welfare state but want to see savage cuts in public spending and the abolition of the welfare state. The mentality is very much the same as could be found in New Zealand and England, with the introduction of workfare programs and draconian cuts in social assistance. Other provinces governed by less conservative parties are facing major cuts to their program expenditures and try to portray themselves as fiscal conservatives. It is in this fiscal climate that postsecondary education is being called upon to spearhead the new information economy and be an engine for increased competitiveness.

A NEW DISCOURSE ON VOCATIONALISM

Federal and provincial policy documents see education and training as a way of making Canada more able to compete in a time of globalization and economic restructuring. A key statement in the discussion paper *Agenda: Jobs and Growth: Improving Social Security in Canada* (Human Resources Development Canada, 1994) is typical: "As the pace of global competition quickens and technological complexity intensifies, the fortunes of individuals and of nations turn increasingly on the skills they already possess or are prepared to acquire" (p. 39). The connection between learning and earning can be seen in titles such as *Lifelong Learning and the New Economy*, a 1994 report from the Ontario Premier's Council on Economic Renewal. The report states, "Lifelong learning, therefore, is the key link between our educational and economic strategies as the 21st century approaches" (p. 2).

Within the new economic imperative, the relationship between postsecondary education and work has become the key issue and a major battleground between competing ideologies and interests. The structure of universities, educational provisions and student options, the curricula, and the governance of the linkages between universities and work are being questioned. Recent policy documents express a strong need to establish closer ties with the labor market and "[to adapt] education to the real requirements of the labour market, . . . making it more relevant, and . . . easing the transition into the workplace" (Gouvernement du Québec, 1996, p. 54). This discussion is set within a broader context of the Canadian training deficit.

A key issue in the debate on education and training is the lack of private sector involvement. The Canadian Job Strategy (CJS), launched by the Conservative government in 1985, and its replacement, the Labour Force Development Strategy (LFDS) from 1989, emphasized market sensitivity and private sector involvement (Haddow, 1995). A cornerstone of CJS was making public funds, which traditionally had gone to community colleges through federal-provincial agreement, available to the private partners for "indirect federal training purchases." Canada Employment Centres could enter into training agreements with firms, private providers, nonprofit organizations, or sectorial committees. These groups might, if they so chose, purchase the education and training from a public education institution. The result was rapid growth in private sector training enterprises and, despite some entrepreneurial approaches by the college system, a reduction in federal training funds going to public institutions.

The LFDS, which was introduced to overcome the shortcomings of CJS, specifically its narrow preoccupation with lower-end skills, approached private sector involvement in a different way. Haddow (1995, p. 344) characterizes the CJS as a pluralist approach to private sector involvement; the LFDS was constructed around a corporatist approach. Following the creation of a federal LFDS board, some provinces set up similar boards. As training increasingly becomes a provincial responsibility alongside education, we see a merger of what traditionally has been two partly separate policy fields. This change has major repercussions on postsecondary education.

In British Columbia, the responsibility of the Labour Force Development Board (BCLFDB) was to provide the Minister of Education, Skills, Training, and Labour with strategic and tactical advice on labor force development, training, and adjustment. In its first report, *Training for What?*, the board presented an analysis of the future of work, skills that will be required, and how British Columbia could best organize its learning system to meet these skill needs (BCLFDB, 1995). Because BCLFDB is a major player in the policy arena, its conclusions cannot be taken lightly. The following conclusion has led to much controversy:

> First, the mix of education and training programs [does] not match labour market needs as well as it might. For example, while there is no gap in the capacity of the province's universities and university colleges to produce the number of university graduates that will be required, there appears to be a relative over-supply of graduates in academic programs and an under-supply of those in applied. (p. 43)

The changing political economy as reflected in the fiscal situation and policies, as well as human resource strategies to improve Canada's competitiveness, has caused concern about the ability of the postsecondary system to respond. Several provinces have or are presently undertaking reviews of their postsecondary system. The purpose here is to briefly review how the changing external factors are being reflected in the present policy discussions.

AN OVERVIEW OF PROVINCIAL POLICY

External Differentiation

To meet the demands for rationalization and differentiation, either provincial intermediary bodies have been created or their powers to intervene have been strengthened (see, for example, Nova Scotia Council on Higher Education, 1995; University Program Review Panel, Saskatchewan, 1993). To meet the financial challenges, the Nova Scotia Council on Higher Education (1995) presented a series of goals and strategies. To increase responsiveness to social, cultural, and economic needs and opportunities, the council suggested a reexamination and a refocus of the institutional mission of universities. The purpose was to define the institutional relationship with the labor market, to improve means for ongoing liaison between stakeholder and university communities, and to promote programs addressing the needs of the economy and society. With these goals in mind, the council recommended consolidation of institutions and "structural changes that would make possible system-wide decisions on major policy and program issues" (p. 27). Teacher education has already been restructured, and currently other programs are under scrutiny. One of the principles underlying the proposed new funding formula for universities in Nova Scotia was to provide incentives for system effectiveness, including institutional differentiation and interinstitutional cooperation (Nova Scotia Council on Higher Education, 1996).

Similarly, recent reviews in Québec and Manitoba concluded that differentiation of university institutions was beneficial and necessary (Gouvernement du Québec, 1996; University Education Review Commission, 1993). The "major" universities in Quebec supported the plan that certain universities would specialize in research, whereas others would concentrate on undergraduate studies. Not surprisingly, the "other" universities were afraid of being left with reduced missions and were not willing to give up their research and graduate programs. As the commission noted, "The restructuring would also require changes in policy with respect to funding, faculty workloads, and faculty assessment to replace the current system that often results in an undue dispersal of funds" (University Education Review Commission, 1993, p. 13). The Manitoba commission concluded,

> In recent times, Manitoba's post-secondary institutions have explicitly defined the mission and roles to which they are committed. This commendable development, however, has taken place without the presence and articulation of the mission and roles of Manitoba's post-secondary system as a whole. The Commission has viewed this as a deficiency, in a context of an environment in which both interdependence and longer term planning for the future are so important. (p. 11)

Ontario's response to fiscal pressures was to restructure the university system and to rationalize professional programs. This involved tightening new program-funding approval criteria, as well as cutting and merging existing programs (Ontario Council on University Affairs, 1995). The provincial legislature authorized the provincial auditor to examine the financial records of three of its universities. This task force issued 47 recommendations, all intended to make universities more accountable to the government and the public at large. Alberta has undergone a joint university-government exercise to eliminate program duplication. Attempts have been made to reduce government expenditures by instituting major transfer payment cuts following a government review. George and McAllister (1995) cite a March 1994 draft of a White Paper that includes as one of its goals "to ensure responsiveness and accountability [by universities] to learners and taxpayers" (p. 311). To fit within an accountability framework, postsecondary institutions in Alberta are required to provide key indicators of performance on enrollment levels, graduation rates, costs per student, measures of student satisfaction, and employment outcomes.

Internal Differentiation

The tensions between teaching and research are particularly visible in professional applied fields. From their inception, universities have been concerned with "vocational" issues. Alongside the provision of what has come to be called a liberal, classical education, universities took responsibility for teaching subjects intended to meet the intellectual requirements for the performance of certain practical professions. The development of the modern university is housed in and has contributed to the professionalization of society. The model of the late nineteenth century included the four traditional faculties: theology, arts, law, and medicine.

The professionalization of society has been mutually beneficial to universities and the professions. While a university education justifies the professions' claims to a knowledge base and therefore to professional status, it also serves to screen entrants to the profession through means that may sustain and improve professional standards. Universities have expanded their client base by offering career-oriented courses and including areas of professional training that were previously outside the university's domain (Eraut, 1992). This is particularly the case in the fields of social work, education, and administrative sciences (business administration, commerce, and public administration). Since the early 1960s, the number of full-time, tenure-track faculty in English-speaking Canadian universities in these fields has expanded enormously. Between 1960 and 1990, the increase was from 58 to 274 (372%) in social work, from 290 to 1,611 (455%) in education, and from 81 to 1,484 (1,732%) in the administrative sciences (Commonwealth Universities Yearbooks). As these fields have reached for legitimacy within the academy, so faculty have emphasized scientific research and have run the danger of separating themselves from their professional communities. This is particularly the case in education where, over the past decade, "academic researchers" account for the large majority of appointments.

Internal differentiation lies at the heart of the strong concerns regarding quality of teaching and the balance between teaching and research. During the past 25 years, the reforms within higher education have concentrated on questions about the expansion and organization of higher education. At the same time, particularly since the early 1980s, there has been a lively discussion of research policies. However, Canadian universities were originally teaching institutions, and only after the Second World War did research become an integral part of their activities. Graham, Lyman, and Trow (1995, p. 12), when discussing the changing professoriate, note that as the research university became the most influential model for higher education, professors defined their work not as their teaching but more as their research. In the standard vocabulary of campuses, teaching was a "load," research an "opportunity."

Financial constraints that inevitably led to differentiation have had an impact on the discussion of the relationship between research and teaching. Several national and provincial reports conclude that the quality of teaching is a major problem and point to the underfunding of teaching in universities, resulting in deficiencies at the undergraduate level (New Brunswick Commission on Higher Education, 1993; Smith, 1991). During public hearings in Quebec, college and university students criticized the overuse of lectures (Gouvernement du Québec, 1996). The Ontario Council on University Affairs (1995) asked, in its Resources Allocation Review,

> Should the balance among teaching, research, and community service be altered? If so, what form of differentiation in roles would be appropriate? Should it be at the level of institution, academic unit, or individual faculty member? Should the funding allocation system be changed to enable any such shifts? (p. 72)

In its discussion paper, the council reviewed the empirical research and concluded that little evidence exists to support links between effective undergraduate teaching and research. The council suggested some caution in the interpretation. However, it seems obvious that without strong evidence for these links, the move toward differentiation at the level of individual faculty becomes more convincing. The concern with quality of teaching is used to frame a more explicit division of labor between teaching and research. At the same time, administrators seem convinced that with the inflation of credentials, the strongest vocational role for the modern research university is through an excellent undergraduate liberal arts program.

CHANGES IN THE VOCATIONAL ROLE
OF UNIVERSITIES IN BRITISH COLUMBIA

Structural differentiation characterizes the relationship between and within the three older universities. Consistent with the historical development of the university system in British Columbia and elsewhere in Canada, each institution continues to carve out its own particular niche. Of the three universities, only the University of British Columbia (UBC) continues to claim the universal functions that go with being a major national research university. As the recipient of about 80% of the total external funding for research coming to British Columbia, UBC can quite properly claim the "right to be irrelevant." The security and status of being the only full medical/doctoral university in the province gives the institution the confidence to claim the traditional vocational ground that goes with the older professions. On the other hand, Simon Fraser University (SFU) and the University of Victoria (UVic) claim with confidence their relevance to community and provincial interests. Both institutions have consciously tried not to replicate existing programs and have attempted to identify unique programs they can develop.

Just as, in the province of Ontario, York University began life as the antithesis to the University of Toronto, so in British Columbia SFU continues to take pride in not being UBC. The focus is on innovation and interdisciplinarity. As one administrator put it, "the ethos of the institution is more open to thinking in different ways, in doing things differently" and developing "a sense of community responsibility." With its strong commitment to continuing and cooperative education and to serving the metropolitan region of Vancouver, SFU, not UBC, took the lead and established the downtown Harbour Centre Campus. Through this campus, the university serves a "bridging" function and has become accessible to the community by location, program/course, and, according to their mission statement, even spirit. Their initiative is perhaps best represented in the outreach degree-completion program designed for employees of B.C. Hydro and Canadian Pacific Rail, which began operation in 1995.

Similarly, UVic has developed a special expertise in cooperative education. UVic mounts the third-largest program in the country, running behind Waterloo and Sherbrooke. The cooperative philosophy permeates the culture and has become the defining characteristic of this campus. Co-op programs operate in over thirty-five departments. Some departments offer an optional program; others make it mandatory. The Faculty of Business Administration began life with a mandatory co-op component at both the undergraduate and graduate levels. In addition, the Faculty of Engineering, which dates back to the early 1980s, has from its inception had a mandatory component. As one administrator put it, "The thought was that in those applied fields of Business and Engineering it would be sensible for all our graduates to have had some work-based learning experience."

All departments at UVic, except anthropology, political science, and psychology, have some work-based learning opportunities, through either co-op, internships, or practicums. UVic's reputation for bridging the gap between the academy and the labor market was a key factor in the university's being chosen as the Canadian location of the Swiss-based program in hotel and restaurant management.

Analysis of policy documents reveals that commitment to adult and part-time study is strongest in the original mission statements of SFU and UVic. Both institutions are strongly committed to the maintenance of access for adult learners and the development of facilities and programs for part-time study. In its original statement of mission, UBC's commitment to adult and part-time study could, at best, be characterized as lukewarm. Not until the 1980s did UBC, in a series of revised and successive statements of mission, become theoretically committed to adult part-time study and lifelong learning. At SFU, continuing education is not so marginalized as it is in other universities, and it has become part of the wider ethos of the university. The faculty agree on the value of lifelong education and the outreach policy. For the group in continuing education, "liberal education is more than education for its own sake—it is education that is relevant to the general public interest." It follows that the MBA Executive program and the Downtown Eastside-City Program should exist side by side.

Although these approaches to vocationalism serve to distinguish the three universities, there exists substantial agreement among the three universities on their "real" vocational function. All three universities have over the past decade expanded to include more applied fields and programs. This trend is nowhere more pronounced than at UVic, which has self-consciously added many professional and applied programs and schools over the past twenty years. These additions were, according to one administrator, "all designed to address the problems of society." Law was added in 1973, followed by a number of programs (nursing, social work, public administration, child and youth care, and health information science) that are now housed in the Faculty of Human and Social Development. Engineering programs were added in the 1980s and computer science later joined the Faculty of Engineering. The addition of engineering was a controversial decision, causing massive division in the Faculty of Arts and Science and a profound split in the Senate. This debate was a turning point in the history of UVic, as the ideal and myth of the university as a liberal arts college were put to rest. Finally, the Faculty of Business Administration was added in 1991. The change has been both massive and drastic. As one faculty member put it, "The whole nature of its [UVic's] operation has changed. Now, with all the applied and professional programs, there's much more focus on students wishing to prepare themselves for specific professions when they leave university.

At UBC, the fastest-growing areas are commerce and computer science. A school of journalism opened in 1997. The new undergraduate programs in occupational hygiene and advanced wood processing were tailored to the needs of profession and industry, involving the cooperation and financial backing of government.

The pressure on universities to respond to external social forces can be observed in the debates on training versus education and the trend toward interdisciplinarity. A clear distinction is made between education and training. According to one administrator, training is, for many faculty, "a dirty word because it's not educational, not cognitive enough for them." The colleges, university colleges, and new universities (Royal Roads University and Technical University) are expected to fulfill training rather than education functions. Whereas the "academic drift" symbolized by the Malaspina Liberal Arts degree and the British Columbia Institute of Technology applied degree is recognized, the three older universities still retain their claim to liberal education. For most faculty, the arts and sciences are still the core of the university. As one faculty member put it,

> Universities are not here simply to train people for jobs. It is a fundamental tenet of universities that they exist to educate. Universities exist to provide people with an opportunity to explore the intellectual world as well as preparing people for the jobs and the workforce.

Senior administrators talk at length about the generic skills (flexibility, critical thinking, problem solving, independence, and the ability to communicate) that are learned as part of a classical liberal education. These skills are regarded as the vocational heart of any institution that claims to be a university and are symbols of the unity between theory and practice. One administrator declared that it was false to make "any distinction between pure and applied research, or between theoretical and vocational education." The Arts and Science One course is held up by UBC as the exemplar of modern vocational education. The liberal arts components of both the cooperative and outreach programs at SFU and UVic are similarly displayed as badges of vocational virtue. SFU is wedded in the broadest sense to the concept of liberal education. All undergraduates take a "general education" program in their first two years. At UVic, which began life as a liberal arts college, all programs have strong roots in the Faculty of Arts and Science.

In recent years, generic skills have received more attention, in part because of the continuing inflation of credentials and the concomitant expansion of graduate work. If specialized vocational preparation is a postgraduate experience, then space is left for a more traditional undergraduate education. This view converges with the conventional wisdom that employers want generalists who can learn on the job. Universities then quite properly should be providing broad, general liberal education not just for students in the arts and sciences, but also for students in professional, applied, and technological fields. According to this view, which is the mirror image of the position taken by the Conference Board of Canada, general education will produce trainable workers who can think critically, work in a team, and solve problems.

The trend across the system is toward more interdisciplinarity and more applied programming. At SFU, the tradition of interdisciplinarity has been extended into new graduate programs such as environmental toxicology, which are geared to provide people with certification or professional requirements for the local job market. UVic has a strong commitment to interdisciplinarity, which is demonstrated by the rise of the applied and professional fields referred to earlier and exciting initiatives such as the computer science master's degree in software engineering. Universities take accountability to the external world more seriously than they have done before. All three universities defined themselves as being more responsive, more willing to take the initiative and be proactive. Inevitably, administrators were aware of the political-economic pressure to change but were clear that neither government or industry had pushed them in a particular policy direction. Rather, financial stringency and government policy stressing the vocational role of the tertiary sector have created a climate for change. For the most part, universities have translated the signals and then taken the initiative, although at times, government direction has clearly been decisive. The Nursing School at UVic was a direct response to government overtures. Similarly, the Faculty of Business idea was renewed in the late 1980s by the government after the initial suggestion was rejected earlier in the decade.

The faculty was established with line funding from the government. The best example at UBC is the advanced wood products program.

Although many of the changes have not been formulated as policy, we can identify clear shifts. The most obvious example is the move toward full cost recovery. This became policy at UBC for continuing education in 1995 and is under active consideration at SFU and UVic. The trend is toward strategic, money-making, diploma and certificate programs. The new climate explicitly rewards entrepreneurship. The boundary separating the academy and industry is much more permeable. As one administrator put it,

> Education is a door opener to industry. They're interested, and if you help them out with their education and training problems, you're going to get to know them better. They'll get to know you better, and then you can start talking about joint research ventures with them, so that your faculty get involved in joint research.

Although administrators would want to deny that their universities are "for sale," the trend toward sale of services and profit-taking is clear and consistent.

The professionalization of university culture has reached a critical stage in the 1990s, as our universities have become more corporate. At one level, administration has become a separate career, producing a culture at odds with the traditional, collegial definition of university life. The division between scholars and administrators is not new, but now the tensions are exacerbated in an extreme way by the external pressure to focus on relevance and accountability. The collegial model of governance continues to be undermined, and the uneasy truce between the two cultures has been broken. Many faculty, particularly within the most established arts and science disciplines, as well as students, are highly critical of these developments. Most faculty regard the work of professional and applied units as legitimate but are concerned about the current vocational trend. For many, our universities have crossed a line that challenges the fundamental autonomy of the university with its "particular character . . . and own institutional esprit de corps and raison d'être." The pursuit of learning, critical thinking, and basic research all come under threat, according to one faculty member, when instrumental and functional objectives displace the concern with autonomy and a separation of powers within society. As one student representative observed,

The dominant political culture [on campus] has created a more atom-
ized, individualistic, competitive kind of atmosphere on campus, and
that cuts in so many different directions . . . student to student, faculty
to faculty . . . people see each other as competitors rather than as
people who are learning in a common environment . . . a market
competition mentality.

Yet, against this background, senior administrators define the new
relationships with industry and government as opportunities rather
than threats.

The definition of professionalism is changing as fields such as
commerce and forestry respond to external pressures and embrace
praxis. For one administrator in commerce, professional schools
should quite properly "link ideas and practical skills." The faculty is
run as "a business on full cost recovery and then some," yet the belief
is that the research mission has been strengthened. The "ivory tower"
definition of the university has been replaced by a "society-problem-
oriented" one where the university is connected to the external world
in a hundred different ways. According to one administrator, the
Faculty of Forestry has thoroughly embraced the new definition:

We are a professional faculty. . . . if society did not have forestry
problems, UBC would not have a forestry faculty, and so we see our
destiny as being linked to the outside world, and, being a bridge
between the outside world and the university to a degree.

Professional faculties that initiate and promote contact with external
agencies provide the best indicator of what has become a "sea change"
in university culture.

CONCLUSION

The foregoing analysis highlights seven overlapping changes in
the external life of Canadian universities. First is the further softening
of federalism. Less involvement will mean less regulation and will
undermine the principle of universalism, which has been at the heart
of the post-Second World War experience in Canada. Second is a
further blurring of the vocational part of the boundary that has
traditionally separated the universities and colleges. The education-

versus-training labels will no longer characterize the binary structure of the postsecondary sector as in the past. On the surface, two contradictory trends seem to be at work: academic drift, as colleges become more like universities; and vocationalism, as universities take on more responsibility for training the highly skilled technical employees in, for example, computer science, and for retraining professionals. The increase in university transfer courses and the extension of degree-granting status to colleges are indicators of the former trend. The long-established trend toward vocationalism is exemplified by the expansion of commerce and business administration over the past two decades. On the boundary between these two sectors are the applied degrees offered by technical colleges or universities.

Third is the increasing differentiation and specialization within the university system. The hierarchy between institutions will become more pronounced. A small number of universities will qualify as national institutions. These elite corporate research universities will continue to attract both corporate and state funding as they become more specialized, yet still retain the character of the full university. Occupying the second rung are two parallel institutional categories that meet both provincial and specialized needs. The two categories are as follows: liberal arts undergraduate and provincial research universities. The third rung includes smaller provincial universities and the technical universities. The final rung is occupied by the relatively small number of university colleges and those with a religious affiliation.

The fourth change will be the higher level of competition for research funding and for students. The new academic industry liaison offices and research service units in our universities are but two indicators of this long-established trend. The new emphasis on marketing universities through the media with glossy brochures is the first major salvo in the new battle for student dollars. The international market seems particularly attractive. Fifth is the continuing decline of the public sphere. Universities will have less autonomy as they establish a closer and more accountable relationship with business and industry. The exchange relation between governments and universities has always been understated. As provincial governments become more directly responsible, we have noted obvious attempts at tighter control over university policy and more emphasis on the strategic needs of the province. Increasingly, profit will become a motive for action, as universities more consciously try to adapt to the needs of business and students. Sixth is the continuing bifurcation in the opportunity structure in the labor market. Universities will explicitly attempt to capture the "good jobs" market and the professional retraining market. The inflation of credentials will continue, so that more jobs will require a degree as a screen for entry. Finally, as a corollary to the previous point, universities will become more the preserve of the elites in our society. The existing relationship between socioeconomic status (SES) and participation in adult education will be reinforced (Fisher & Rubenson, 1992). We can expect to see a tightening of the tie between class and levels of participation in different levels of the system. The barriers to access will increase, so that people from lower SES backgrounds will be pushed into lower echelons of the system. The participation of females at the top of the hierarchy is in danger of dropping, as the lower-status semiprofessions such as nursing and teaching are pushed onto the lower rungs of the system. With less public regulation, the market will punish the weaker members of our society.

If we now turn to the internal life of Canadian universities, we can highlight four overlapping changes. First is a change in the culture of our university. Canadian universities are becoming more commercial and more entrepreneurial. The *bildung* part of our academic tradition, which emphasizes the cultivation of inward and external criticism and a "richness of mind and person," will be further undermined (Ringer, 1992). What might be called the "civilizing mission" of universities will be less central than in the past, except for a privileged elite. The current tendency of some university administrators to define liberal education as the vocational heart of the modern university might best be regarded as the modern version of "vocationalism of dominant groups" (cited in Wright, 1992, p. 219). It follows that the critical function of universities will also be threatened. The tradition of academic freedom has been tied to and colored by the profound distrust of utilitarianism and utilitarian forms of knowledge. With less "relative autonomy" guaranteed by the state, academics will take fewer risks.

Second is an intensification of the current trend toward organizational models that are bureaucratic, corporate, and directed to the market. As administrators become corporate managers and strive for more efficiency, we can expect certain costs. Our results confirm the conclusions drawn by Ball (1990), who claims that academics will experience the following changes in their work: an intensification of work practices, a loss of individual autonomy, closer monitoring and appraisal, less participation in decision making, and a lack of personal development through work. The division between administration and research will become wider. Third is an increase in the commodification of education leading to more internal differentiation by program. Differential fees, full cost recovery, and the establishment of programs for profit are all part of this trend. Finally, the increasing emphasis is on short-term individual experience at the expense of long-term collective contributions. According to the OECD (1993), this is the real danger of educational policy making in the 1990s, because the long-term contributions are often more indirect than direct and less easy to measure than by merely what it costs.

The most pronounced change in our universities is the continuing trend to more and more differentiation. This is occurring across the Canadian system between and within provinces. We can expect variations on the California Plan as the functions served by our higher education institutions are divided along lines of education and training, or "pure" versus applied/professional. The pressure to rationalize program offerings within the province will increase as provincial governments look for ways to save money. Although British Columbia is somewhat of an anomaly because provincial spending on the system has been maintained rather than reduced, we do see a very clear hierarchical division of labor. Similarly, we already see a greater degree of differentiation within our universities along the "teaching/research" divide. Universities have come to rely on part-time or sessional instructors to do much of the teaching work once done by tenure-track professors.

Privatization continues to be the overwhelming trend. Institutions are changing their practices to accumulate power. Our universities are becoming more corporate, more technocratic, more utilitarian, and far more concerned with selling products than with education. Jointly designing curriculum with private donors, the differentiation between teaching and research internally, and the reliance on non–tenure-track sessional or part-time labor are already established trends. Full cost recovery is a major theme. The marketing of programs at profit-making rates to foreign elites will become the norm. In short, the very essence of the university in Canada will change in ways that undermine some of the best parts of the tradition that emphasized national norms and public service.

REFERENCES

Abele, F. (1992). The politics of competitiveness. In F. Abele (Ed.), *How Ottawa spends, 1992-93*. Ottawa: Carleton University Press.

Ball, S. J. (1990). Management as moral technology: A Luddite analysis. In S. J. Ball (Ed.), *Foucault and education: Disciplines and knowledge* (pp. 153-166). London: Routledge.

Barlow, M., & Cambell, B. (1991). *Take back the nation*. Toronto: Key Porter.

Bourdieu, P. (1969). Intellectual field and the creative project. *Social Science Information, 8*(2), 89-119.

British Columbia Labour Force Development Board (BCLFDB). (1995). *Training for what?* Victoria: Author.

Clark, B. R. (1983). *The higher education system: Academic organization in cross-national perspective*. Berkeley: University of California Press.

Commonwealth Universities Secretariat. *Commonwealth Universities Yearbook* (Selected Years). London: Author.

Department of Finance, Province of New Brunswick. (1996). *Budget 1996-1997*. Fredericton: Queen's Printer for New Brunswick.

Eraut, M. (1992). Developing the knowledge base: A process perspective on professional education. In R. Barnett (Ed.), *Learning to effect*. Buckingham, UK: The Society for Research into Higher Education and Open University Press.

Fisher, D., & Rubenson, K. (1992). Polarization and bifurcation in work and adult education: Participation in adult education in British Columbia. *Policy Explorations, 6*(3), 1-19.

George, P. G., & McAllister, G. A. (1995). The expanding role of the state in Canadian universities: Can university autonomy and accountability be reconciled?, *Higher Education Management, 7*(3), 309-327.

Gouvernement du Québec. (1996). *The state of education in Quebec, 1995-1996*. Québec City: Author.

Government of Canada, Human Resources Development Canada. (1996). *Federal and provincial support to post-secondary education in Canada: A report to Parliament, 1994-1995*. Ottawa: Author.

Graham, P. A., Lyman, R. W., & Trow, M. (1995). *Accountability of colleges and universities*. New York: The Trustees of Columbia University.

Haddow, R. (1995). Canada's experiment with labour market neocorporatism. In K. Banting & C. Beach (Eds.), *Labour market polarization and social reform*. Ontario: Queen's University School of Public Policy.

Horry, I., & Walker, M. (1994). *Government spending facts two*. Vancouver, BC: The Fraser Institute.

Human Resources Development Canada. (1994). *Agenda: Jobs and growth: Improving social security in Canada*. Ottawa: Author.

Johnson, A. F., McBride, S., & Smith, P. J. (1994). *Continuities and discontinuities: The political economy of social welfare and labour market policy in Canada*. Toronto: University of Toronto Press.

McBride, S., & Shields, J. (1993). *Dismantling a nation: Canada and the new world order*. Halifax: Fernwood.

Mullay, R. (1994). Social welfare and the new right: A class mobilization perspective. In A. F. Johnson, S. McBride, & P. J. Smith (Eds.), *Continuities and discontinuities: The political economy of social welfare and labour market policy in Canada*. Toronto: University of Toronto Press.

New Brunswick Commission on Higher Education. (1993). *New Brunswick Commission on Excellence in Education*. Fredericton: Author.

Nova Scotia Council on Higher Education. (1995). *Shared responsibilities in higher education*. Halifax: Author.

Nova Scotia Council on Higher Education. (1996). *Government support of universities in Nova Scotia: A proposal for a new funding formula*. Halifax: Author.

Ontario Council on University Affairs. (1995). *21st annual report*. Toronto: Author.

Ontario Premier's Council on Economic Renewal. (1994). *Lifelong learning and the new economy*. Toronto: Queen's Printer for Ontario.

Organization for Economic Cooperation and Development. (1993). *Employment outlook*. Paris: Author.

Organization for Economic Cooperation and Development. (1996). *Education at a glance: OECD indicators*. Paris: Author.

Ringer, F. (1992). *Fields of knowledge: French academic culture in comparative perspective, 1890-1920*. Cambridge, UK: Cambridge University Press.

Scott, P. (1995). *The meanings of mass higher education*. Buckingham, UK: The Society for Research into Higher Education and Open University Press.

Smith, S. L. (1991). *Report on the Commission of Inquiry on Canadian University Education*. Ottawa: Association of Universities and Colleges of Canada.

Stanbury, W. T. (1989). Privatization in Canada: Ideology, symbolism, and substance. In P. W. MacAvoy, W. T. Stanbury, G. Yarrow, & R. J. Zekhauser (Eds.), *Privatization and state-owned enterprises: Lessons from the United States, Great Britain, and Canada* (pp. 273-329). Boston: Kluwer.

University Education Review Commission. (1993). *Post-secondary education in Manitoba: Doing things differently*. Winnipeg, Manitoba: Author.

University Program Review Panel. (1993). *Looking at Saskatchewan universities: Programs, governance, and goals*. Regina, Saskatchewan: Author.

Wright, P. (1992). Learning through enterprise: The enterprise in higher education initiative. In R. Barnett (Ed.), *Learning to effect*. Buckingham, UK: The Society for Research into Higher Education and Open University Press.

CHAPTER 5

The Service University in Service Societies

The Norwegian Experience

Arild Tjeldvoll

Norway has four research universities. The University of Oslo (UO) is the oldest of them, having just reached its 175th anniversary.[1] However, the next 25 years may hold even greater challenges than those faced in the previous 175. Changes in societal structure, relations to the international community, standards of living, and dramatic shifts in public expectations for education and research have consequences that can only be guessed.

The Norwegian government's recent policies on higher education are in accord with international trends that favor the market economy, decentralization, and greater accountability from public institutions. Universities are receiving signals that they should prepare for a leveling out of public support. These signals have been a catalyst for internal discussions at various levels.

Important clients in the Oslo region express strong expectations about using the research capacities of the UO for their purposes: for example, for internationally oriented businesses, for the Oslo Municipality Government's economic development work, and for the Norwegian Environment Protection Organization. But they find the UO to be "a closed door" and do not know how to identify what it might offer. They are hoping that the UO will soon start informing them. On the other side, the central leadership of the UO wants to provide the region with research-based services, but it faces two problems: (a) motivating their own production workers (the professors) and (b) not knowing what the regional clients want to buy. Prominent public actors in Norway generally support the central administrative leadership's policy of trying to carefully adopt a "service" orientation without harming the UO's position as a research university of quality.

How will the UO as a research community react to this policy direction? Following a brief summary of the Norwegian context, this chapter will seek to answer this question by drawing on a documentary survey and interviews with key leaders both inside and outside the university.[2]

CHANGED NORWEGIAN HIGHER EDUCATION POLICIES

Recent changes in higher education policy make up the new context within which the UO must now construct its future. These include:

1. Decentralization and differentiation. The recent decentralization of higher education in Norway has created a system with two parallel sectors: the university sector and the regional sector. Both compete for the same resources. The goal of decentralization is to develop an integrated knowledge network for higher education and research. The result is a clear division of activities: The universities are responsible for basic research and researcher education, and the regional colleges are responsible for professional education and applied research important to their region. Also, the nation's resources do not permit every institution to offer every program. A recent White Paper states,

> The goal for the further development of the regional college system is to make more of the regional institutions into national centers in special areas, so that the institutions can mutually benefit from each other. . . . The distribution of decision-making power must unite the need for national political control with the institution's academic independence within the given limits. (KUF, 1988, p. 22)

2. A common regulating framework. In 1996, a new law gave the universities, the scientific colleges, and the district colleges a unified legal foundation for the first time. A common frame of reference has thus been established for the regulation of student issues, as well as for the institution's internal management and organization (KUF, 1995a, p. 7). The new law delegates much power to the boards of the individual institutions (KUF, 1995a, p. 139).

3. Research coordination and funding. Predating efforts to rationalize educational programs, in 1991, the five foundations supporting research in distinctive areas were merged into a single national research foundation, among other things, to increase political influence on the distribution of resources (KUF, 1991). Also, the distinction between pure and applied science has been blurred by enhancing the interplay between basic and applied research and reducing the time between research breakthroughs and their practical application. Political authorities therefore consider it no longer useful to maintain an organizational divide between basic and applied research (KUF, 1991, pp. 51-52).

Consequently, universities are being challenged to find new ways of financing so-called free projects and recruiting researchers. They must compete with research institutions abroad to get the best researchers and to receive funding from the programs of the newly established National Research Council (UO, 1995c). Moreover, estimates of university funding are uncertain. In the past couple of years, universities have been granted more money to accommodate an increasing number of students. However, the increase in students has been greater than the corresponding increase in financial support. The UO expects that the latter will be temporary and that new activities will have to be financed largely through internal rationalizing and reallocation or through new sources of income (KUF, 1991). From this perspective, the reduction in funds distributed by the National Research Council is of considerable concern. A new model for the financing of research could also affect the UO's ability to use its academic staff for teaching and tutoring.

THE UNIVERSITY OF OSLO

How has the UO responded to these trends and the government's policy shifts? As though to defend itself against being seen primarily as an educational institution and being expected to increase applied research, its stress on pure research rather than education has been strong. Paradoxically, the educational aspect has been the government's criterion for support because funds are allocated to the university up to now on the basis of student enrollment. Moreover, an important backdrop to the changes in policy of both the government and the leadership of the UO is the historical legacy that research has been seen as an individual duty of the professor.

Generally speaking, the political authorities are expected to continue the national coordination of higher education within Network Norway. The new demands for national coordination, and especially for further standardization, could represent new challenges for the UO as it seeks to share in the distribution of activities within the National Network while maintaining its own academic standards and academic autonomy (UO, 1995c).

University Policies

The UO is responding on different levels to these challenges from government and from Norwegian society. At the macro level, the UO wants to play an active role in national policy making on research and education. The UO ought to use its large amount of knowledge to work for a better society. Highly specialized, technical knowledge increases the number of options for action, which forces the political and executive sectors of society to make choices. The goal-oriented use of knowledge to induce growth and prosperity gives less room for the long-term, non–goal-oriented obtaining of insight (UO, 1995c).

At an operational level, UO sees itself as having the most diverse research environment in Norway. It emphasizes both the preservation and development of academic breadth and the use of this diversity to promote cooperation between researchers and research students from different academic disciplines. To promote interdisciplinary cooperation, the UO aims to loosen the ties between the academic and administrative structures and also to convene new interdisciplinary forums. The UO wants to make it easier for faculty to divide their research and education time between different subjects according to their competence and interest.

These expressions are seen as a constructive response to the government's challenges. For the immediate future, the government has emphasized the following areas: researcher recruitment, basic research, applied research, and specifically research on environmental issues. Of the four, the government especially stresses the importance of the technological part of basic research and applied research, because these forms of research are important to create new jobs, to foster economic growth, and to secure the nation's future revenues. The government also wants to give research in the humanities a high priority (UO, 1994a).

An essential part of the country's research potential is accumulated in the Oslo area. This is seen to facilitate an extensive cooperation between the UO, businesses, cultural institutions, and various public offices. The UO aims to play a key role in this cooperation (UO, 1994a). The present priorities of UO may be simply summed up as (a) to continue doing what has been done up until now, and (b) to do more applied work in order to meet the needs of the society.

Governing Structure

Norwegian higher education institutions have an elaborate decision-making system for educational and administrative matters. On the other hand, the decision-making system for research is not as well developed. As a result, research often suffers, especially during periods when, or in fields where, there are high student-staff ratios.

A characteristic common to governing systems in the university sector is the colleague-based decision-making structure at each level—central, faculty, and department levels. Each level's governing system has an academic leadership with a parallel administration. It has been argued in many studies that too much time is spent on detail at the top level while the departments do not have enough freedom to make the necessary decisions at the operative level (UO, 1995b).

In general, the UO is very democratic, and every level can find clear directions in the law. Organizational changes at the UO in the 1970s brought about a transition to a system where all groups of employees, as well as the students, came to be represented at all levels. Elections are held for all important academic positions at least every third year. All boards and councils are constituted in a way that ensures that all groups are represented when important decisions are made. Administrative positions are permanent, with job security similar to that of the tenured professors. In 1996, UO employed 1,238 professors (499 full professors) and 400 part-time academic teaching personnel. Technical and administrative personnel (librarians included) fill 1,691 positions.

So far, there are no clear indications that service is an important criterion for hiring either academic or administrative personnel. This is a crucial observation. Whatever the positive phrasing about the service function found in the policy documents, it remains to be seen whether this attitude will materialize in the job descriptions.

Academic Degrees

The Norwegian doctoral degree program in the humanities and social sciences is organized differently from that of most other countries. Compared with the Swedish Faculty of Social Sciences, there is a difference of two years in the required time to reach a Ph.D. During this period of internationalization, this relative lack of compatibility with most other countries' systems of higher education is increasingly putting pressure on UO in terms of student exchange and research cooperation. In fact, the Faculty of Social Sciences is now participating in a European experiment with a study program for an international master's degree. Because offering educational programs (e.g., M.A./Ph.D.) to foreign students might be one of the future products that could create new revenues, a streamlining of the degree structure might be one important measure to create budget accountability and cost-effectiveness. Such programs would also be an efficient way of tapping the solid competence in the use of the English language found among all faculty at UO. So far, the academic plans are traditional and do not use UO's full potential for creating more tailor-made teaching programs for clients of the region.

Institutional Research Policies

At the present time, the UO does not have a research program of its own. As a whole, the university has primarily been concerned with the task of education, with research being left to individual faculty members. The general work contract for scientific positions says, "for the institution as a whole, and over the course of a year, the distribution of time should be 50% on research and 50% on education. The time spent on administration should not affect this distribution principle." This formulation allows for more flexible use of the total scientific labor force. However, in practice, almost every single faculty member follows the standard time distribution and spends much more than 50% of his or her time on education activities. Neither department, faculty, nor central level has been able to use the flexibility intended in the work contract. Therefore, when specific research interests have come up, normally from circles within the UO, the solution has been to create a research center.

A number of such centers exist within the university. The five independent ones are the Biotechnology Center in Oslo; the Center for Development and the Environment; the Center for Women's Research; the Center for Technology and Culture; and the Norwegian Institute of Human Rights. The Faculty for Medicine has several centers. Within the Faculty for Law is the Center for European Union Law. The Faculty for History and Philosophy and the Faculty for Social Sciences both have two centers; the Faculty for Mathematics and Natural Sciences has its Center Component for research.

Hardly any of these centers can be said to have been established from a service perspective. Generally, they were created to attend to "pure" research interests or else have arisen out of a strong social policy orientation, such as human rights issues. Data from the Finance Division at the central administration of UO give the following figures for 1994 and 1995. Total revenue in 1994 was $350 million, of which $55 million came from external and service-oriented activities, which is 15% of the total revenue for 1994. In 1995, the total revenue was $415 million, of which externally funded activities provided $81 million or 20%. This is a substantial increase. Comments from an informant in the Finance Division suggest that this might be partly due to pressure from the central level for more effective reporting of departments' external activities and revenues. The increase both in service-based revenue itself and in the central level's interest in departments' external activities may be seen as indicators that the service university movement has reached Oslo. Yet an assessment by deans and department chairs stipulates that their staff's average earnings from informal or out-of-duty activities (moonlighting) approximates $6 million.[3]

Reduced Funding From the State?

The university today faces a historically new situation. The establishment of the Norwegian Network for Higher Education and the new Research Council structure, on the one hand, clearly leads the

UO in the traditional direction of pure research and education. But, on the other hand, the UO has received more freedom to create its own research policy. An openly stated goal for the UO is to put more of its attention on industry and business. However, at present, little or no information about concrete plans for such activities exists centrally at the UO. Furthermore, the government describes its own research policy and long-term investments as follows: "The Government will give research a high priority, but wants to emphasize that new funding should primarily come from private sources. The public support should be used to initiate more extensive private investments" (KUF, 1991).

The UO's central administrative leadership is already sensitive to the new financial reality. At the same time, the leadership recognizes the growing pressure from demands on teaching. Reduced public support for independent research projects is thinning out the resources available for research. To improve this situation, the UO wants to (a) critically evaluate its internal resource allocation with the aim of freeing resources for research, (b) go through internal priorities and cooperate with the authorities to modernize the equipment in the experimental disciplines, and (c) strengthen the effort to obtain external project funding, especially from the European Union's research programs. Furthermore, the UO stresses that it should emphasize actions that improve the research environment, such as strengthening academic leadership at the departmental level and stimulating cooperation on larger projects or long-term programs (UO, 1995c).

The Broader Research
Context of the University

Norway's universities are all supported by the Ministry of Church, Education, and Research, but most strategic issues affecting the university are decided by the university's board. The 1996 law assigns new responsibilities to the board, particularly stressing that of the development and execution of a strategic research plan. This represents a change from the previous situation, in which the university had no institutional research policy and, instead, responded to the initiative of individual faculty and outside agencies. In that this law requires universities to take greater responsibility for their finances, it is expected that the UO will exercise greater initiative in clarifying its research goals.

In devising a research plan, the university has to take account of the research policy at the national level, as devised by the Parliament, the government, and the ministries. The government's research committee mildly coordinates the research policies. In 1988, the Research Policy Council was dissolved, and since then, Norway has not had a specific council dealing with research policy. All ministries are responsible, in principle, for the research in their sector, but the interpretation of what this means varies greatly among them. The most important research ministries are the Ministry of Church, Education, and Research and the Ministry for Industry and Business (KUF, 1991). Other important connections are the Ministry of Foreign Affairs and the Ministry of Social Welfare. The National Research Council provides funding for many research projects, and its decisions are also an important part of overall research policy.

The Research Park, Inc., is a company owned jointly by UO, other research and educational institutions, research institutes in the Oslo area, the City of Oslo, and a number of larger industrial companies. It has 31 private and public shareholders, with UO being the single-largest one. Its purpose is to put ideas and results from the research environment to use and to facilitate increased cooperation between research and industry. More of the resources in the research system are used to promote renewal and increased growth in Norwegian business and industry. The company is responsible for the leasing and daily management of the research park in Oslo and the development of the center. Its users can be grouped in three categories: industry, research institutes, and newly established businesses. Newly established businesses are located in an innovation center, where there are suitable buildings and the necessary service and support functions (Forskningsparken, 1994).

The Partner Forum, originally a cooperative venture between the private Business Administration and Management Institute and the UO, has recently involved new partners from the public sector. So far, eight public offices have joined, and each pays an annual membership fee of $11,500. These partners are the Ministry of Administration, the Ministry of Children and Family Issues, the Ministry of Finance, the Ministry of Defense, the Ministry of Environmental Issues, the Pollution Control Agency, the Directorate for Public

Management, and the National Social Security Service. With money from these institutions, the UO and the Business Administration and Management Institute seek to solve problems posed by the members.

UO also has limited arrangements with large partners, such as the petroleum companies Hydra and Saga. But the most important connections between UO and other institutions are those initiated and maintained by individual researchers. Researchers meet at conferences, and these meetings often lead to cooperative agreements for individual projects that usually involve the university in a formal contract (UO, 1995a).

INDICATIONS OF DEVELOPMENT
TOWARD A SERVICE UNIVERSITY

Strong academic environments tend to attract the best researchers and the best students, and hence to have the best results. Also they have the best chance of receiving funding from external sources. UO clearly wants to be an institution in which curiosity and free thinking are legitimate reasons for conducting research, a place that gives its researchers the opportunity to try out new ideas or challenge commonly accepted truths. In principle, the UO expects society (taxpayers) via the government to make this possible without forcing the researchers to try to generate revenues by offering services to clients of the region. Nevertheless, it is clear that the desire to find better solutions to practical problems may be an important motivating factor for research and that research can contribute substantially to the accumulation of material wealth, as well as improving the quality of life. The UO takes the position that it is possible to combine its responsibility to protect the free search for knowledge with an active involvement in putting research results into practical use (UO, 1995c).

In cooperation with the National Research Council and the Research Park, among others, the UO wants to facilitate the transformation of its own research results into new products and practical solutions (UO, 1995c). The UO's long-term strategy ought to be "to play an active part in the research co-operation in the Oslo area." The Oslo Area Research Foundation (FOSFOR) and the Research Park represent interesting forms of cooperation with business, industry, the city, and public institutions; the two institutions have the ability to facilitate considerable growth in the total research effort in the Oslo area (UO, 1987).

On the one hand, the leadership of the UO is obviously concerned about its service function. It wants to direct resources for research toward business and industry, and it realizes that it is necessary to move out and compete for external funding for research. But to date, it is difficult to see any substantial initiatives in this area. The term *service function* is rarely heard. Instead, phrases such as "research directed toward industry" or "externally financed research" are used. Concrete action in this area is usually in conjunction with cooperation projects where the Research Park, Inc., plays an important part.

Adult education programs as well as psychiatric and dental clinics offer regular services for users and clients outside the UO. The treatment of patients is a necessary part of the education for these disciplines. However, the question naturally arises: Does the UO make a profit from this activity? The answer is simply no. The fees charged by the clinics cover only the cost of the materials used. The rest of the clinic's expenses are covered by the institution.

A structural expression of service is the Science Store, an initiative by the student committee at the Faculty for Social Sciences. In this store, organizations, businesses, and research institutes can "buy" research services from the students. The Science Store has become a popular clearinghouse, where clients with evaluation or investigation needs meet with advanced degree students (Norwegian *hovedfag*) who are interested in doing their empirical work in a related area. The revenues involved vary up to one, two, or three semesters of full salary for doing the field studies and report writing. Sometimes, the arrangement will also involve a student's supervisor and also imply some payment for him or her (ISO, 1995, p. 104).

So far, it seems fair to conclude that the UO has taken two steps related to the idea of service within a university. First, in policy, the necessity of taking initiatives to create new revenue is clearly acknowledged. Second, the UO has taken direct action through forming public research foundations that expect to do applied research for regional clients while using the university's scientific manpower. The traditional nonprofit services are still provided (e.g., odontology and psychology). The most visible new action in this field is the one taken by students who organized the Science Store. Also, it is fair to believe that moonlighting by (market-attractive) faculty has increased, not least because of the relative decrease in professors' salaries. In sum, the service function is still essentially latent at the UO.

ACADEMICS, CLIENTS, AND SERVICE

The policy documents issued by the UO and referred to above express clear intentions of offering services to the region. But policy documents are only formalized opinions. What about the personal opinions of the main actors in the UO? To what extent are their views consistent with the policy documents? And what about the clients' views? How are the service ambitions of the UO experienced on the clients' side, and what are the structural conditions necessary for the UO to implement its policy goals regarding service to the region?

Views From Inside

There are differences between what key actors see as the UO's service function at present and what it ought to be ideally. This variety is found both within the central leadership and between the different levels of the university structure.

General statements from all respondents at the central level confirm that UO already is part of, or on the point of joining, the international trend of creating more autonomous financial conditions for the traditional research universities. This acknowledgment is followed by positive expressions from all respondents at central level regarding the necessity of an active investment of energy in the service function. One of the central leaders stated it is "extremely important" for the university "because we are dependent on external revenues in order to keep up the existing level of activities both regarding research and teaching, and even regarding some of the administrative support services." Successful investment in the service function is seen as crucial for keeping up real university autonomy in the future.

One reason for stressing this policy now is that the UO leadership has been given clear messages from the national political authorities that grants from the state will be stagnating and even decreasing, because the demand for higher education is expected to level out. For the UO to fulfill its legal obligations of being part of and serving "the knowledge society," the university has to be innovative in finding new sources of revenue. If it is not successful in this matter, the UO might see its legitimacy at risk in the future. Two possible sources of new revenue are seen to be of particular importance: to tap European Union sources and to sell services to Norwegian corporate life in general and to the Oslo region in particular. It is evident, given the size of UO, that there must be a huge unused potential for commissioned research and services for its region. If the university is not successful in finding new financial sources, the consequence might be a reduced level of activities, in both the traditional pure research and teaching programs.

Although these views and assessments of the current situation of the UO are consistent with the policy documents referred to previously, a more restricted, not to say slightly reluctant view is also expressed within the central leadership. Acknowledging the coming necessity of finding new sources of funding, leaders simultaneously stress that such sources ought to be limited in size and "should not affect the independent research"; "it is the strength of the university, that we do not govern our researchers," and "the single researcher has complete autonomy, and nobody should interfere in what a researcher chooses to research." The function of the university leadership is to inform the researchers about needs expressed by external institutions and actors and to encourage scientific staff to respond to these needs. These rather reluctant views in relation to the service idea are expressed by the Rector. Central administrators claim that it is necessary to be more active in developing the service capacity—the "market value"—of UO. To find new sources of revenue is simply necessary to be able to keep up the traditional autonomy. The political framework has changed. However, university budget policies ought at the same time to be very careful not to become too vulnerable to the quick shifts of market forces. This is a difficult balance to keep.

Out of the eight faculties, five deans, two pro deans, and one faculty's Chair of Research Committee were challenged to assess the principle of moving toward a service university, the institutional consequences of such a development, and the steps that might be taken to find out about regional clients' needs. Of these key actors, three were definitely negative to the principle, four expressed a neutral attitude and one was positive. In summary, their reasons for being against a service development were the following: It would develop a negative working environment, with rich and poor colleagues; there would be less leisure time for the faculty; and pure research and research-based teaching would be threatened. The four neutral deans saw two possible tracks of development. External activities, selling of research-based services, might strengthen the general work of the university. Then "going service" would be a good development. On the other hand, if a service development would harm the traditional character of the university, then they would be against it. The neutral deans seemed to see a service development as positive if it would be under clear academic control. Given this, the UO ought to take the offensive and actively go out into the region and the country and make its services visible for its clients.

The positive view at the faculty level is first pragmatic, and then more principled. The selling of services gives important extra money to the faculty. This activity promotes good contact with both public and private clients. Without service-selling opportunities, the faculty might risk losing its most talented professors, which in a short time would harm the faculty as a research institution. Looking at the internal conditions of the UO for this new challenge, it is claimed that some of the faculties already have a more developed apparatus to handle services. The general lack of an administrative instrument, a marketing department at the central level, is the main hindrance to enabling faculties to take up profitable service activities. While taking into account that, at the department level, there are mixed opinions about this issue, to say the least, this sort of organizational development is seen as a crucial task. The UO, as an operating organization, has to play a much more active role in relation to external funding agencies, such as the Research Council of Norway. The university must be visible as something more than a number of interesting individuals; it must become an accountable organization, led like other organizations that have an aim, that become visible as agents having something to offer to clients or customers. Then something in return—revenues—may be expected. The UO needs an apparatus in its own structure to take care of this function. One dean wondered why there seemed to be an absence of thinking about effective policy for the university as an organization in its own right.

Eight department chairs were interviewed, one selected from each faculty. Three of them wanted to be anonymous. Four were negative, three were neutral, and one was positive. The one positive toward the principle of service belonged to the faculty with a positive dean. The seven others all had a view different from their dean. If the dean was negative, the department chair was neutral, and the other way around. The negative and neutral arguments, respectively, were the same as found for the deans. The negative chairs claimed that this was not really a question for university initiative. It would be the clients of the region that had to take the first step.

Except for the one positive chair, both the negative and the neutral respondents were fairly outspoken in their reluctance to promote the principle of service. The UO should not, in any significant manner, move away from its traditional role of pure research. The individual researcher should continue to have the right to decide what to research. The negative chairs held that pure research and money making can never coincide at a research university. At the department level, it is taken for granted that the main function of a research university is research, pure research. For this purpose, society via its government is expected to pay. Such activities can never find a market that will make them financially profitable.

Listening to voices at the department level, it is easy to notice contradictory opinions between different levels at UO regarding what the service function is, what it ought to be, and what would be its consequences. Differences of opinion are also found concerning what should be the accountability of a research university. Most representatives at the department level have not registered any directives from central or faculty levels about any new situation requiring new external sources of funding, or that the service function has become of importance for the university as a whole. As one department chair expressed it, "There have been a lot of fashion and buzz words about what the [UO] now ought to do . . . which has luckily carried very little meaning for our reality." Although both central level and some faculty level actors express concern about contact with clients of the region not being good enough, the department level expresses the least interest in fostering relations between regional clients and the UO as an organization.

Summarizing the most important findings revealed by the interviews, one might conclude that the written plans to a large degree have ritual value. They represent a written confession to a new funding agenda of the 1990s and beyond. The sense of ritualism is created by the contradiction between what is declared as necessary action, for example, in the field of offering services, and what is actually seen as proper follow-up actions. The contradictions are found within the central leadership and between the levels. One of the faculty-level respondents had the sharpest perception of the schizophrenia and danger of this situation—if proper attention is not given to the financial needs of the UO as an organization, in view of the new way of framing university finance, the legitimacy and future autonomy of the institution may be threatened.

The data seem to illuminate a somewhat shaky university policy toward its organizational conditions. Why? The proper understanding of the situation and the necessary actions are clearly visible in the policy documents and the oral expressions of the central leadership. These seem to represent the rational analysis of the UO in its regional and national financial context. Contradicting this rationality is the tradition of seeing the university's main task as pure research, and what is pure research is decided by the individual researcher at the department level. The governing structure of the UO as a whole seems still to be a function of this tradition. The department-level individual scientists still seem to have the decision-making power to defend and keep up their traditional position. The higher levels of the governing structure seem mainly to have administrative and ritual functions for the UO as an organization. The new agenda of external funding has so far not reached the production workers—the professors at department level. As long as the funding situation does not negatively hit daily life among professors at this level, it is not likely that there will be new awareness about the necessity of finding new revenues.

So far, the organization development strategy of the central level seems to have worked mainly as an attitude campaign. Well-written policy documents and program speeches to selected audiences of professors, students, and administrative personnel have been carried out, with the expectation that these messages would be understood by the professors and result in actions in favor of common university goals and strategies to improve the financial context. But so far, there are few indications that the department level has been influenced by this campaign. For the time being, the central level seems to be lacking real executive power on behalf of the university as a whole. As long as fairly generous grants are continuing to flow in from the state, and the local level professors retain the most effective control of these resources, there is likely to be little reason for implementing a shared, goal-oriented, institutional policy for the UO as a whole.

Regional Clients' Expectations

What are the service expectations of important clients in the Oslo region toward their university? As part of the study, the following were selected as important representatives of the clients: the Oslo Department of the National Employer Association (NHO), the Norwegian Environment Protection Association, and the Oslo Municipality Government. Centrally positioned executives of these three organizations gave their opinion about the present situation and future need of services from UO. All three claimed that the general contact with UO was poor and that this was a matter of serious concern. A common view of the three is that they do not know "which door to knock on" at UO. The university is seen as a closed and distant institution. No active public relations are seen to be initiated by the university. The clients see their interests and the university as "two different worlds."

The clients indicate that in the past several years, they have become increasingly sensitive to where they may buy knowledge-based services within the region. Several other research-based environments in the region have shown a lot of interest in the new needs of actors, such as business and industrial companies, for research-based information. Those other research institutions are actively reporting their possible contributions. The UO is not seen as being actively informative about its available services.

Regional institutions mentioned as examples of importance for these clients are the Agricultural University at Aas, the Research Foundation at Kjeller, and the Eastern Region Research Foundation (Oestlandsforskning). Institutions outside the Oslo region seen as actual sources of research-based services are the Research Foundation of Rogaland (Rogalandsforskning) and SINTEF, Trondheim. These institutions are telling clients of the Oslo region about what they can offer. UO is not. A respondent expressed his wish: "I would like to see a contact forum where we could meet—enterprises with development and research needs—and universities with their knowledge environments."

Another respondent clearly states that the responsibility for initiating contact has to be with the university. "The [UO] is the superior and powerful actor. It has to invite us for communication in a way that creates credibility among us as customers." The representative of the Environment Protection Association expressed a critical opinion about the UO's role, in the area of nature protection and knowledge about nature, energy, development, and the environment. The UO seems to have abandoned the cross-disciplinary and applied orientation in which it previously was strong. But such an orientation had more promise for attacking practical problems. From an environmental protection point of view, there is an urgent need today for creating cross-disciplinary environments within the UO in order to meet the need for applied knowledge production made necessary by huge environmental problems.

Summing up, the interviewed clients seem generally aware of a future where research-based services will be increasingly important for success in their activities. They also have a clear expectation that UO could provide services relevant for their needs.

Well-Known Public Actors
in Favor of Service Development

To illuminate the Oslo case from angles other than those of the UO and the region, some actors, seen as important representatives of Norwegian public opinion on higher education, were asked to give their views on the principle of the service university.

Steinar Stjernoe, president of Oslo College (the fourth-largest higher education institution in Norway), holds that taking into consideration the increased pressure from the society and the current financial factors of Norwegian universities, it will not be possible for them to stay away from external activities required by business life and public authorities. However, it would be a pity if the university's responsibility for basic research in the long term should be reduced, because external service activities became a dominant part of the university's total activities.

Inge Loenning is a professor of theology at the UO (and has also been a former president of UO, national campaign leader of the Pro-European Union Movement, former member of the National Research Council, and a prominent conservative politician). Loenning does not see any problem with the selling of research-based services, within certain limits. It is positive if clients find competence at UO of interest. The alternative would be that clients' needs would be directed toward the sector of institutes established for applied research in particular. It is generally assumed that research competence is best in the university environment and that the quality of research-based services would be best when carried out by the university. A common concern in relation to this issue is negative dependence of the clients, their possible influence on the research process, and, in the worst case, "influence on the results." Generally, this is a bigger problem for the institutes of applied research and consultancy companies. However, UO participates in international debate and critique. Dubious research at the university will always be brought to light.

Dag Kavlie, director at the Norwegian Research Council, Department of Strategical Planning, confirms that the service university movement has also reached Norway. From the point of view of the National Research Council, constructive cooperation between the research universities and the sector of institutes for applied research is the ideal. Direct contacts between UO and regional clients are also seen as positive, given that these are not done solely for pure commercial reasons. The UO is expected to continue being a stronghold of pure research.

Frode Onarheim is president of the Norwegian Institute of Business Management (and former president of the Norwegian Employer Association). The Institute of Business Management is a nonpublic higher education foundation, which has now established formal cooperation with UO. Onarheim claims that it is healthy for an institution to be capable of taking responsibility for its own financing. To be sensitive to market needs may give new impulses and stimulate creative thinking within any organization. Taking for granted the qualities of institutional autonomy, it looks, however, like the UO could be even more sensitive to the rest of our societal system. A minor part of the activities of the UO ought to be exposed to market judgment. That way the professors and researchers would get more direct impulses to do research on topics of great interest for our nation.

CONCLUSION

Formally and administratively expressed opinions by the central level leadership of UO seem to indicate that more active efforts will be made to offer knowledge-based services to its region and to the nation. But these opinions of service policy are weakened when the central leadership elaborates this issue. Both faculty and department leaders are split in their assessment of the service approach. Comparing their positions to the attitudes found at the central level, roughly half of the respondents may be seen as supporting the reluctance of the rector, whereas the other half are pretty much on line with the central level administration.

How are these findings to be interpreted? Are the statements of the political and administrative bodies just an epiphenomenon of the 1990s? Do they express a market rhetoric reflecting the general change of ideological climate in the direction of liberalization, privatization, and market economy? Or do we face indications of changed frameworks that might have serious long-term effects on the role and function of the autonomous university in the division of labor in society?

Political and administrative pressure toward a service university model could be an effect of changed power relations both within the university and between the university and significant actors outside. If such changes have taken place, they would most likely be the result of an interplay between different political forces. Historically, the Norwegian university via its faculty has maintained a strong autonomy vis-à-vis the political and administrative state and corporate life.

There can be no doubt that during the past ten years, the state has tried to increase its control over the universities considerably. Due to a series of legal acts passed in this period, the universities are now integrated into a national planning system and a higher education network, with the aim of standardization and increasing efficiency. This is a distinct political move toward more centralized power over the universities. At the same time, decentralizing of decision making in some areas has taken place. The universities now have the mandate to appoint professors, and as shown in this study, budget responsibility is being transferred to the single institution. However, it may be questioned whether decentralization measures like these have favored scientific autonomy or the opposite. Institutional autonomy does not necessarily mean scientific autonomy.

Looking at the university as an institution, it can be seen that at least two organizational changes may have altered the balance of power in decision making against independent research and for a service university development. First, in the name of democratization, the composition of the governing bodies has changed. Once, the senior professors had the real say; now, all bodies have a functional representation, including academic staff, administrative and technical staff, research fellows, and students (both undergraduate and graduate). These groups have different frames of reference and different agendas when discussing and deciding on university, faculty, or department policies. Since 1996, external representation (from the spheres of state bureaucracy and corporate life) on university boards has been required. At present, this representation may not be significantly influencing the decision making, but the symbolic effect is quite obvious. According to the political authorities, external representation on university boards is a means to make the universities more accountable to the problems of real life. When these two measures of democratizing the decision-making bodies of the university are seen in relation to the changes in the budgetary system, it seems fair to assume that the powerholders of the political, administrative, and corporate spheres may be paving the way for the service university.

Corporatist influence on changes is a typical phenomenon of many political arenas in Norway. However, such influence has up to now been next to absent in the field of higher education. In neighboring Sweden, it is obviously quite different. There, corporatist influence has been heavy on higher education, as well as in other fields. Why has this been different in Norway? A tentative answer would be that the professors socialized in the Danish-German university tradition have not had their autonomy challenged until recently. In that respect, such a culture has hardly made it natural for the trade unions of people working within the university to seriously try to affect university policy making. The unions have normally not involved themselves in other areas than working conditions and wages. As part of the government's efforts to centralize and integrate higher education and research into a single more efficient tool for the nation's overall interests, corporatism may now also be affecting the sector of higher education.

Summing up, two types of power relations have been changed. Internally, the administration, other employer groups, and external representatives have reduced the professors' role and power in decision making. Second, the state has taken much clearer command of higher education policies, through legislation and budget guidelines. These changed power conditions seen together suggest that Norwegian universities may be carefully moving in the service direction. The unanswered question is, however, how will the traditionally strong scientific labor force of the universities—the tenured professors—react strategically to these pressures and the changed central level policies affecting their traditionally autonomous territories?

The Norwegian situation is rather open. Norway is different from many other countries today, particularly in two respects. First, the country has a favorable economy due to its oil. This makes budgetary constraints less problematic than in most other countries. Second, the position and status of the autonomous university is still strong in the population at large. Both of these factors could slow down the development in the service direction and could even counteract it.

The paradox that observers of Norwegian university development are left with consists of the double effect of changes frequently justified by the norm of democracy. On the one hand, internal changes reducing the power of the scientists in favor of students, administrative/technical staff, and external groups are claimed to be important measures in creating a more democratic university, both internally and in relation to the rest of the society. On the other hand, reducing the influence and power of the scientists of the universities means reducing the capacity for independent critique of the political, administrative, and corporate powerholders in society. This may reduce democracy in society at large.

NOTES

1. In 1994, the UO had a budget of $285 million. In comparison, the budgets for the University of Bergen, the University of Trondheim (NTNU), and the University of Tromsoe were $164 million, $198 million, and $105 million, respectively (KUF, 1995b). The total number of students at the UO was 36,000 in the fall of 1994. The total number of students in Bergen was about 17,500; in Trondheim, 17,700; and in Tromsoe, 7,000. At the undergraduate level, 12,684 examinations were recorded at the UO in 1994. At this point, admission to most programs was restricted. The UO admitted 6,000 out of the 29,000 students who applied to one of the undergraduate programs.

2. The data collection for this study is based on two main strategies; document analysis and open-ended interviews with key actors of the UO and the region, as well as some prominent public opinion actors. The policy documents reviewed are (a) legal acts about Norwegian universities and higher education, the Ministry of Education's White Papers preparing the acts and amendments to acts, and budget proposals from the Ministry of Finance; (b) annual reports, policy documents/strategic plans, and working papers from the UO; and (c) the UO's internal paper, *Uniforum*, for 1995. In this paper, debates on the role of the UO in general and its "efficiency project" in

particular have revealed opinions by ordinary faculty and key actors within the university system.

3. It ought to be stressed that this amount is not necessarily reliable. The informants stressed their uncertainty about what was going on. Based on several other bits of information, a fair hypothesis would, however, be that the actual amount of moonlighting is substantially higher than the reported amount and percentage.

REFERENCES

Forskningsparken, A. S. (1994). *Aarsberetning 1994*. Oslo: Annual Report of the Research Park, Inc.

ISO (Department of Sociology, University of Oslo). (1995). *Notat nr. 3 1995 hovedfagsguide* (Working document No. 3, 1995—Guide for advanced degree students). Oslo: University of Oslo.

KUF. (1988). *NOU 1988, No 28 Med viten og vilje* [By knowledge and will]. Oslo: Author.

KUF. (1991). *NOU 1991, No 24 Organisering for helhet og mangfold i norsk forskning* [Organizing for totality and plurality in Norwegian research]. Oslo: Author.

KUF. (1995a). *Lov av 12. mai 1995 nr. 22 om universiteter og hoeyskoler* [Legal Acts of May 12, 1995, No. 22—on universities and higher education]. Oslo: Author.

KUF. (1995b). *Stortingsprp. nr. 1 95-96* [Parliament White Paper No. 1, 1995-96]. Oslo: Author.

UO. (1987). *Perspektiver mot Aar 2011* [Perspectives towards the year 2011]. Oslo: Author.

UO. (1994a). *Aarsplan 1994* [Annual plan 1994]. Oslo: Author.

UO. (1994b). *Aarsrapport 1994* [Annual report 1994]. Oslo: Author.

UO. (1995a). *Aarsplan 1995* [Annual Plan 1995]. Oslo: Author.

UO. (1995b). *SODA-rapporten* [The SODA-Report]. Oslo: Author.

UO. (1995c). *Strategisk plan 1995-99* [Strategical plan 1995-99]. Oslo: Author.

NOTE: In Norway, documents written by organizations are usually referenced by the acronyms of these organizations. In these references, KUF refers to the Ministry of Church, Education, and Research, and UO refers to the University of Oslo.

CHAPTER 6

The Last Decade of Higher Education Reform in Australia and France

Different Constraints, Differing Choices, in Higher Education Politics and Policies

Richard DeAngelis

Higher education institutions, especially universities, are remarkably international, diverse, flexible, adaptive, and enduring phenomena (Organization for Economic Cooperation and Development [OECD], 1987, pp. 7, 91). Very few cultural inventions of the European medieval period have persisted so continuously and so long. Very few have been so widely adapted and adopted globally, across traditional barriers of time and space. Universities, ideally, balance many competing claims: tradition and conservation with creativity and intellectual contention; universal and objective standards with the values of local and national communities; institutional autonomy, academic freedom, and "truth-seeking" for its own sake with service to society, economy, and polity. Universities do all this more or less well, in different ways, in differing systems, with different names and rules. But they also maintain a robust capacity to protect their own self-constructed identities against outside threats, despite internal squabbling that can take the form of anarchical but collegial interchanges.

Globalization is a relatively recent concept, referring to a variety of socioeconomic and cultural processes that seem, increasingly, to integrate diverse local and national entities into a single global whole (Albrow, 1993, p. 248). Over the past decade, a hegemonic version of globalization has stressed the empirical dominance of neo-classical economics and ideologies (in Australia, so-called economic rationalism), as well as the commanding and competitive pressures of the global financial and production markets.

Most policymakers in the OECD countries, with varying degrees of enthusiasm, have accepted the reality of such pressures, at least in trade, industrial, and macro-economic policy. Some endorse laissez-faire liberalism and market capitalism both externally and internally and across all policy sectors. Some attempt to foster but also regulate or guide market activities. Others accept external, international, free market liberalism but compensate with interventionist domestic policies as much as possible, especially in welfare and labor market areas (Katzenstein, 1985; Lijphart, 1984). Increasingly, if unevenly, both right-wing and left-wing governments have engaged in major restructuring and reform, to the benefit of central bureaucracies and strategic policymakers, at the expense of government public outlays and protected economic sectors (Schwartz, 1994, pp. 528-531, 553).

Not surprisingly, the same trends are increasingly apparent in higher education policies. These have shifted emphasis dramatically from the 1960s to the 1980s. Most have moved away from generous, government-funded, and planned higher education expansion along democratizing lines and toward cost-cutting, privately funded, market-driven agendas with slower expansion and diversification plans. However, in this policy sector too, there are crucial divergences of policies, such as in the areas of student fees, degree of government funding and control, internal higher education management structures, curricula and pedagogic innovations, quality, and social equity (OECD, 1990).

Australian higher education policy is not unique in paying increasing attention to global economic pressures and opportunities or to domestic pressures for the new market principles (e.g., austerity, "user pays," efficiency, and accountability). Australian policy is rather unique and unprecedented, however, in the suddenness, the scope, and the degree of reversal of previous policies and the vigor that characterizes the revolutionary reform process begun in 1987 by the then-Minister for the Department of Employment Education and Training (DEET; a new and enlarged department), John Dawkins (1988). Similar trends have continued or accelerated under subsequent ministers, even after a change of government in early 1996.

> Dawkins' broad policy objectives [were] four: ... to raise participation in higher education and to widen access to it ... ; to improve institutional efficiency and effectiveness, and to increase the responsiveness of institutions to Australia's economic and social needs. ... Our institutions ... have ... been pressured to conform to policies laid down by the central government; ... they have generated much uncertainty and many tensions, and some have done great damage. However, they have produced some positive results and established conditions which will facilitate deregulation, ... to free our universities ... so that they can entirely manage ... their own affairs. (Karmel, 1992, pp. 55, 70)

Dawkins was a key player in the wider, ambitious government policy framework for major socioeconomic change. This process deliberately began to reverse and reconstruct the inward-looking, regulated, and protectionist Australian Settlement of 1900, the uncontested grounds of public policy for three generations (Kelly, 1992). (See Chapter 2 by Dudley for discussion of the settlement.) Instruments of change were policies of internationalization of the economy; tariff reductions; enhanced exports and trade, especially in the Asia-Pacific region; bureaucratic managerialism; and reductions in government programs and spending.

In higher education, Dawkins pursued a micro-economic reform agenda to harness the sector to "national needs." He overturned previous Labor policy and reintroduced student fees (only partial fees for Australians, paid by deferred, indexed Higher Education Contribution Scheme loans, but full fee recovery for an increased number of foreign students). He also abolished the expert-policy buffer organization, Commonwealth Tertiary Education Commission (CTEC), and exerted greater direct and strategic government control on university specialization profiles while devolving operational and managerial responsibility and implementation to institutions. Finally, he very strongly "encouraged" mergers for efficiencies and economies of scale and significantly expanded student places, while steadily cutting per capita operating grants. And all this without major public or electoral controversy. More recent policy guidelines from Australia's Higher Education Council (HEC) identified current and future characteristics of the context in which universities will operate, including the following:

- increased application of public sector reforms;
- ongoing pressures for performance or output-based funding;
- greater constraints on the amount of public funding available;
- increased competition and contestability;
- restructuring of the workforce and other economic reforms;
- ongoing pressures for retention of diversity . . . to cater to all groups;
- potential for changed regulatory environment; and
- impact of communications technology. (HEC, 1996, p. 16)

Prior to Dawkins's revolution, the Australian higher education system had operated on a very different consensus: a collegial, arms-length-from-politics, internationally privileged, high-quality, free, and publicly funded education ideal. Thus, all these changes constituted a real shock for most in higher education.

Government reformers argued, however, that such changes were inescapable and in line with global trends and necessities; "free education" for all who qualified and protected autonomous higher education systems were no longer viable or practical. Alternative strategies, other than those of the United Kingdom or United States, which were predominately laissez-faire and market-oriented, were not seriously considered. It is at least plausible that some of the difficulties inherent in such a massive change, obsessively focused on government fiscal restraint, could have been avoided if other models had been canvassed. Although the Australian system is still in many ways an enviable one, it has undoubtedly lost some of its preeminence and quality in recent years, perhaps because of excessive adherence to neo-classical economic theses, justified as necessary by globalization. The French, however, have taken a different path in response to the same pressures, suggesting that alternatives are possible.

In the same period in France, with the exception of more student places, the trends and policies are almost totally the opposite: free education for all and no unmet student demand; greater decentralization of administration and more university autonomy; creation of new, stand-alone campuses and the continuing breakup of older mega-universities; increasing government resources and steadily rising standards of pedagogical practice and innovation; and continuing public controversy and interest group mobilization. Such substantial differences deserve to be explored to test the limits of the uniformity of the globalization hypothesis.

This chapter argues that although the forces of globalization are often seen as qualitatively new, inevitable, constraining, and leveling (and especially reinforcing a neo-classical, smaller government paradigm across the developed capitalist nation-states), there are very real limits to such forces. Thus, there is considerable scope for diversity and choice in policy responses, both within and across different political systems. In short, globalization is still susceptible to countervailing trends and resistance. Other factors that can influence these globalizing processes are local traditions; bureaucratic/policy networks and shared habits, knowledge, and familiarity; interest group mobilization; policy creativity (or ineptitude); and coalition construction and political calculation (often involving values such as social justice and equity, public order, and cultural quality, identity, and ambition). The Australian and French examples are, in many respects, nearly polar opposites in political system, politics, and higher education policy reform. They illustrate the considerable diversity and resistance to globalizing uniformity in a critical sector of evolving cultural traditions.

GLOBALIZATION

Some commentators view the power of globalization as unique to these times and quite strong, as the following quotes indicate:

> The serious diminution of the power of individual nation states over fiscal and monetary policies . . . has not been matched by any parallel shift towards an internationalization of politics. (Harvey, 1990, p. 305)

> The G7's role has dwindled . . . partly . . . due to new factors, including the consensus which says that "globalization" has removed the power

of governments to steer their economies. ("Can the G7 Ride Again?", 1996, p. 76)

The contribution of the [National Commission of Audit] report is to provide an intellectual framework for evaluating the efficiency and effectiveness of government programs at a time when the public sector is coming under increased pressure from . . . demographic change and rising expectations . . . and intensifying global competition to attract capital . . . (Mitchell, 1996, p. 4)

Within an increasingly global context, Australian universities carry out a multi-faceted role . . . the international context focusses attention on new challenges. . . . The globalization of communications and transport . . . and the growing interdependence of countries and regions have brought increasing recognition that the world needs people who can operate across national boundaries. (Australian Vice-Chancellors' Committee, 1992, pp. 1-2)

For Francis Fukyama (1992), world history has consistently exhibited a teleological purpose; it has now reached its "end" in the global spread of liberal-democratic capitalism. For international relations theorists such as Hedley Bull (1977), the twentieth century has seen the uneven and hesitant but cumulative emergence of world society, an increasingly global set of dense interchanges and shared experiences, values, and moral codes. Other international relations theorists speak of international interdependence and global "regimes" that regulate arms control, finance, trade, migration, environmental problems, and financial and economic activities (Keohane, 1989).

Economists of a determinist bent, of both left and right, speak of a world system or global economy with emergent properties and a causative structure of its own (Wallerstein, 1974). Thus, in Australia, we read of "the recession we had to have and the relentless competitive pressure from the global marketplace" (McCrann, 1996, p. 23).

Clearly, all these phenomena suggest the plausibility of the generalization that there is a complex if eclectic reality in fields such as economics, technology, communications, politics, and culture that can be referred to under the concept of globalization. At the same time, it is also clear that the term *globalization* has acquired a mythical (frankensteinian?) life of its own in recent years (Holton, 1996). Like other useful but ambiguous concepts, such as *modernity* and *postmod-*

ernity, globalization as a concept can be both a misleading, analytical shortcut and a dangerous caricature for normative evaluation. Too often, it suggests determinist, impersonal forces that eliminate political or economic alternatives, as argued in Margaret Thatcher's slogans: there is no alternative; There is no other way (Barry Jones, 1995, pp. 13, 15, 101, 256). Too often, there is confusion (or fusion) of different ideas of globalization (as description, analysis, prescription, and/or method) and, even more, between different levels (financial, productive, technological, civil, cultural, political), with the economic and normative discourse given undue prominence.

Although global forces and structures constrain choices of agents, it is rare for such globalization processes to be so strong and unrelenting, so uniform and all-pervasive, as to eliminate diversity, resistance, and different policy processes and outcomes (Gourevitch, 1986; Moore, 1966; Scharpf, 1987). In fact, it seems that the greater the external global context, the more likely that compensatory and offsetting processes may be provoked by subjects seeking to protect local identities and cultural or political investments (Harvey, 1990). For example, the small, liberal-democratic capitalist states of Western Europe have for several decades offset their integration into the global market by developing compensatory welfare and political protections for their citizens (Castles, 1988, 1996; Katzenstein, 1985). These differences can be systematized. In contemporary politics, for example, we can distinguish several alternative types: liberal/pluralist, statist/mercantilist, and consensual/neo-corporatist, for example. In higher education policy, there are similar choices: market/economic rationalist, managerial/bureaucratic, and collegial/democratic (OECD, 1990, pp. 10-11).

Moreover, the link between globalization and neo-classical economics and a particularly austere, financial, cost-cutting form of policy is often unnecessary and counterproductive. Furthermore, in the main, it is practiced in only some (especially Anglo-Saxon) political economies in any pure form, and even there is rarely successful for very long (as John Major, George Bush, and David Lange/Roger Douglas have learned through political rejection).

Globalization, therefore, can be a useful but also a slippery concept. It can help to remind us of a new and as yet imperfectly achieved level of commonality and shared fate across national and cultural borders. However, it can also too easily be employed as an irresistible force that causes and explains all, without contradiction or contest.

At one level, university life has always been inherently global, universal, and cosmopolitan, at least as compared to other social institutions, allowing constant interchanges of personnel and ideas across boundaries of time, space, and types of knowledge. But, at the same time, universities are repositories of tradition and culture; they conserve knowledge and habits and are therefore also inherently conservative. Language, culture, religion, and knowledge are multiple, complex, and diverse, and thus, higher education institutions are never merely a network of ivory towers responsible to each other and themselves alone, but they are also socially embedded structures with particular local and national contexts. There is no reason to suppose that such cultural richness and openness to novelty and creativity will ever be eliminated by global uniformity.

In this instance, Australia and France illustrate some of the range in higher education policy and structures of universities. Both are liberal democratic, capitalist, and affluent, and both have experienced the expansions of elite systems of higher education into mass systems, with many similar problems. However, instructive differences remain.

A COMPARISON OF FRENCH AND AUSTRALIAN SYSTEMS OF HIGHER EDUCATION

Similarities in Higher Education

France, a unitary state, and Australia, a pluralist federation, despite some quite significant differences, are alike in being leading members of the OECD club of affluent, postindustrial, liberal democratic, advanced capitalist societies. Their higher education systems also share many characteristics. Both have created "mass" systems of higher education in just over forty years. They started from very small, select, male, upper-class elite student and staff populations and traditional, classical, humanistic, and even proudly "ivory tower" pre-World War II starting points. Their systems expanded more or less systematically, but in cyclical bursts of effort, under both left- and right-wing governments. Ironically, much of the biggest growth spurts in both countries occurred in the 1950s and 1960s under modernizing conservative intellectuals, Charles De Gaulle and Sir Robert Gordon Menzies.

In both nations, pressures have existed for a variety of conflicting ends in their higher education systems: social mobility and equity, economic modernization, and vocational and professional training, as well as traditional concerns for cultural conservation, teaching, and research. Resources usually have not fully kept up with student numbers, needs, or rising expectations and capital requirements—especially in France (Jallade, 1991; OECD, 1990). However, in both (although until only recently in Australia), most students have usually had to pay only a very small fraction of the administrative costs of their education; and employers in both countries pay very little toward the cost of higher education. The bulk of university financing has traditionally come from central and/or regional public authorities. For many years, both governments believed that more and better education was affordable, desirable, and a necessary investment in human capital (Marginson, 1993).

Currently, pressures for further tertiary expansion persist in both countries, as pools of potential students widen to include mature age, female, and disadvantaged students. Higher education has broadened its curricula and diversified teaching methods to cater for more diversity, more applied and interdisciplinary programs, and new subjects (especially the more commercially and professionally relevant). Its systemic structures, therefore, have become more complex, multilayered, and difficult to coordinate, partly due to the considerable autonomy of most units of teaching and research and the wider participation by staff, students, and outside "stakeholders" (Perkins, 1972).

Both Australia and France have also increased high school retention rates to very high levels (about 80%) and recruit to higher education overwhelmingly via impersonal national or statewide public exams (Matriculation, Baccalaureat), which technically constitute the first level of attainment at university studies. Although both have democratized their access considerably in absolute numbers, neither has succeeded in doing so relatively, particularly with respect to rural, ethnic, or working-class minorities. Thus, there is reason to expect further growth in student numbers, unless public expectations for social mobility change dramatically.

Unfortunately, for students who might appreciate them, neither country has a widespread tradition of green fields and live-in campuses, for full-time students with an intense and nearly self-sufficient student life, as in the United Kingdom or the United States. Instead, French and Australian universities are predominantly urban or suburban/commuting in orientation, with staff and students isolated from each other and among themselves. Both systems are controlled by national and subnational bureaucracies and emphasize *equal status* and *national degree equivalence*, keeping competitive and market pressures (although growing) still in a subordinate role.

In both, most institutions, and the respective systems as a whole, are internationally perceived as ranking high in quality, with considerable appeal for foreign students (and much more student movement into than out of the country). Yet, the universities are also relatively monolingual, often aggressively so. Both systems prize, and usually practice, a healthy amount of academic freedom. Yet, despite their internationally comparative virtues, both systems are marked by controversy and complaints of conservatism, malaise, and crises; the difficulties of reform; and the contradictions of balancing the traditions of academia with the claims of the market and the state for training, relevance, and efficiency. Finally, neither is particularly good at integrating its activities with apprenticeship or technical training agendas.

Differences in Higher Education: Structures, Policies, Politics

France's higher education system differs, however, from Australia's in many aspects, reflecting different historical inheritances, differing policies, and divergent political dynamics, making Australia's system much more egalitarian, malleable, and amenable to a reform process, when firmly and skillfully conducted. Ironically, the relative ease of recent reforms may be to Australia's long-term detriment if, as argued here, it has adhered too strictly to an excessively global, small-government form of change.

Higher education change, especially university policy, has been a highly contentious and politicized issue for over thirty years in France. By contrast, in Australia, until only recently, higher education policy has rarely been discussed by nonspecialists, political parties, or the general public. French students have traditionally taken leading roles in French political life, much more so than in Australia. In May 1968, student groups provoked massive student street protests, strikes, and occupations of the universities. This wave of protest nearly sparked a "new kind of revolution" politically and socially (DeAngelis, 1985), when students triggered the massive strikes and events of May as nonstudents and workers also joined in the struggle against the Gaullist regime. The 1968 protest also led to the major university reforms of the eminent Education Minister Edgar Faure, to open up, democratize, and modernize the system (which passed parliament unanimously).

Implementation of the Faure reforms, however, was uneven, contested, and less than satisfactory. Subsequent and spasmodic reform attempts from on high to rationalize, restrict, restructure, or make the system more selective and efficient have, so far, invariably failed, except at the margins. In fact, education and higher education ministers have almost become an endangered species. Periodically, riots or mass demonstrations under different ministers of education (as in 1984 under Pierre Mauroy, 1986 under Jacques Chirac, or in 1993-1994 under Edouard Balladur) have often forced humiliating government backdowns. As a result, student fees are still very modest, and students still have a right to enter a university if they pass the baccalaureat, without formal selection. Most of the funding and controls are still by grants from central public authorities in Paris. Pressures for equal treatment and resistance to market pressures and competition are very high, and the themes of globalization, smaller government, economic rationalism, and laissez-faire are minority phenomena and seen as politically dangerous, even on the right. The recent referendum on the Maastricht Treaty to strengthen the European Union via monetary integration deeply divided the French. It was passed by a narrow majority, with a large minority rejecting the more global economic perspective assumed to be a part of the treaty.

Thus, the diverse attitudes of students and staff (representing both conservative and leftist anti-capitalistic viewpoints), belief in educational entitlements, and also contested government policies have made and continue to make the higher education system of France very different in some key respects from Australia's, despite global pressures from the markets. Undoubtedly, many of the same factors explain why France's level of government spending in gross domestic product (GDP) (at about 45%) is much higher than Australia's, which is at a comparatively low level (about 30%) for an OECD affluent democracy ("What the Taxman Takes," 1993, p. 81). Ironically, it is in the low-spending Australian community that tax reductions and small government are dominant themes of public debate, with little effective dissent.

Other aspects of the uniqueness of France lie in its historical development. The higher education sector is much more diverse than in Australia. In addition to old and prestigious institutions, such as the Collége de France and the various specialized scholarly *instituts* and academies, there are also the Napoleonic legacies of the largely state-run *grandes écoles* (usually for the civil service professions of applied science, school teaching, administration, and management), which nearly monopolize the recruitment paths into the highest segments of French society. Only a small percentage of the higher education students are admitted into these great schools, after one or two years of special preparatory classes in select high schools with highly competitive exams (where only a tenth of candidates succeed in gaining a place). The rewards for graduates are guaranteed success, prestigious placements in state jobs at graduation, and privileged-for-life positions in society for closely knit alumni networks. Generous funding and staffing set these schools apart from the rest of the struggling university sector (Ardagh, 1982).

Furthermore, the French basic research effort, which is quite substantial, is concentrated in a separate national institution, the *Centre National de Recherche Scientifique* (Marginson, 1993, p. 138). Finally, a network of quite successful University Technology Institutes, drawing on the separate stream of technical high schools, coexists with the much more wasteful, inefficient, and underresourced general university institutions. Thus, paradoxically, despite its formal federalism, Australia's higher education system is probably much more uniform and unified than the French system. That system is entrenched, and its unequal structural diversity has always been controlled by the highly centralized bureaucracy in the unitary state, run from Paris, with little scope for local experimentation in pedagogy or entrepreneurial activity.

The French system, at its best and for most students, is of high academic quality, especially in engineering and theoretical areas (such as philosophy, mathematics, science, and history), with considerable scope for individual opinion and academic freedom and creativity. Oral presentation, organization, and writing skills are highly prized and developed. New exchange programs within Europe, such as ERASMUS, have opened up the previously excessively French-centered academic system. Fortunately, pedagogic innovation, increased resources, and a more participatory and consultative style of reforms seem to be the order of the day in France. The trend is clearly toward a looser, more decentralized system of more autonomous and responsible and innovative university institutions, which can begin to emulate the successes of the more manageable University Technical Institutes (IUTs) and "great" schools. Also, foreign students can still study in France virtually for free.

However, the French system is still in need of major improvements. It is overstretched, scandalously overcrowded (with staff-student ratios as high as 1:60 in some areas), excessively unequal, rigid, without enough sports or accommodation facilities, excessively theoretical and highly competitive, wasteful and inefficient in the first two years (where nearly half fail in large lecture classes without tutorials), and unnecessarily contentious and divisive. Academics in France, since 1968, no longer have to prepare two theses, one in Latin; but they still are overwhelmingly civil servants, whose nationality must be French and whose appointments are made or approved in Paris. Certainly, the balance between its good and bad features is very different from that in Australia, and its policy making and politics have prevented the kinds of economic rhetoric and managerial reforms that John Dawkins and his successors succeeded in bringing about in Australia. In spite of its problems, the French system seems to be improving, heading in the right direction, whereas the Australian system since Dawkins seems to be unnecessarily losing some of its previous strengths and advantages.

CONCLUSION

Many of our [U.S.] universities are very good, but they are hardly perfect. They lead the world . . . because their counterparts abroad possess still greater failings. Even in the most advanced countries, universities are typically overcrowded, overregulated, undercompetitive, and underfunded. . . . Most of the charges [against universities] are . . . flawed because they ignore basic contradictions in the demands society makes on universities. (Bok, 1990, p. 59)

The massive changes under way [in Australia] are evident and will incur some costs. . . . International experience suggests that everywhere the current transition to a mass from an elite higher education system is fraught with tensions and frustrations. (Marceau, 1993, p. 36)

In a period of decline, resource allocation decisions become more difficult, participation is intensified, decisions are complicated by considerations of equity and entitlement, and morale plummets in declining organizations. . . . governments tend to . . . denial and simplification, . . . to externalize and transfer the problem, . . . they feel a need to act, sometimes embarking on a "policy making stampede." (Pratt & Silverman, 1988, pp. 114, 116)

Comparisons of these two higher education systems highlight considerable similarities, as well as vast differences, in inherited policy choices and outcomes. France's higher education system represents a different set of choices and constraints than Australia's. Although neither can simply transplant particular features or policies from the other in isolation, there are modest lessons each could learn from the other to make the best of differing circumstances. Both could also widen their intellectual horizons to include comparisons with other similar systems, especially in the OECD, such as the German experiences with binary higher education and apprenticeships; Dutch generosity in student spending levels; Swedish policies of decentralized administration, additional local government funding of higher education, and mandatory language requirements for students; or creative American traditions of combining public and private sectors and balancing collegial and managerial modes of governance within university institutions (OECD, 1980, 1990).

The French could certainly profit from many Australian and British traditions: a higher level of funding per student; lower staff-student ratios; more pastoral care and pedagogic intimacy, accountability, and innovation; a greater diversity and equality of treatment of different kinds of students; more sports facilities, autonomous institutions, and vigorous student activities. In sum, a more informal, pleasant, flexible, and less wasteful university experience has been the goal of recent and increasingly bipartisan reform proposals by dynamic French Education Ministers, socialists Lionel Jospin and Claude Allégre, and centrist François Bayrou. At the same time, by looking closely at the costs of Australian reforms to quality and morale, the French might also be reinforced in their distrust of an excessive emphasis on cost-cutting, market competition, and economic rhetoric at the expense of cultural and democratic agendas.

The Australian system could certainly benefit from a broader, truly global, and comparative understanding of the full range of options practicable in public policy and especially in higher education, instead of limiting its thinking primarily to one set of models (United States, United Kingdom, New Zealand) and one ideology (economic rationalism/managerialism). From France, despite the very great differences in history, structure, and political dynamics, Australia could learn that very small government and penny-pinching on per student funding is neither inevitable nor without long-term cost; that successful reforms can be very difficult and require time, respect, and consultation; and, most of all, that a desirable higher education system requires diversity, balance, and continuity with the best of a nation's own experience and history.

Over a generation, after World War II, Australia created a remarkable achievement in its higher education system, especially for such a new, small, and peripheral country. By most world standards, and despite its limitations, it was well funded, international in scope and staff, arms-length from political demands, balanced and diverse in goals and types of autonomous, self-governing institutions, innovative and high quality in research and teaching, and open, on merit, to increasingly large portions of the total population.

Narrow and extreme views of globalization pressures can make the maintenance and improvement of this system very difficult, and especially so if governments endorse a low-tax, austerity, and managerial/bureaucratic approach while also insisting on the goals of a rapidly expanding student body in a system of internationally competitive quality. However, such global pressures can also be reacted to in different ways—resisted or compensated for—rather than being employed as an excuse for narrowing the policy agenda and imposing an ill-thought-through agenda, instead of more sensible and consensual long-term reform (DeAngelis, 1992, 1993, 1996).

REFERENCES

Albrow, M. (1993). Globalization. In W. Outhwaite & T. Bottomore (Eds.), *Blackwell dictionary of twentieth century social thought* (pp. 248-249). Oxford, UK: Basil Blackwell.
Ardagh, J. (1982). *France in the 1980s: The definitive book.* Harmondsworth, UK: Penguin.

Australian Vice-Chancellors' Committee. (1992, May). *Australian universities in a changing world*. Canberra: Author.

Barry Jones, R. J. (1995). *Globalization and interdependence in the international political economy*. London: Pinter.

Bok, D. (1990, May-June). What's wrong with our universities? *Harvard Magazine*, pp. 44-59.

Bull, H. (1977). *The anarchical society*. London: Macmillan.

Can the G7 ride again? (1996, June 22). *The Economist*, p. 75.

Castles, F. (1988). *Australian public policy and vulnerability*. St. Leonard's: Allen & Unwin.

Castles, F. (1996). On the credulity of capital: Or why globalization does not prevent variation in domestic policy-making. *Australian Quarterly, 68*(2), 65-74.

Dawkins, J. S. (1988, July). *Higher education: A policy statement* (White Paper). Canberra: Australian Government Publishing Service.

DeAngelis, R. (1985). France, May 1968: A new kind of revolution? In D. Close & C. Bridge (Eds.), *Revolution: A history of the idea* (pp. 203-221). London: Croom Helm.

DeAngelis, R. (1992). The Dawkins revolution. *The Australian Universities Review, 35*(1), 37-42.

DeAngelis, R. (1993). Funding the Dawkins' revolution in higher education: The first five years—policy, problems, prospects. *Flinders Studies in Policy and Administration*, No. 9, 43 pp.

DeAngelis, R. (1996). Universities. In A. Parkin (Ed.), *South Australia, federalism, and public policy* (pp. 217-230). Canberra: Federalism Research Centre, Australian National University.

Fukyama, F. (1992). *The end of history and the last man*. London: Hamilton.

Gourevitch, P. (1986). *Politics in hard times: Comparative responses to international economic crises*. Ithaca, NY: Cornell University Press.

Harvey, D. (1990). *The condition of post-modernity*. Oxford, UK: Blackwell.

Higher Education Council (HEC). (1996, May). *Tenth report to the National Board of Employment, Education, and Training (NBEET)*. Canberra: Department of Employment, Education, Training, and Youth Affairs (DEETYA).

Holton, R. (1996, June 6). *Four myths about globalization*. Flinders University Professorial Inaugural Lecture, Bedford Park, South Australia.

Jallade, J.-P. (1991). *L'enseignement supèrieur en Europe: Vers une evaluation des premiers cycles*. Paris: La Documentation Francaise.

Karmel, P. (1992, Autumn). The Australian university into the twenty-first century. *Australian Quarterly*, pp. 49-70.

Katzenstein, P. J. (1985). *Small states in world markets: Industrial policy in Europe*. Ithaca, NY: Cornell University Press.

Kelly, P. (1992). *The end of certainty*. St. Leonard's: Allen & Unwin.

Keohane, R. (1989). *Power and interdependence*. New York: Scott Foresman.

Lijphart, A. (1984). *Democracies*. New Haven, CT: Yale University Press.

Marceau, J. (1993). *Steering from a distance: International trends in the financing and governance of higher education*. Canberra: Australian Government Publishing Service.

Marginson, S. (1993). *Education and public policy in Australia*. Cambridge, UK: Cambridge University Press.

McCrann, T. (1996, June 21-22). For single-minded fiscal crusaders, a trap awaits. *Weekend Australian*, pp. 55, 58.

Mitchell, A. (1996, June 24). NCA report signpost on the road to recovery. *Australian Financial Review,* p. 4.

Moore, B., Jr. (1966). *Social origins of dictatorship and democracy.* Boston: Beacon.

Organization of Economic Cooperation and Development (OECD). (1980). *Educational policy and planning: Goals for educational policy in Sweden.* Paris: Author.

OECD. (1987). *Universities under scrutiny.* Paris: Author.

OECD. (1990). *Financing higher education: Current patterns.* Paris: Author.

Perkins, J. A. (Ed.). (1972). *Higher education: From autonomy to systems.* New York: International Council for Educational Development.

Pratt, J., & Silverman, S. (1988). *Responding to constraint: Policy and management in higher education.* Milton Keynes: Open University Press.

Scharpf, F. (1987). *Crisis and choice in European social democracy.* Ithaca, NY: Cornell University Press.

Schwartz, H. (1994, July). Small states in big trouble: State reorganization in Australia, Denmark, New Zealand, and Sweden in the 1980s. *World Politics, 46,* 527-555.

Wallerstein, I. (1974). *The modern world system.* New York: Academic Press.

What the taxman takes. (1993, March 13). *The Economist,* pp. 70-72.

PART III

GLOBALIZING PRACTICES: CORPORATE MANAGERIALISM, ACCOUNTABILITY, AND PRIVATIZATION

Jan Currie
Janice Newson

Parts I and II provide theoretical and empirical mappings of the social, political, and economic changes associated with globalization. They focus on the manifestations and effects of these changes within local institutions as well as entire national systems of higher education. They expose assumptions that underlie the model of globalization that has recently come to dominate higher education policy discourse in most nations across the world. They display this model as a historically grounded political and economic project that is being promoted by particular agents to serve particular interests. They suggest that globalization should not be conceived as a single, logically coherent package of social, political, and economic changes, leading inevitably to a more advanced stage of human history. Rather, globalization should be seen as a more fluid and less determinate process that has often contradictory and contingent sets of possibilities.

Part III addresses the question of how these changes associated with globalization are being brought about in the historically divergent national systems and local institutions of higher education. What are the concrete social, political, and economic practices that bring them into being? After all, public policy statements, position papers, and even the pronouncements of the most economically and politically powerful lobby groups do not leap from the page directly into material reality. Moreover, many of the changes that are described in Part II involve fundamental changes in higher education practices and orientations that have not been publicly debated, either on a national scale or in local institutions. Nevertheless, they are being accomplished, if on a piecemeal basis, in a broad range of national and local arenas. In Part III, we explore the practices through which these changes are being accomplished. We move from the macrolevel policies to the microlevel analysis of practices within institutions. The three practices we investigate are managerialism, accountability, and privatization.

Managerialism represents more than the expansion of administrative personnel in universities and more than a style of leadership. It involves entire institutions in new ways of conceiving of and accomplishing their business: indeed, of defining its activities in terms of business rather than of education. Managerialism represents changes in practice that have a profound impact on the nature of higher education itself. There is evidence that in many countries, the increased emphasis on managerialism in higher education rose to prominence in the mid-1980s and has been implemented in many universities in the 1990s—for example, in Canada (Newson, 1992), New Zealand (Fitzsimons, 1995), the United Kingdom (Middlehurst & Elton, 1992), Europe (de Boer & Goedegebuure, 1995), and Australia (Angus, 1994; Bessant, 1995; Meek, 1995). The decline in collegiality has appeared in direct relationship to the rise in the corporate reforms facing universities. Presidents and vice-chancellors no longer think of themselves as "first among equals" or as operating through consensual leadership (Karmel, 1991; Yeatman, 1993) but as chief executive officers of corporate enterprises with multimillion-dollar budgets (Brown, 1996).

As these various studies demonstrate, managerialism has been central to a very significant transformation in the practices and structures of locally based institutions of higher education. Universities in Third World countries are being transformed because of the economic stringencies applied by the World Bank. The World Bank's (1994) higher education paper suggests that universities change their governance to be managed more autonomously, rather than controlled by central governments. It urges governments to adopt more indirect, incentive-based policies for managing higher education systems. Marceau (1993) describes this type of relationship between government and universities as "steering at a distance." This also links management of universities with the use of certain accountability measures, such as performance indicators. Institutions are made to compete for funds, and this gives managers a greater rationale for managing without consultation, stating that they need to act quickly to be able to better position their institutions within the new competitive environment. In the Australian context, Rees (1995) has described managerialism as an ideology in which financial accountability should be the criterion to measure performance, managers should be given room to manage (most often in secrecy), and other groups should accept their authority. Yeatman (1993) has identified in greater detail the characteristics of corporate managerialism that have invaded Australian universities:

> The Vice-Chancellor becomes the Chief Executive Officer of a higher education commercial enterprise. His or her job is to . . . get the employees of this enterprise to perform at an optimal level, not to bestow on them his/her collegial respect. The committee system is replaced by a system of centralized executive management combined with devolution of budgetary management to the School or Faculty level. This means that Deans of Schools/Faculties become the equivalent of a branch manager. . . . Their job now becomes one of monitoring the performance of the academic staff in their unit in relation to standardized performance criteria produced by the centralized executive management level of the university. (p. 5)

Corporation managers are also thought to "bracket" their values and to follow the lead of more senior managers (Watson, 1994). They aim to be good team members and adopt the firm's values as their own. This notion of the "organization man" is well portrayed by a senior manager at Murdoch University, who described those who don't get ahead as those who don't want "to be on the team . . . their goals are so tiny that they can't see the global picture." This senior manager's analogy of the university also shows the new emphasis on management as where the action is: "I sometimes find myself looking at the analogy of this university to an Australian Football League match—there are 36 players, and there's a few reserves on the bench, and 20,000 spectators watching the game." He went on to say that the players were management and the academics were the spectators, often "whistle blowers" calling the bad plays that impeded managerial imperative. He identified the main university business as what the managers were doing and the chancellery as the center of the university, where all the action was, not teaching and research, which have been considered the core activities of universities since their inception.[1]

Jan Currie and Lesley Vidovich, in Chapter 7, "Micro-Economic Reform Through Managerialism in American and Australian Universities," describe the process of dwindling collegiality in six case studies of American and Australian universities. They note the use of similar practices in these six universities: the restructuring of universities into larger divisions with the appointment of executive deans, the widening gap between management and academics, the increased salaries of managers, and the lack of trust that has developed and continues to develop between managers and academics. In the responses in both the United States and Australia, there was no doubt that decision making was becoming more managerial. These changes appeared to be getting worse, rather than better. The group that was seen as the most powerful in these universities was the senior management group. Currie and Vidovich call for greater debate within universities about the kind of governance needed for the twenty-first century.

It is clear from this chapter that the move to create more autonomous, entrepreneurial universities has been accompanied by a move to managerial governance. This may be necessary for the competitive environment of neo-liberal societies, but it does challenge the conception of a university as a community of scholars. It also raises questions about the extent to which this new market orientation of universities stimulates creativity in the pure search for knowledge and the extent it generates critical thinking about society in general. It makes the universities more accountable to governments in a financial sense, but it appears that governments do not demand any accountability in terms of how democratic universities are or how they function, beyond being economically viable. This also suggests that rather than operating in a free market undeterred by government regulation, universities are in a managed market where the government acts as an intervening player.

Closely related to the development of managerialism in universities is the increasing adoption of performance-based measurements and assessments of quality, designed, ostensibly, to render higher education "more accountable." As Claire Polster and Janice Newson argue in Chapter 8, performance indicators and quality assessment are technologies of management that provide the basis for linking local institutions national and global networks of control—enabling the steering at a distance that Marceau (1993) describes.

Chapters 8 and 9 explore this relationship between globalization and accountability. They provide us with another window through which to view processes of change that are associated with, or are interwoven as strands of, globalization itself. Both chapters proceed from the view that the various strategies of applying accountability practices to academic work and academic workers are based on a conception of accountability that draws meaning from the discourses identified in Parts I and II—discourses such as economic rationalism, neo-liberalism, and vocationalism. Both chapters argue that this conception of accountability can be neither assumed nor taken for granted. In fact, they demonstrate in some detail the extent and nature of the debate that has been taking place over the meaning and relevance of particular conceptions of accountability to academic work and over the ways it should be practically implemented. These two chapters therefore make a strong case for concentrating scholarly inquiry on the political agendas that are attached to the quest for accountability, rather than on debating and refining definitions of the term itself, and for analyzing accountability practices, not in terms of their technical qualities or as measurement fads of the moment, but rather as social and political mechanisms for advancing the objectives and values of these agendas. Most important, the two chapters together illustrate an important theoretical proposition that runs throughout this book. That is, that globalization does not constitute a unidirectional, invariable, and unalterable package of social, economic, and political changes, as much literature by advocates and critics alike tends to imply.

In Chapter 8, Polster and Newson maintain that the relationship between the variety of political agendas currently at play in higher education policy and globalization is contingent. They consider three domains in which accountability practices in the form of performance indicators are currently under development: the local-national domain, the international domain, and the knowledge-workers-in-general domain. Rather than focusing on "real" or confirmed effects of accountability practices in these domains, they construct their discussion around the possibilities that are brought into play simply by the development of performance indicators: that is, by the convergence of interests via new organizations at the national and international level, the development of data collection capacities and measurement technologies, and the expansion of professional specializations. For example, whether or not it is currently taking place, they argue that performance indicators make it possible to standardize aspects of academic work, such as teaching styles and formats, and through standardization, to classify institutions within national and international ranking systems. Also, they foresee the possibility of creating and ultimately imposing international regulation over the mobility, pay scales, certification standards, and so on of academic workers, in much the same way that such regulations have begun to exist for other kinds of workers.

Polster and Newson argue that performance indicators should be analyzed as conceptual technologies that help to accomplish a reorganization of the social relations of academic work. Moreover, they conclude that the scope, range, and complexity of the social technology that is emerging around performance indicators, along with other globalizing practices, point toward an emerging globalized knowledge industry. However, although this is a possibility, given the current intersection of social, political, and economic forces, they insist that its realization in the material world remains fluid and is subject to intervention. The political and economic interests that are actively promoting this development are not monolithic. For example, Polster and Newson point to emerging tensions between managerial forms of corporatism and entrepreneurial forms of corporatism in higher education. They conclude their chapter with a discussion of strategy, outlining some of the ways that the divisions, inconsistencies, and contradictions within the constellation of forces currently promoting performance indicators can be exploited by politically active social agents who are concerned about their negative effects on higher education.

In Chapter 9, Lesley Vidovich and Jan Currie focus on the implementation of accountability practices in Australia since the Dawkins' educational reforms of the mid-1980s. They document not a fixed process that moves into institutions straight off the policy page, but rather one that is open to contest, reformulation, and even resistance, and thus a process that must "negotiate" its intended results into existence. For example, even though operating in a similar economic climate, and even though advocating a similar package of microeconomic reforms in order to maximize Australia's global economic competitiveness, two governments over the past decade adopted different approaches toward accountability. Whereas the Dawkins' approach of the 1980s—much like the approach taken in Britain by the Thatcher government—represented an aggressive, government-led strategy that proposed to tie the funding of institutions to performance-based quantitative measurements, the Baldwin approach that followed was more cautious about relying on quantitative measures or on using funding as a lever for securing the desired institutional changes. Baldwin displayed a more subtle touch and greater shrewdness in his attempt to make accountability practices "palatable" to academics who were concerned about maintaining professional autonomy, implicitly acknowledging that academics were not entirely ineffectual or without power in the face of government initiatives. Also, Vidovich and Currie's account shows how members of an "elite group of university administrators" (Bessant, 1995) can be instrumental in attempts to secure academics' compliance and cooperation. They serve as a pool of bona fide members of the academic community who can be strategically placed on committees that are advisory to the government to satisfy demands for consultation and to formulate approaches that can claim the marks of an academic viewpoint even though they fundamentally advance the government's position.

Finally, Vidovich and Currie's case studies of three universities provide evidence of the affects of accountability practices on academic work, as perceived by academics themselves. As well as confirming that academics in pre-Dawkins universities experience a loss of autonomy in spite of government's (claimed) contrary intentions, the findings also interestingly expose serious contradictions in the discourses that underlie accountability exercises. For example, despite claims that such exercises will improve the productivity and efficiency of universities, respondents consistently report that increased paperwork and attention to record keeping distracts them from getting their "real" work done. In fact, although advocates of accountability practices presume that a more rational approach to university functioning will result, Vidovich and Currie's rich interview data attest to the actual irrationality of various measurement and quality assessment exercises, each of which is often designed and redesigned to counteract the negative consequences flowing from the others.

Privatization involves another constellation of changing practices in higher education that are interwoven with globalization. By *privatization*, we refer to more than the sources of funding for universities and their activities. In fact, privatization can take forms that involve the continuation of primarily public funding while the uses of university activities become privatized. For example, matched funding of university research involves public funding for half the cost of the particular project being funded; but the research is accomplished through the operations of universities—their faculty and staff, their laboratories and buildings, their libraries and computer resources—that continue to be funded through public money. Yet, matched funding and other forms of private-sector research support open the door to patent and licensing agreements that shift ownership of the research results to the private sector sponsor. Similarly, students are increasingly encouraged to view a university degree as providing them access to a particular level of income and, hence, to accept increased tuitions as investments or even equity in their future financial security. Education is thus conceived as a private commodity for the individual degree holder rather than a public good that serves the interests of citizens of the society as a whole.

Privatization can thus encapsulate a range of practices through which knowledge is commodified and universities' services and activities become commercialized and offered for sale to private owners. The forms of privatization vary from nation to nation and institution to institution, depending on location, the quality and prestige of the institution or system, historically developed patterns, and many other factors. Packaging knowledge for overseas consumption, recruiting "foreign" students into specially designed programs that charge full cost recovery or even profitable tuition fees, and selling self-teaching, do-it-at-home course modules to local students are forms of privatization as we have defined it. These forms are increasingly being adopted in First World university systems in relation to less-developed nations' institutions and students. Although students have always traveled abroad to study, and private universities in particular have traditionally appealed to an international student contingent, public universities and governments are now relying, more than in the past, on the foreign exchange and the differential tuition rates they receive from nondomestic students. Whereas several decades ago, programs to assist foreign students to study abroad were sponsored by governments and foundations, the latter now play only a small part in bringing foreign students to Western countries. Moreover, the rationale for attracting these students has changed. Although cultural and intellectual exchange remains a by-product of attracting international students, it is much less emphasized while greater emphasis is placed on foreign exchange to increase export earnings.

There is mounting evidence that the World Bank, the International Monetary Fund (IMF), and the Organization for Economic Cooperation and Development (OECD) have had considerable influence in encouraging governments to move toward privatization. They have urged governments to change public policy based on the social good to one based on the economic good, leading toward greater deregulation and privatization. To carry out these market practices, governments have moved to corporatize public sector organizations to make them function more like private businesses. As other writers in this book have indicated, privatization appears to be the overwhelming trend affecting universities in many parts of the world. For example, Fisher and Rubenson (Chapter 4) noted that, in Canadian universities, full cost recovery is a major theme. However, in addition to existing in many forms, privatization is very much affected by the local context.

In some countries, such as China, Australia, and Canada, where public higher education has exercised a monopoly, privatization comes through deregulation, to allow for-profit institutions to enter the marketplace. The greater reliance of government institutions on corporate sponsorship—thus creating hybrid institutions that are mainly publicly funded but significantly open to corporate sponsorship for specific research and teaching projects—is another form of privatization, which is detailed in Chapter 10 by Edward Berman. Berman begins by describing the transformation of American higher education through a "revolution of markets and management." The most notable pressure on higher education in the United States has come from severely reduced government funding. He also notes the pressure of increased institutional and faculty accountability. These pressures have led to downsizing and restructuring. The pressures have also led to stronger ties with for-profit ventures. Berman details a number of linkages between prestigious universities and powerful corporate bodies. He then describes some of the scandals that have led to conflict of interest charges, legal suits, and recriminations.

Other corporate influences on universities have come through endowment of chairs (such as the Reliance Professorship of Private Enterprise) and revenue-generating athletic programs (through sponsorship by clothing, footwear, and food companies and broadcasting on major TV networks). In addition, international development, notably teaching business and computer courses in rapidly growing economies such as Hong Kong and Saudi Arabia, is another source of revenue. Berman argues that in linking themselves to corporations, American universities are providing a source of revenue for the corporate sector. This results from the alliances between corporate board members and the governing bodies of universities (boards of trustees and regents). Of course, these alliances are not always easily maneuvered; political conflict sometimes emerges when either presidents or faculty members resist the penetration of capital when it takes the form of unhealthy, corporate influence.

Berman's analysis is largely on the experiences of a relatively small, regional university with a third-rate research capacity. He ends by questioning the kind of university that this institution of higher learning should become, given the high cost of establishing high-quality research universities and the limited tax base a university in a poor state can draw upon. The quest for increasing the research prestige of the university has led the university to seek ever more revenue from dubious sources. Berman asks whether this trend is healthy for society.

NOTES

1. This interview formed part of a study on gender and organization culture (Harris, Thiele, & Currie, 1998).

REFERENCES

Angus, L. (1994). Sociological analysis and education management: The social context of the self-managing school. *British Journal of Sociology of Education, 15*(1), 79-91.

Bessant, B. (1995). Corporate management and its penetration of the university administration and government. *Australian Universities' Review, 38*(1), 59-62.

Brown, G. (1996). *2000 and beyond—the university of the future.* Unpublished manuscript, Sydney University.

de Boer, H., & Goedegebuure, L. (1995). Decision-making in higher education: A comparative perspective. *Australian Universities' Review, 38*(1), 41-47.

Fitzsimons, P. (1995). The management of tertiary educational institutions in New Zealand. *Journal of Education Policy, 10*(2), 173-187.

Harris, T., Thiele, B., & Currie, J. (1998, June). Success, gender, and the academic: Consuming passion or selling the soul? *Gender and Education, 10*(2), 133-148.

Karmel, P. (1990). Higher education—tensions and balance. *Journal of Tertiary Educational Administration, 12*(2), 329-337.

Marceau, J. (1993). *Steering from a distance: International trends in the financing and governance of higher education.* Canberra: Australian Government Publishing Service.

Meek, V. L. (1995). Introduction: Regulatory frameworks, market competition, and the governance and management of higher education. *Australian Universities' Review, 38*(1), 3-10.

Middlehurst, R., & Elton, L. (1992). Leadership and management in higher education. *Studies in Higher Education, 17*(3), 251-264.

Newson, J. (1992). The decline of faculty influence: Confronting the effects of the corporate agenda. In W. Carroll, L. Christiansen-Rufman, R. Currie, & D. Harrrison (Eds.), *Fragile truths: 25 years of sociology and anthropology in Canada* (pp. 227-246). Ottawa: Carleton University Press.

Rees, S. (1995). *The human costs of managerialism.* Leichardt, New South Wales: Pluto Press.

Watson, T. (1994). *In search of management: Culture, chaos, and control in managerial work.* London and New York: Routledge.

World Bank. (1994). *Higher education: The lessons of experience.* Washington, DC: Author.

Yeatman, A. (1993). Corporate managerialism and the shift from the welfare to the competitive state. *Discourse, 13*(2), 3-9.

CHAPTER 7

Micro-Economic Reform Through Managerialism in American and Australian Universities

Jan Currie
Lesley Vidovich

The legislators have tried to micro-manage, and it's very clear that over the past five years, each year there is some kind of initiative that constrains or in fact structures the faculty collegial making process.

—*Florida State University Professor,*
United States

W hether it is described as micromanaging, micro-economic reform, or increasing managerialism, there is a definite feeling among academics that both external agencies (government departments, legislators, and politicians) and managers internal to their universities are shifting the balance of power and autonomy away from academics. Academics perceive these moves as a bid to centralize power in the hands of a few senior managers who make decisions more quickly, and as a result, academics are consulted on fewer decisions, mainly those dealing with curricular issues. This

AUTHORS' NOTE: The study on which this chapter is based was funded by an ARC Large Grant and Murdoch University. We wish to thank the academics who were interviewed; our colleagues, Anthony Welch (Sydney University) and Ed Berman (University of Louisville), who were involved in conceiving the research and interviewing; and the research assistants, Harriett Pears, James Bell, and Jim Breadmore.

153

phenomenon has been identified in Australia (Bessant, 1995; Moodie, 1994; Scott, 1995; Terry, 1995), the United States (Berman, 1996; Rhoades, 1993), Canada (Fisher and Rubenson, Chapter 4, this volume; Newson, 1992), and other countries. Along with this shift in power, a new kind of fundamentalism has developed where business practices are adopted by university managers with an earnestness that makes these practices almost above criticism (Rees, 1995). Exemplifying this trend, Hecht quoted a University of California at Los Angeles (UCLA) administrator as stating, "Can a university be run more like a business? You bet it can. . . . Most universities can do a significant job of cutting costs through the same re-engineering of processes and work that have characterized the best for-profit corporations" (Hecht, 1994, p. 6).

Another idea coming from business is that change has to be the order of the day and that decisions should be made quickly. In describing visionary companies, Collins and Porras (1994) quote Sam Walton as saying, "You can't just keep doing what works one time, because everything around you is always changing. To succeed, you have to stay out in front of that change" (Walton, 1992, p. 249). Collins and Porras also point out that not all businesses they studied operate on this assumption and that some of the most visionary companies have some very traditional ways of operating, ways that have not changed with the times.

Certain myths pervading current thinking advocate that corporate managers should make the most important decisions and make them quickly. Managers who adhere to this idea of corporate decision making have a penchant for restructuring institutions and molding them into streamlined operations that allow only a few people access to the information base on which decisions can be made. Books tell managers how to bring about reforms quickly. A New Zealand academic whom we interviewed in 1997 talked about one such book. He said that it could have been describing changes that have occurred in a number of American and Australian universities:

> If you read Roger Douglas' [former Treasurer in New Zealand] book, *Unfinished Business,* he talks about the politics of successful reform, and he articulates a number of principles for successful reform. I quote them to you off the top of my head. One of them is institute the reforms in quantum leaps, big packages neutralize opposition, once you start the ball rolling never let it stop, speed is essential, just keep on going,

and consult with the community only to improve the detailed implementation of decisions that have already been reached. (University of Auckland, New Zealand)

And in the voice of another academic across the world from the University of Auckland, the rapidity of change was noted in response to a question about the current style of decision making in the University of Louisville.

It seems that bureaucratic tendencies are increasing. The faculty has a lot less control over the institution. There were a number of changes imposed on the faculty: not electing deans; changing the definition of what we do, making teaching-only and research-only streams; a post-tenure review, evaluating what you do which could lead to termination; increasing the proportion of faculty without tenure. The faculty met for the first time in donkey's years and voted against these proposals, like 495 to 15—and these were faculty from all the colleges—the medical school, the law school—they all said "this sucks." The Board of Trustees said "we don't care, this is what is happening." There is a contempt for the faculty. But also a sense that they are running a business. You know when you are running an auto plant, you don't ask the workers how to run the plant, at least in America, and if you are running a university, you don't ask the faculty how to run the institution. (University of Louisville, United States)

At Murdoch University in Australia, the newly appointed Vice Chancellor began enacting a change agenda within months of arriving on campus in 1996. Within the first three months, he eliminated thirty-two committees. Within the next six months, he wrote a new vision statement, *Murdoch 21* (Schwartz, 1996), preparing the university for the twenty-first century. This was brought to a new academic council (with increased representation from staff to make up for the loss of collegial input from committees). He wanted twenty-three actions to be voted on within three weeks, which among other things would restructure the university into divisions, create a hierarchical management structure with appointed executive deans, and eliminate small programs and courses. Before the end of the year, the vice chancellor had achieved most of his objectives. To continue the momentum for change, he (along with the chancellor of the university) initiated a merger with another university. This was brought to a vote in the academic councils at both universities at the beginning of 1997 and was defeated. However, the pace of change at Murdoch University has not halted as major new initiatives are debated at each council meeting.

During 1997, Murdoch's senior management tried to "take over" a campus owned by a rival university. This takeover bid was never discussed by Academic Council. It was initiated secretly by the pro vice chancellor of development, who talked with staff on the other campus and gained the endorsement of local politicians. He did not negotiate this takeover with the senior management of the other university. Through a State Review Committee, it was decided that the campus should remain with the current university.

In 1998, the vice chancellor initiated a management review by two outside consultants; academics fear this may diminish the policy role of Academic Council and lead to a tighter rein on decision making by senior management. The other major initiative that senior management has undertaken in 1998 is to lease a sizable portion of university land to Mobil for a gas station and fast-food outlet (probably a McDonald's or Hungry Jack's). These are the business tactics that the current management feels are necessary to be a competitive university in the late 1990s in Australia.

In the process of making such changes in universities, management often delineates which aspects of decision making academics can be involved in and which aspects the administration should control. A memo from an American university administrator to one of his deans noted, "Matters such as curriculum belong to the faculty but decisions about the development and monitoring of resource allocations are the responsibility of administration" (Glidden, 1993, p. 12). Several decades ago, this was not the case in many American universities. The Council of the American Association of University Professors endorsed a statement in May 1972 that made it very clear faculty should participate in budgetary matters: "The faculty should participate both in the preparation of the total institutional budget and in decisions relevant to the further apportioning of its specific fiscal divisions" (Council of the American Association of University Professors, 1973, p. 170). The statement also emphasized the importance of having an elected representative committee of the faculty deciding the overall allocation of institutional resources.

Control among faculty over budgetary matters is decreasing in both the United States and Australia. Scott (1995) argues that university managers have fallen under the spell of public choice theorists who assume the superiority of private sector approaches to management. The administration is perceived as no longer thinking of universities as primarily educational institutions, as can be seen in a statement adopted in the form of a motion at the University of Newcastle, Australia:

> The general perception is that academics are generally excluded from significant decision-making, that a great deal of money is expended on salaries and ancillary costs at senior- and middle-management levels and that an administration designed to serve the academic function of the university has succeeded in having that function made secondary to managerial imperatives. (Jones, 1992, p. 40)

These changes are not unique to universities. Other public agencies have been urged by governments to undergo micro-economic reform, or what has been termed in some countries *public sector reform*. The aim is to remake these public institutions into organizational cultures that will serve a more competitive state (Knight & Lingard, 1996; Yeatman, 1993). The person who has been saddled by government with changing the culture of universities has been the chief executive officer (CEO). These CEOs are busy developing corporate images for their universities that will help develop their niche markets. The images created are of efficient businesses selling university places both overseas and at home, cooperating with industries, and selling research products and professional services. Many academics are willing to buy into this new conception of their universities. However, others are more suspicious of these changes and the "new managerialism" that is sweeping into their universities. This next section allows the voices of academics to be heard as they respond to these changes.

THE PROJECT: "CHANGING NATURE OF ACADEMIC WORK"

This chapter reports on findings from a larger project studying the impact of globalization practices on the work culture of academics. Here, we focus on the governance of American and Australian universities and how it has changed over a five-year period. We wanted to discover the extent to which universities were described by academics as either *collegial*, which can be defined as having shared decision making along with trust, openness, concern, and cooperation (Miller & Findlay, 1996), or *corporate managerial*, which features "leaner and meaner" decision-making structures and processes with smaller groups at the top reacting quickly to changing external imperatives, with little consultation beyond senior management and greater secrecy (Bessant, 1995; Coaldrake, 1995; Fitzsimons, 1995).

We interviewed academics about decision-making structures and processes within their institutions, following Foucault's (1991) suggestion that power should be studied at the microlevel of society to see how it circulates. We started at the bottom and studied power in an ascending way. We reported our findings to the vice chancellors and presidents and have received feedback from them on our *Trends Reports*. In 1997 and 1998, we interviewed Australian senior managers about their views on the future of their universities, especially in light of the budget cuts and the more competitive policies of the Australian Liberal government. We followed the aim of Foucault's "microphysics of power," which is to investigate the effective practices and techniques (often borrowed from business in this case) used by government (or in this case by CEOs along with the Commonwealth government in Australia and boards of regents/trustees and state legislatures in the United States) to control and shape behavior.

The Australian universities chosen for this study represent a range of different contexts evident in the higher education sector (enrollments given are approximate sizes in 1996):

- University of Sydney—a large, old, traditional university established in 1850, which has an enrollment of 30,000;
- Murdoch University—a small, alternative university established in 1975, which has an enrollment of 8,000; and
- Edith Cowan University—a new university, which began as a postsecondary college in 1902 and, after a series of amalgamations, became a university in 1991; it has an enrollment of 17,000.

The institutions from the United States represent state universities in different geographical locations; they also have different ranks within what has been termed the 100 "research" universities by the Carnegie Foundation:

- University of Arizona—in the first third of research rankings; established in 1885, it has an enrollment of 34,000.
- Florida State University—in the top part of the second third of research rankings; established in 1857 as a women's college, and later became a coeducational university; it has an enrollment of 30,000.
- University of Louisville—in the lowest part of the second third of research rankings; established in 1798, it has an enrollment of 22,000.

We make comparisons between the total samples in Australia and the United States. We also comment on some differences evident between universities and present typical quotes from academics interviewed both to highlight general trends and to provide context for specific issues.

There were 153 respondents at the Australian universities and 100 at the American universities, although not all respondents answered all interview questions. Respondents represented a range of discipline areas across education, social sciences, and the sciences and a range of academic ranks from professor to associate lecturer. About one third of both samples were female academic staff. The NU•DIST software program facilitated the analysis of responses into tables presenting numbers and percentages of respondents and responses in the different categories that emerged from the data.

General Impressions on Changes Within These Universities

Before looking specifically at the three questions on decision making, it is informative to reflect on some of the general issues raised by a number of respondents. An issue that seemed to be most irritating to many academics was the gulf that had grown between academics and administrators, particularly in the area of salaries and benefits. One professor remarked quite vehemently,

> The university administration is approaching corporate managerialism. If you look at the salaries of administrators, they're paid enormous salaries comparatively speaking; they're in the top 10% and the faculty is in the bottom 25% nationally. There is a lot more of the

administrative fiat being passed down to faculty. (Florida State University, United States)

Staff at Australian universities echoed these feelings, where administrators are being paid higher and higher salaries with more fringe benefits and corporate managerial tendencies are exhibiting themselves. Staff in both American and Australian universities also talked about how their universities were being run like businesses. This is captured in the following quotes:

You want to talk about the one thing that has changed; it is striving to put industrial-driven productivity models into a service and scholarship profession. Productivity models as applied to education are terribly misplaced and terribly abused. They do nothing but promote a labor versus management concept. That's one thing that has been more complicated and different, as I think we have been striving to meet the Legislature's push for industrial and production models into the educational process. (Florida State University, United States)

The central administration has gained more control. The President has attempted to centralize decision making. He has a business mentality. He's a CEO, a jargon term used in business. A lot of the vocabulary and rhetoric used is deceptive because he may say we want to achieve equity, but there are such disparities between the different units. He suggests that he is looking for some kind of social justice but I think it is an attempt to run things from the central administration. (University of Louisville, United States)

Of course, much of the Dawkins (Australian labor minister responsible for education, 1987-1991) agenda was an argument about the lack of accountability of institutions. The inappropriateness of their governance structures demands that they be run much more like business corporations and the "knock on" effect of that right down from reduced numbers in the Senate to the kind of line management universities are adopting. (Murdoch University, Australia)

Findings on Decision Making

To determine the kind of decision making that existed in their universities, we asked respondents this interview question:

Would you describe decision making at your university as bureaucratic, democratic, collegial, or something else?

As respondents used a variety of labels to describe decision-making styles, responses were categorized into the broad groupings of *more centralized, more consultative, combination* of these two styles, and "don't know." Individual academics differ on how they perceive a more centralized system such as managerialism or a more consultative process such as collegiality. Their perceptions are shaped by their past experiences of different styles, their cultural origins and knowledge of different democratic styles, the history of their institutions, and the form of managerialism or collegiality they have experienced as academics. For example, in many of the older Australian universities, a more traditional form of collegiality persists where power rests with the heads of departments or the so-called god professors. In these situations, only some academics have power, and these are usually not the female or junior academics. Some observers may question whether that could actually be called collegiality. In some of the newer universities, a style of decision making has developed where committees of academics debate policy, and there is greater transparency in how decisions are made.

However, no matter which university is studied, it becomes readily apparent that decision making is complex, involving different power groups in the policy process (trade unions, staff associations, powerful individuals such as key professors, formal academic bodies, and informal lobby groups). Currently, in American and Australian universities, the power of these academic groups (whether unionized or nonunionized, whether powerful professors or not) appears to be waning as the attempt by managers to capture power in the universities has been strengthened by the policy decisions of governments.

Table 7.1 summarizes the pattern of responses to the above question. The predominant response for both the Australian and American samples was more centralized decision making, with this effect being more marked in the United States (73% compared with 59% in Australia). The next most frequent category was a combination of decision-making styles (17% in the United States and 19% in Australia), followed closely by more consultative decision making in Australia (18%). In the United States, more consultative decision making

TABLE 7.1   Decision-Making Style (1994-1996): Frequencies (and Percentages)

Country	More Centralized	More Consultative	Combination	Don't Know	Total
Australia	84 (59%)	26 (18%)	27 (19%)	6 (4%)	143 (100%)
United States	72 (73%)	6 (6%)	17 (17%)	4 (4%)	99 (100%)

(6%) was cited only marginally more frequently than "don't know" (4%).

Although there was some variation between individual universities, more centralized was the predominant response for each of the six universities in the study. Murdoch University was the only one to record less than half (44%) of respondents in the more centralized category, which could well be reflecting some of its alternative 1970s foundation ethos of more consultative decision making. Murdoch, Sydney, and Florida State respondents were more likely to describe a combination of more consultative and more centralized decision making (27% for Murdoch, 25% for Sydney, and 23% for Florida State) than the other universities, which recorded less than 15% in this category. More consultative decision making was cited most frequently at Edith Cowan and Murdoch in Australia (24% and 23%, respectively), but less than 10% of the time at the other universities in the study.

The following quotes have been chosen to add some flavor to the numerical results and to represent the predominant response category of more centralized decision making in both countries.

It is more managerial. It is less democratic as a result. Any sense of a coherent university has been lost by the production of fiefdoms, where the different faculties are run by robber barons who call themselves Pro-Vice Chancellors and who get motor cars and so on. They are called senior management. It came with the previous Vice Chancellor and the appointment of the Boston Consulting Group and the throwing of at least a million dollars at them to produce a bunch of flow charts.... It had almost no beneficial impact but it gave the green light to restructure or managerialize. (Sydney University, Australia)

Important decisions are passed down from the top I think, although there's quite a lot of flexibility about how people can allocate resources at the school and departmental level. It's certainly a lot less dictatorial than in some universities. . . . This university has made a decision about extending to another campus at Kwinana. . . . I think that was probably one of the least democratic decisions, but it had to be made quickly because we were in competition with other institutions. . . . So we were driven very much by outside forces. (Murdoch University, Australia)

It's close to corporate managerial, and it's moving down to the level of the deans, who used to be much more collegial. The idea that one can manage a university in terms of accountability and productivity is a carryover from the corporate world of the 1980s. I don't think it can work, and it only alienates the faculty from the administration. (Florida State University, United States)

It's as autocratic as is possible for the central administration to make it. It maintains a facade of consultation, but the President makes it very clear that he does not feel himself bound by any consultation. . . . He made himself chair of the last provost search committee. He said the only thing he was mandated to do was consult with the faculty advisory committee, and that he was not bound by their decision (which previous presidents had considered themselves bound by) nor by the search committee. In short, he could go to someone never considered by the committee and name that person provost—that's about as authoritarian as you can get. (University of Louisville, United States)

The next interview question focused on changes:

> Have there been any changes in the decision-making process over the last five years?

The responses to this question were categorized according to whether the respondent perceived an increase in more centralized or more consultative decision making, no change, or didn't know.

Table 7.2 reveals that an increase in more centralized decision-making was the predominant experience for respondents in both Australia (53%) and the United States (63%), with this effect again being more pronounced in the United States. In Australia, the second most frequent category was an increase in more consultative decision

TABLE 7.2 Changing Decision-Making Style Over Previous Five Years: Frequencies (and Percentages)

Country	Increase in More Centralized	Increase in More Consultative	No Change	Don't Know	Total
Australia	65 (53%)	28 (23%)	15 (12%)	15 (12%)	123 (100%)
United States	52 (63%)	3 (4%)	11 (13%)	16 (20%)	82 (100%)

making (23%), whereas this was the least frequent response in the United States (4%).

The response pattern in Australia has been distorted by the findings from Edith Cowan University, where over three quarters of respondents (77%) perceived an increase in more consultative decision making. The other two Australian universities, in contrast, recorded only small percentages (3% and 7%) in this category, consistent with the American pattern. Edith Cowan's historical context as a former college, with a highly bureaucratized structure, is pertinent here. As a result of the combination of the new vice chancellor of 1992, the appointment of new professors with substantial research records and more collegial expectations, and the devolution of financial administration, a greater sense of more consultative decision making was created, in comparison with the college era.

In the United States, Florida State revealed a pattern slightly different from the other two universities in that at least some respondents recorded an increase in more consultative decision making (6%, compared with 0% at the other universities) and about one fifth (18%) recorded no change (less than 10% at the others). Furthermore, there was a relatively high percentage of respondents at Florida State (28%) who did not know about changes in decision-making styles over the previous five years, perhaps suggesting an influx of new staff. When staff were interviewed at Florida State, a new president had just been appointed, and staff were uncertain of how his style would affect collegiality. The union president had also been elected to the executive committee in the Faculty Senate, which still operates as a viable, collegial body. Thus, there was still a feeling among some faculty that a collegial voice was being heard within the university, but some cynicism about its real power was also expressed by faculty, coupled with their sense that the president was still an unknown quantity.

The following quotes represent the predominant response category of an increase in more centralized decision making in both countries, except for the first quote from Edith Cowan (Australia), where there was an increase in more consultative decision making.

A lot of it has devolved down to the schools. Much more than we ever had before. Much, much better. (Edith Cowan University, Australia)

It's changed because the sheer increasing size of the university has meant that more decisions are being made by smaller groups of people. For example, there was no Planning and Management Committee or anything that even looked like it four years ago. (Murdoch University, Australia)

It's moving to top-down management on a corporate style that almost deliberately elicits hostile relations, adversarial, I guess I would say. (Arizona University, United States)

For the worse. More bureaucratic, less accessible, and less responsive to the central mission of the university—students, faculty, and the curriculum. Much more responsive to the Board of Regents and the Legislature. It's become an outward process rather than inward. We simply become conduits to feed data upward and that's accountability. (Florida State University, United States)

The final question asked respondents to identify particular loci of control of decision making in their universities:

Who or which group of people would you say makes the most important decisions at your university?

The responses were grouped using six categories. The *senior executive group* includes positions such as vice chancellors, deputy vice chancellors, pro-vice chancellors (in Australia) and presidents, vice presidents, and provosts (in the United States). Perceived control by this group could be identified as top-down decision making, relating to the more centralized category. The *middle managers* refer to the deans and committees of deans. *Powerful committees* was a more diffuse category employed usually when respondents referred to particular committees other than those dominated by deans, or when respondents had not been specific about the type of committee. The *commu-*

nity governing board refers to the Senate or University Council (in Australia) and the Board of Regents or Legislature (in the United States). The *Academic Council/Senate* is also known as the Academic Board (in Australia) and the Faculty Senate (in the United States). *Community or lay boards* have mostly appointed members in both countries but with some elected student and staff members on the Senates or University Councils in Australia.

Table 7.3 shows that respondents perceived the senior executive group to be making the key decisions more often than other groups in both countries. Consistent with the responses to the previous two questions, respondents in the United States (60%) were more likely to describe a top-down model of decision making than those in Australia (42%). Australian respondents chose middle management (deans) as the second most powerful group (30%), whereas respondents in the United States ranked the community governing board (Board of Regents or Legislature) second (22%). Generally, there is a much longer and larger tradition of community involvement in educational decision making in the United States than in Australia, and the more decentralized organization of education in the United States may well facilitate this more extensive community participation (albeit appointments are mainly from the business and professional sector). The size of the "don't know" category in Australia suggests that some staff are perhaps not as informed as they should be on decision-making structures/processes, perhaps due to the rapid rate of change or the lack of appropriate induction. Alternatively, they may feel that they cannot influence decisions, and it is better for their careers to just "get on with their work."

As deans are increasingly seen to be part of the administrative structure of universities, the first two categories in the table might be combined to reveal a perception by a large majority in both countries that management, as opposed to academic peers, makes the important decisions. In both Australia and the United States, almost three quarters (72%) of respondents identified either the senior executive group or middle management as making the key decisions.

Within Australia, there was a somewhat different pattern for Sydney than for the other universities. At Murdoch and Edith Cowan, the predominant response was the senior executive group (44% at both), but at Sydney, middle management played the predominant role (39%). This difference was a result of Sydney's 1992 reforms (recommended by an external management consultancy) to devolve power

TABLE 7.3 Key Decision-Making Groups (1994-1996): Frequencies[a] (and Percentages)

Country	Senior Executive Group	Middle Management	Powerful Committees	Community Board	Academic Council/ Senate	Don't Know	Total
Australia	80 (42%)	58 (30%)	14 (7%)	12 (6%)	12 (6%)	16 (8%)	192 (100%)
United States	71 (60%)	14 (12%)	0 (0%)	26 (22%)	8 (7%)	0 (0%)	119 (100%)

a. Maximum of two responses coded per respondent.

from the vice chancellor to the next level down the line management structure: the pro-vice chancellors or deans, who were no longer elected but appointed. Also at Sydney, respondents identified the Senate (community governing board), and the chancellor, in particular, more often (18%) than other Australian respondents. On the other hand, at Murdoch, powerful committees featured relatively more often (15%) than at the other universities, consistent with the stronger evidence of more consultative styles at that university. (As noted in the beginning of this chapter, all these committees were abolished, so the degree of collegiality was altered in one fell swoop.)

Within the United States, Florida State revealed a slightly different pattern than the other universities. Respondents described the senior executive group as key decision makers less often (56%) than the other universities (64% at Arizona and 66% at Louisville). Florida State respondents were the only ones to identify the Faculty Senate as being involved in key decisions (11%); as mentioned earlier, this collegial body is still seen as having an important, if declining, role in the governance structure.

The following quotes reflect the strong tendency for management (senior executives or middle managers) to dominate decision making in both countries.

> I'm not sure what they're called, the deans of the faculties come together with the vice chancellor and the deputy vice chancellor and the representatives of the major service organizations, effectively that's where the power is, and then their decisions are passed along to the Academic Council, which effectively is a rubber stamper. (Edith Cowan, Australia)

> They have created a set of feudal fiefdoms by devolving finances to the deans and the VC [vice chancellor] finds himself unable to break

through these feudal fiefdoms, and he probably got so frustrated that he decided to go. . . . The restructuring got people half way across the river and there is no clear vision of how we are going to proceed. (Sydney University, Australia)

The provost and vice provost—that level just below the president. It is never very clear whether these people are the hired guns, and they do the nasty stuff and he wears a smile and blesses everyone, or if he is a creep, too, you never know. The decision makers at this place are those line administrators, and they can exert enormous, persuasive power on us by manipulating our finances and by not promoting people. There are a lot of power games to be played in a place like this. (Arizona University, United States)

Beginning with the president and taking into account the president's influence over the Board of Trustees, individually and collectively, and then expanding that to include a core group, and I don't know if I want to use the term *elite* administrators. (University of Louisville, United States)

CONCLUSION

We do not want to give the impression that either consultative forms, such as collegiality, or centralized forms, such as corporate managerialism, are unproblematic or pure types about which there is common understanding. Collegiality does not represent a "golden age" of more consultative decision making that existed sometime in the past. The realities of hidden hierarchies (Brown, 1996) and autocratic styles of god-professors (Moodie, 1995) contrast with the rhetoric of a community of self-governing scholars. Collegiality as a style is also problematic for those wishing to make fast and decisive decisions. Likewise, corporate managerialism is a complex entity, with competing discourses of centralizing control for policy directions (ends), yet devolving responsibility for spending (means). This new relationship between devolved means and centralized ends has been referred to as "steering at a distance" (Ball, 1994) or for universities, in particular, "steering from a distance" (Marceau, 1993). Some commentators argue that both the intended and actual effects of corporate managerialism are to increase accountability (Angus, 1994) and surveillance (Meadmore, Limerick, Thomas, & Lucas, 1995), rather than offer enhanced participation. Furthermore, other commentators, such as Treuren (1995), maintain that there is little evidence that line management has led to greater productivity or efficiency, which its proponents claimed as its principal advantage.

Despite the lack of clear consensus on definitions, across the six universities observed in this study, there was a convergence toward a more common, corporate managerial model of decision making. There is no doubt that according to a majority of those interviewed, this type of management and the resulting micromanagement of academic work has led to increased alienation of academics from their institutions. There is also evidence of a widening gap between administrators or managers and academics, and in many cases, this has resulted in a lack of trust within the universities.

By studying one of the globalizing practices, corporate managerialism, in the familiar proximity of our workplaces, it became clear that a lively debate needs to be generated within universities about decision-making practices, with the objective of ensuring that forms of participatory democracy are maintained. Our data provide evidence of the retention of significant collegial fragments in three of the six universities studied (Florida State, Murdoch, and Sydney), where a combination of centralized and consultative decision making was identified by about one quarter of the respondents. From such a base, collegiality (in the form of transparent, democratic decision making) is more readily retrieved (or developed in the case of a more traditional university like Sydney) and strengthened. It is ironic that businesses, which supposedly provided the model for more efficient, effective, and productive higher education institutions, are moving to increase more consultative decision making, and especially to reduce middle management, when universities are still initiating moves to build management hierarchies (Middlehurst & Elton, 1992), especially with the strengthening of middle management in the form of appointed (rather than elected) deans.

Slaughter (1993) urged American faculty who were concerned with restructuring to begin preparing for it through debate within their own universities and at open forums in which community and political groups can interact with professionals to form new coalitions built around concepts of the public interest (p. 249). Retaining tenure is an important plank in this resistance strategy, because few contract academics would take the risk of speaking out against management and challenging them on what management sees as their managerial prerogative. Yet it is important to keep up the pressure and not lose ever more ground in the collegiality stakes.

Jones (1996, p. 8) proposed the development of charters of collegial autonomy for Australian universities, which would ensure greater accountability of academic middle managers to their colleagues. He also suggested making collegial skills essential criteria for middle management appointments. Charters would thus register the dual accountability of academic middle managers: upward to the university management primarily (and increasingly) via budgetary responsibilities and laterally (not downward) to their colleagues, primarily as practitioner/advocate of the collegial norms and procedures articulated in the charters.

Within their recently enhanced roles as chief executives of corporate universities, vice chancellors and presidents might consider preserving and extending the fragments of collegial, more consultative decision making identified in this study. Otherwise, universities and their clients are likely to suffer in the long term. It is salient to heed the advice of Ken McKinnon, a former Australian vice chancellor, who advocated that universities be run not like businesses but more like legal partnerships where all constituencies, including students, staff, governments, and taxpayers, participate in the decision making. He reminds us that "the university is one of half a dozen institutions that has lasted for a couple of thousand years so that form of governance is not one you would give up lightly" (quoted in Armitage, 1995, p. 30).

REFERENCES

Angus, L. (1994). Educational organisation: Technical/managerial and participative/ professional perspectives. *Discourse, 14*(2), 30-44.

Armitage, C. (1995, November 15). Are our university councils fit to govern? *The Australian Higher Education Supplement*, p. 30.

Ball, S. J. (1994). *Education reform: A critical and post-structural approach*. Buckingham and Philadelphia: Open University Press.

Berman, E. H. (1996, July 1-6). *The entrepreneurial university: Macro and micro perspectives from the United States*. Paper presented at the Ninth World Congress on Comparative Education: Tradition, Modernity, and Postmodernity, Sydney.

Bessant, B. (1995). Corporate management and its penetration of the university administration and government. *Australian Universities' Review, 38*(1), 59-62.

Brown, G. (1996, September 4). *2000 and beyond—the university of the future.* Inaugural lecture as vice chancellor, Sydney University.

Coaldrake, P. (1995). Implications for higher education of the public sector reform agenda. *Australian Universities' Review, 38*(1), 38-40.

Collins, J. C., & Porras, J. I. (1994). *Built to last: Successful habits of visionary companies.* London: Century.

Council of the American Association of University Professors. (1973). The role of the faculty in budgetary and salary matters. *AAUP Bulletin, 58*(2), 170.

Fitzsimons, P. (1995). The management of tertiary educational institutions in New Zealand. *Journal of Education Policy, 10*(2), 173-187.

Foucault, M. (1991). Governmentality. In G. Burchell, C. Gordon, & P. Miller (Eds.), *The Foucault effect: Studies in governmentality* (pp. 87-104). London: Harvester Wheatsheaf.

Glidden, R. (1993). Internal memorandum to deans. Florida State University.

Hecht, J. (1994, November). Today's college teachers: Cheap and temporary. *Labor Notes,* No. 188, 6.

Jones, C. (1992, October 7). FAUSA urges inquiry into management "bias." *The Australian,* p. 40.

Jones, P. (1996, July 3-9). Time for charters of collegial autonomy. *Campus Review,* p. 8.

Knight, J., & Lingard, B. (1996). Australian higher education 1987-1995: Some notes on a Labor policy regime and its dilemmas. In M. Warry, P. O'Brien, J. Knight, & C. Swendson (Eds.), *Navigating in a sea of change* (pp. 4-15). Rockhampton, Queensland: Central Queensland University Press.

Marceau, J. (1993). *Steering from a distance: International trends in the financing and governance of higher education* (Higher Education Division of Department of Employment, Education and Training [DEET], Evaluations and Investigations Program). Canberra: Australian Government Publishing Service.

Meadmore, D., Limerick, B., Thomas, P., & Lucas, H. (1995). Devolving practices: Managing the managers. *Journal of Education Policy, 10*(4), 399-411.

Middlehurst, R., & Elton, L. (1992). Leadership and management in higher education. *Studies in Higher Education, 17*(3), 251-264.

Miller, E., & Findlay, M. (1996). *Australian thesaurus of educational descriptors.* Melbourne: Australian Council for Educational Research.

Moodie, G. (1994, November 9). Consultation process must encourage staff consensus. *Higher Education Supplement, The Australian,* p. 34.

Moodie, G. (1995). The professionalisation of Australian academic administration. *Australian Universities' Review, 38*(1), 21-23.

Newson, J. (1992). The decline of faculty influence: Confronting the effects of the corporate agenda. In W. Carroll, L. Christiansen-Rufman, R. Currie, & D. Harrrison (Eds.), *Fragile truths: 25 years of sociology and anthropology in Canada* (pp. 227-246). Ottawa: Carleton University Press.

Rees, S. (1995). *The human costs of managerialism.* Leichardt, New South Wales: Pluto Press.

Rhoades, G. (1993). Retrenchment clauses in faculty union contracts: Faculty rights and administrative discretion. *The Journal of Higher Education, 64*(3), 312-347.

Schwartz, S. (1996, April 17). *Murdoch 21: Achieving the vision.* Discussion paper presented at Academic Council Meeting, Murdoch University, Perth, Western Australia.

Scott, R. (1995, June 15-21). Bureaucracy and academe: Crossing the divide. *Campus Review*, p. 8.

Slaughter, S. (1993, May/June). Introduction to special issue on retrenchment. *The Journal of Higher Education, 64*(3), 247-249.

Terry, L. (1995, July 6-12). Corporatism—spectre for tomorrow. *Campus Review*, p. 9.

Treuren, G. (1995, May 24). Award pits collegiality against managerialism. *The Australian*, p. 29.

Walton, S., with Huey, J. (1992). *Sam Walton: Made in America*. New York: Doubleday.

Yeatman, A. (1993). Corporate managerialism and the shift from the welfare to the competitive state. *Discourse, 13*(2), 3-9.

CHAPTER 8

Don't Count Your Blessings

The Social Accomplishments of Performance Indicators

Claire Polster
Janice Newson

A*ccountability* is a banner word of higher education policy in the 1990s. In diverse local and national arenas,[1] the public policy discourse has been converging toward a common conception of accountability and its achievement through performance indicators. Although this conception gained currency in the United States in the early 1970s (Bowen, 1974; Kogan, 1986), efforts have intensified in the 1990s[2] to apply it more widely not only to local institutions but also to entire national systems of higher education.[3]

This renewed attention to achieving accountability through performance indicators is not surprising. Governments have imposed deep cuts in public funding, and education ministries have actively promoted and, in some cases, unilaterally implemented performance indicators to increase the efficiency and cost-effectiveness of higher education systems (Johnes & Taylor, 1990; McNeil, 1995; Trow, 1994).

Generally speaking, responses from within universities and colleges to this policy direction have focused on technical aspects of the proposed measurements rather than questions about the notion of accountability as a basis for decision making. Even individuals and organizations representing the interests of the academic staff, who are openly critical of the policy, have not tended to intervene in ways that fundamentally disrupt the measured performance conceptualization of accountability. The strategy most frequently recommended by them is to participate in developing the measures so that they will be more meaningful or less harmful: Rarely if ever is their use resisted outright.[4] Although critics may believe that government and administration demands for accountability are little more than a cover story to justify further budget cuts, their interventions more typically follow a strategy of accommodation.[5]

Our approach differs in two important respects from these earlier discussions of performance indicators. First, we engage in a conceptual, as opposed to technical, examination of performance indicators. Second, we attempt to display the potential weaknesses, if not dangers, of accommodation strategies and argue for strategies that address the political and economic relations that have promoted and are promoted by a performance-based conception of accountability.

Our interest arises out of separate investigations of the reorganization of academic work that has taken place over the past two to three decades. Newson's work has focused on changes within universities—particularly managerialism and corporatism[6]—that are coincident with changes in government funding policy. Polster has focused on the role of federal governments and of intellectual property rights instruments that are contained in international trade agreements, in reorganizing academic research. We are both interested in how these processes at the institutional and national government levels articulate with, and become part of, broader projects that contribute in complex ways toward developing a *globalized knowledge industry*. Hence, we examine performance indicators as potential facilitators of these broader projects.

PERFORMANCE INDICATORS AS CONCEPTUAL TECHNOLOGIES

Drawing from Dorothy Smith's (1990) work on the social organization of knowledge, we conceive of performance indicators as technologies for managing and controlling the academic activities that flow within and through institutions of higher education. As such, they are conceptual devices that link academic judgments to budgetary and policy-sensitive constructs. Performance indicators open up the routine evaluation of academic activities to other than academic considerations, and they make it possible to replace substantive judgments with formulaic and algorithmic representations. For example, judgments of teaching quality and pedagogical formats, which previously emerged through face-to-face discussion and debate in collegial bodies, can be replaced by mechanically produced, standardized "facts" such as class size. These can be compared across departments, faculties, and even universities in association with other facts—for example, student output—to assess the cost-effectiveness of a given institution's deployment of its teaching resources.

We are not so much interested in the measurement protocols of performance indicators as in the way they intrinsically reorder the social relations of academic work. They not only displace the interactive, face-to-face process of forming academic judgments as a basis for decision making. They also reconstruct the relationship between those who perform academic activities, on the one hand, and, on the other, those who determine how to evaluate them, the criteria of evaluation, and the interpretation and consequences of the evaluation.

We will build upon this conceptualization of performance indicators to anticipate some of the ways in which they may play a role in the further development of a globalized knowledge industry. Although performance indicators are not new to higher education, we believe that they are taking new forms and being deployed in more complex ways. We examine their use in three different contexts to offer different insights into the reordering work that indicators may accomplish, particularly as they assume these new and more complex forms. Our aim is to identify the forms of reordering and the reorganization of people's activities that are made possible by performance indicators and the implications that flow from them.

THE LOCAL/NATIONAL CONTEXT

In describing the transformation in the work environment of the professoriate in their own Canadian university, Cassin and Morgan (1992) include "methods of describing and quantifying those aspects of the professoriate's work . . . deemed capable of accountability, and deemed 'relevant' to the mission of the university" (p. 253). The use of standardized measures to make visible the aspects of the professoriate's work that are most and least "effective" and "cost-efficient," and therefore, most and least worthy of financial support, has a variety of effects on the work environment:

- An emphasis on research that will increase the revenues of the university
- Increased expectations that research will produce quantifiable results (publications)
- Shifts in the activities of individual faculty members and of academic units toward those that are most productive in managerial terms
- Divisions within the professoriate based on the greater value of some (individual's or unit's) work over others
- Higher workloads in teaching for some faculty members, whereas others have reduced teaching loads to carry out "valued" research
- Comparison of teaching units with each other based on quantified measures

Cassin and Morgan (1992) also show how increasingly complex measurement systems can be used to make comparisons with other institutions as a basis for deciding upon the allocation of resources within their university as a whole (pp. 255-256). These measuring systems and their relevancies have begun to transform both the context and the appraisal of professorial work, insofar as they make the usual collegial criteria and mechanisms of evaluation (such as tenure and promotion appraisals) less relevant and managerial considerations and mechanisms more relevant to budgetary and programmatic planning (see also Buchbinder & Newson, 1990, 1988).

Most important, Cassin and Morgan (1992) demonstrate how these standardized evaluative measures and systems of measures have contributed to the centralization of management. Among other things, the "accounts of work organization" that are necessary for producing performance indicators provide "the basis to structure decisions about programme, work priorities, and allocation *outside the settings* [italics added] in which the work is actually conducted" (p. 255).

As illustrated by Cassin and Morgan (1992), performance indicators can be used to base local level decision making on comparisons with other institutions and to shift control upward and outward, by making it possible to decide on and control priorities and activities from "the outside." Also, these accomplishments illuminate and inform our thinking about the increasing activity around developing performance indicators beyond the level of local institutions. For example, in Canada, this activity is occurring in various education ministries and involves institutions at all levels of education (Bruneau, 1994). Also, the three research councils[7] that distribute public funds to support the research activities of Canadian academics are using performance indicators to "track" the results of the research projects; to monitor the use of and allocate funds to learned societies, their related federations, and scholarly journals; and to monitor and allocate funds to their own internal operations.[8]

Similar consequences are attributed to the use of performance indicators in British universities and colleges. Less than ten years after Maurice Kogan (1986) declared that "highly managerial systems of accountability" are "alien" to the British (school) system (p. 76), Maureen McNeil (1995) reports that performance assessment systems have become almost a routine feature of decision making in British higher education (p. 9). McNeil describes effects within British institutions similar to those that Cassin and Morgan (1992) report in Canada: the invention of an accounting system for rating faculty members' and academic units' publication productivity, the favoring of research that attracts funding, competition within institutions and among institutions for "high producers" of fundable research, increasing teaching loads of less "productive" faculty members to allow the "more productive" to concentrate on research, and an associated deterioration of the conditions of teaching.

Other reports on British universities describe how these more complex systems of performance measures have been used by the government, via a reordered system of councils and agencies, to differentially allocate funds in ways that link funding to specifically approved research and teaching programs (Johnes & Taylor, 1990). The activity profiles not only of individual faculty members and individual academic units but also of entire institutions have become more directly and specifically oriented to policy relevancies and criteria that are established outside the institutions themselves.

Universities and colleges that have been drawn into these processes no longer operate as self-governing and autonomous institutions in the way they did even a decade ago.[9] Performance indicators provide the possibility of regulating the programmatic activities of these institutions and of their members, internally through an on-site administration, externally through various government funding agencies, and also through the competitive instruments of "the market."[10] Moreover, this regulation can apply separately to each aspect of academic work—teaching, research, and even service activities—or it can recombine them in ways that are relevant to the policy priorities and criteria of the regulating agency.

From this brief consideration of the local/national context, we can see how performance indicators accomplish much more than measurement. Contrasted with former situations in which on-site academic committees of departments, faculties, and senates identified problems, then interpreted and resolved them as integral parts of a single process, performance indicators make it possible to separate the work of identifying and conceptualizing issues or problems from the work of interpreting and resolving them. Regardless of what they measure or how well they can be made to measure it, performance indicators help to reorder relations within and among institutions of higher education and between the various levels within systems of higher education. Moreover, they enable these relations to extend to realms that are not directly present. They can be constructed to embody nonacademic considerations and priorities such as budget priorities, as well as corporate priorities such as the commercial exploitability of a particular research project or the job relevance of skills that are taught in a particular course or teaching program.

In sum, performance indicators have opened up the possibility of gaining control over the academic work process: that is, of shifting from collegial forms of control within autonomous institutions to managerial forms that give priority to objectives that are not necessarily academic. Also, they provide a means of standardizing aspects of academic work—for example, teaching styles and formats—and, through standardization, of producing classifications of institutions within national and international systems.

THE INTERNATIONAL CONTEXT

Increasing attention and energies are being devoted to performance indicators by university administrators, educational quality consultants, and government bureaucrats internationally. Various international bodies and conferences, such as the International Conference on Assessing Quality in Education, are engaged in producing and disseminating new knowledge about performance indicators and their application, and, perhaps most significantly, in developing an internationally oriented "profession" of performance assessment experts. It is only reasonable to expect that such a profession will increasingly exhibit an interest in perpetuating and expanding the value of its knowledge and expertise.

Again, we will consider what is made possible and/or transformed, in this case by international cooperation and convergence on this issue. We first draw an analogy to other professions. For some time, Louis Orzach has been tracking the implications of international developments for professional workers, both in the context of the European Community and in the context of the newer multinational trade agreements such as the General Agreement on Trade and Tariffs (GATT) and the North American Free Trade Agreement (NAFTA). His focus is on various ongoing processes that are oriented toward developing common standards and means of regulating professionals and the provision of their services across national borders (Orzach, 1992). These processes are seen by some commentators as eroding local and national professional control, insofar as they involve the transfer of standard setting and other powers to supranational bodies composed of a plurality of actors (including but not restricted to professional associations), many of whom have a more entrepreneurial rather than professional ethos or orientation.

Although they are members of professional associations and learned societies, academics—unlike other professional groups—have tended not to develop or accede to national standards. Instead, their anarchic forms of self-regulation afford a greater degree of international mobility and freedom than many other professions enjoy. However, international collaboration and convergence around performance indicators makes it possible to create and impose criteria and mechanisms through which academics' professional practices can be brought under external, international control. For example, international indicators allow for categorizing academics into different levels (research academic, research/teaching academic, teaching academic), which could in turn be used to regulate their mobility, pay scales, and so forth.

More commonly, performance indicators have been used, or proposed to be used, to categorize and differentiate institutions rather than individuals (although it is important to understand that this possibility is inherent in them). For example, they are currently being used in various countries and in various kinds of institutions, such as hospitals,[11] to develop categories of institutions and ostensibly to more rationally and effectively allocate resources to them. Although different countries have had varying degrees of success at rationalizing their higher education systems, arriving at an international consensus around university performance indicators may allow for the creation of a single global system (or world trade region systems) of categorizing and funding higher educational institutions. In other words, they may allow the production of a tiered higher education system extending horizontally across countries as opposed to simply vertically within them. A multilateral tiered higher education system may be seen as a more efficient means of providing multinational corporations with a smaller but more broadly distributed skilled workforce. Finally, this tiered higher educational system would be well served by a matching tiered system of academic workers whose production we alluded to above.

A second possible implication of these international discussions and conceptualizations of performance indicators is to dilute the input of academics, even into local decisions about performance indicators. This calls into question the assumption that with enough effort, academics and their associations can shape performance indicators in their own interest and according to their own priorities—an assumption that underlies the accommodationist strategy we previously discussed. Indeed, it may be fair to say that these international discussions not only dilute academics' contribution to the formulation of indicators, but actually serve to circumscribe the parameters within which they may contribute to this process, thus further restricting their power and efficacy within their local institutions as well as in their national contexts.

Knowledge Workers in General

More insights about the workings and accomplishments of performance indicators may be available to us through considering some important developments that have begun to arise for the burgeoning category of knowledge workers in general, particularly in the 1990s context of economic and political restructuring that many scholars associate with globalization. Policy and academic research literature has begun to seriously take up the question of knowledge-based work as a central ingredient of postindustrialism and globalization. It is not unthinkable that many established forms of organizing knowledge workers—professionals and academics, for example, who until now have exercised considerable autonomy in their work organizations—might become increasingly subject to greater control. To put it another way, as their work is viewed as being increasingly central to economic development and political reorganization, it is reasonable to assume that economic and political concerns will be brought to bear on the way it is accomplished.

There are at least four possible reasons for this new interest in regulating the activities of knowledge workers. First is the increase in knowledge workers proportional to other categories of workers, particularly in the advanced industrial societies of which we have been primarily speaking. Second is the perceived[12] importance of knowledge workers in achieving industrial and national competitiveness in the context of globalization (Reich, 1992). Third are emerging employment patterns in which industrial organizations—particularly multinationals—search in a global rather than national context for labor pools to produce aspects of their products and services, and workers become more internationally mobile in seeking employment. Fourth are characteristics of knowledge itself and their implications for the utilization of knowledge for specifically economic purposes.

One such characteristic of knowledge is its "leakiness"; that is, it is difficult to "trap" knowledge so that it can be used and applied in the interests of those who may acquire a proprietary stake in it.[13] A second characteristic is that, given its perceived centrality to economic competitiveness, knowledge has acquired increasing economic and political value. Finally, and perhaps most challenging to effective regulation, is the fact that the ability to produce new knowledge resides in the person; in other words, while knowledge already developed can be separated from the producer, the ability to produce it cannot. Consequently, it is especially important and difficult for firms to maintain the involvement and commitment of their workforce. Performance indicators offer a solution to this problem. Through them, even professional workers such as academics may become psychologically and materially preoccupied with institutional requirements rather than with their own interests and projects.

A pointed illustration is provided in an article reporting on a significant change in the working conditions of researchers, engineers, and technicians—knowledge workers—at the National Research Council (NRC) of Canada. The change involves instituting time sheets, the reason for which is straightforwardly presented: "The time sheet tells NRC researchers, *in a way that mere words don't* [italics added], that their time is no longer their own" (Strauss, 1993, p. A11). The introduction of the time sheet is linked to the NRC's recent efforts to change its focus and to transform itself into an institution that specializes more in applied research and partnership projects in contrast to its past emphasis on pure research. The following quotation makes the connection:

> The agency's highly educated, curiosity-driven scientists and engineers also had to be convinced that the change from a research establishment to a more applied one fit their personal ambitions. For most of the agency's history, the research agenda was driven by the personal interests of the researchers, the significance of their publications, and the approval ratings garnered from peer reviews of other scientists. Changing this went not only against NRC's recent history but also against several hundred years of international scientific tradition. . . . NRC managers had to decide how to convince "workers" who might be smarter, more satisfied with their lives and some cases even better paid than they, to alter the focus of their work. (Strauss, 1993, p. A11)

The report describes a transformation of NRC scientists from being oriented toward a traditional conception of pure and basic research to a more market-oriented conception. Various "carrots and sticks" were used to achieve this transformation, and performance-based assessments were prominent. Biologists, for example, were subjected to eleven strategic assessments in a single year.

The NRC example illustrates well how performance indicators can be used to introduce new criteria of judgment into an organization, which, in turn, begins to reorient even highly trained scientists to work in new ways. The constant ratings and the making of resource allocation decisions based on them keep people on their toes, so to speak; they introduce new opportunities for reward and sanction. Moreover, rather than being judged by one's peers, who may share understandings of dry periods, shifting research interests, and the passion to pursue a particular line of inquiry until answers are found, workers are judged by criteria that are set and interpreted by managers, consultants, government officials, or even individuals who claim to represent "the public." Thus, workers may be less inclined to pursue their own agendas and more inclined to perform in terms of the new criteria, whether to keep their job or to maintain the value of their own expertise or, perhaps more important, to retain a sense of personal security and pride in their accomplishments.

These accomplishments of performance indicators resonate with the reports provided by academics of the changing nature of their conditions of work within the academy. On the one hand, they speak of increasing workloads, heightened competition for resources, and hence division and fragmentation within and among campus-based academic communities, declining morale, and less and less ability to influence the overall objectives and *modus operandi* of their institutions (Currie, 1996). On the other hand, they also speak of the new opportunities for teaching and research innovations that have opened up through various industry- and government-sponsored initiatives, of more opportunities to link up with international research teams and teaching programs, and of the benefits of new models of collaborative research that involve them with industrial scientists, practitioners, and community groups. But whether they speak in negative or positive terms or a combination of both, their comments highlight new models of decision making in local institutions and in the overall system of higher education of which they are a part. Through these new models, performance-based assessments of various kinds are used to determine the resource allocations from which academic workers may alternately, or even at the same time, benefit or suffer.

We have enumerated a number of possibly related, possibly contingent, and possibly mutually reinforcing projects that may foreshadow the development of a globalized knowledge industry that will be regulated through international employment standards and accrediting bodies, trade agreements containing intellectual property rights clauses, supranational higher education councils, and the like. However, an important caveat is in order. We have been careful to state that we have been exploring potentialities rather than realities. Even though we have based our exploration on applications of performance indicators that have been proposed and in some cases implemented, describing possibilities is not to predict that any particular "effect" will necessarily come to pass. In order for these possibilities to appear "in the material world," so to speak, they must be taken up by social agents.

When we take into account the various agents that constitute the social relations of academic work, the processes that we have described or to which we have alluded may be problematic, if not contradictory, in a number of important respects. For one thing, it cannot be assumed that knowledge workers will readily accede to the forms of regulation in which performance indicators are embedded,[14] particularly those who have a strong sense of political entitlement and resourceful organizations to represent their interests. They have the skill to take apart the technical grounds of performance indicators and the political base from which to challenge the legitimacy of managements that seek to impose them (Buchbinder & Newson, 1988). In fact, the current debate about performance indicators, at least in part, is the evidence of these kinds of challenges.

Furthermore, the recent activity around performance indicators is contextualized both by managerialism and by corporatism. Although mutually reinforcing in many respects, managerialism and corporatism reference potentially conflicting and contradictory social projects, especially when we take into account the interests that are served by them. For one thing, regulation through institutional and political administration—in other words, the exercise of managerialism—is not necessarily in the interest of those who would benefit from regulation through the market. So, for example, university administrators may have an interest in controlling the research activities of the faculty to ensure that the financial benefits of university-corporate collaborations fall to the university while, on the other hand, the "entrepreneurial spirit" being encouraged in the faculty of universities may lead faculty members to want to pursue corporate linkages independent of institutional interference.[15]

For another thing, particularly in the international context, the corporate community is not a monolith. For example, in the United States, university collaborations with foreign-based corporations have been strongly opposed by domestic industries and politicians who represent their interests, on the grounds that their businesses may suffer from the benefits to foreign competitors of gaining access to leading-edge science and the expertise of highly skilled scientists (see Noble, 1989).

Because our consideration of the social accomplishments of performance indicators points not to closures but only to possibilities, exposing lines of slippage and room for interventions that could disrupt, as much as enable, the economic and political reorderings to which we have pointed, we return in the conclusion of this chapter to the issue of strategy.

CONCLUSION

Our interest in strategy arises from our concern that the economic and political reorderings that are reflected in and propelled by the application of performance indicators contain inherent dangers[16] to public-serving systems of higher education. Because the levels and range of the activity around performance indicators are complex as well as extensive, a serious and detailed consideration of strategies deserves an entire chapter of its own. Here, we will make only a few brief suggestions.

We see only further danger in a strategy that advocates that academic workers themselves become involved in improving performance indicators so that they more adequately measure what universities and colleges do. Regardless of the "good" intentions of those who design the measures, and regardless even of their content, once they are put into place as the basis for decision making in higher education, they can be changed, modified, and implemented in ways that would serve other purposes. Although this same concern applies to other forms of decision making—for example, academic senates and faculty councils have been used to carry out the agendas of their most influential members—the process by which performance indicators are designed and applied is less transparent and less accessible to political intervention and debate (Newson, 1992). Nor do we see value, as some have argued, in applying performance indicators more broadly, for example, turning the spotlight on the efficiency and cost-effectiveness of university administrations. Such an approach may have short-term rhetorical benefits, but in the long run, it legitimizes the notion of accountability on which they rest. That is, it accepts the idea that, if enough effort is given to it, complex issues of quality can be assimilated into standardized measures, making it possible to resolve complex issues and problems from outside the contexts in which their meaning can be assessed.

We believe that strategies to mitigate against the dangers of performance indicators must be located in the social foundations of performance indicators rather than in their technical foundations, because their potential for reordering the social relations of academic work is contained in social rather than technical processes. We have pointed to a number of contradictions and conflicts in these social relations as the reordering process unfolds. Effective strategies will be those that can successfully exploit these conflicts and contradictions as points of intervention, to disrupt the reordering processes or to alter them in ways that will remove or minimize the dangers.

One potentially fruitful strategy flows from the particular problems that knowledge workers present to those who carry the responsibility for managing their work. Because knowledge workers possess the skills of analysis and expect (as well as need) to exercise independent judgment in creating new knowledge, managers of knowledge workers may be more vulnerable, or vulnerable in different ways, to legitimacy challenges than are managers of other types of workers. The interviews with British university administrators reported by Buchbinder and Newson (1988) and the newspaper article on NRC scientists referred to above suggest that to retain the cooperation, if not the respect, of those whom they manage, managers of knowledge workers may need to use techniques and methodologies of management that are more credible to the workers.

These insights can inform a strategy for dealing with the implementation of performance indicators in higher education. Rather than helping to solve this problem of credibility through designing "better" and "more appropriate" indicators—and for the very reason cited, it is very likely that higher level managers and government officials would welcome the participation of academics in this process— exposing the weaknesses of these techniques for solving the problems that institutions are facing would pose a strong challenge to the legitimacy of those who are attempting to apply them.

One important contradiction that can be used strategically applies to the objectives of achieving cost-effectiveness and cost-efficiency, which are assumed to be desirable objectives and are used to justify the use of performance indicators. Developing measurements (which in any event won't adequately address the problems that institutions are facing) will hardly involve cost savings and will almost certainly involve additional costs in both time and money to local institutions and to systems of higher education. It will require, on a routine and recurring basis, that measures be constructed of complex phenomena such as educational quality, that data be collected that will make the measures operational, that a capacity be developed to continually update the data, that the applications be monitored, and that reports be made to the various bodies within the accountability structure. Once the financial justifications for their use is challenged, it will then be possible to focus critical attention on the social reordering consequences that we have outlined.

A long-term strategy would be to engage in well-designed research about the effects of applying performance indicators on (a) the goals that they are purported to achieve—for example, ensuring meaningful accountability to the public, improved effectiveness and efficiency in institutional operations, and improved quality of education from the point of view of students—and (b) such things as the breadth versus narrowness of an institution's research programs; the range of publics to which an institution's research is directed; the diversity of teaching formats in relation to student composition, levels of study, and program variations; the morale and commitments of the faculty, staff, and students; and so on. Such research could also be used to advocate a different, more robust notion of an institution's accountability to its publics.

All these lines of strategy—and there are others like them—have the potential to reconstruct the terrain on which the struggle around performance indicators is being waged, rather than ceding that terrain and challenging only the content of indicators and the choice of contexts to which they are applied. Also, all of these lines of strategy require academics and educators to take a far more aggressive approach toward confronting the underlying conditions that have given rise to the application of performance indicators to higher education. To be sure, less aggressive and more accommodationist proposals for action may be based on the best of intentions. However, although they consume a great deal of time and energy, they often arise out of a sense of powerlessness to do anything but cooperate. They may also arise out of an opposite sense, however. They may arise out of an unwillingness to risk the loss of power and influence for refusing to cooperate with what appears as a "legitimate" demand for accountability.

There are both contradiction and irony in this situation. On the one hand, knowledge workers are perceived to be increasingly valuable to the economic advancement of their societies, especially in the context of global competition. Yet the claims of academics to be self-governing autonomous professionals are being seriously challenged. Paradoxically, many academics fear that refusing to cooperate with the current initiatives of governments and administrations will lead to the loss of privileges and influence. Yet their cooperation risks the greater danger that the processes that threaten their interests will be further enhanced. Moreover, to cooperate with initiatives such as achieving accountability through performance indicators out of a sense of powerlessness to intervene more meaningfully is to not take advantage of the leverage that knowledge workers hold as influential social agents who possess resources of great value at this moment in history.

We believe that the present situation is replete with opportunities for academics to exert their influence. Most important, we believe that their responsibility for preserving universities and colleges as places where knowledge is freely produced and disseminated for broadly defined social purposes requires them to do so.

NOTES

1. The application of performance indicators to higher education is being debated and/or acted upon in highly developed societies such as Australia, Britain, Canada, Japan, New Zealand, countries in Western Europe, and the United States, and in developing societies such as the countries of Latin America.

2. For example, two reports in our own country (Canada) detail the growing involvement of a number of organizations in this effort (see Bruneau, 1994; "Performance Indicators," 1996, pp. 1-2).

3. We are mindful that academics have been central to developing the research and expertise on which many of the procedures of assessment are based. The "contradictory" position of academics as professionals will not be addressed here but only noted.

4. For example, see *CAUT Bulletin,* Special Edition, May 1996; *OCUFA Forum,* Special Supplement, May/June 1996: 2-4.

5. By *strategy of accommodation,* we are referring to responses to political, social, and economic pressures that, rather than confronting the prevailing circumstances in

order to change them, maneuver within the limits set by these circumstances to permit individuals and groups to at least protect themselves and their interests, if not to advance them. For an expanded discussion of the idea of accommodationist strategy, see Polster (1996b).

6. We cannot elaborate here on our understanding of managerialism and corporatism. We use these terms to reference two distinct but mutually reinforcing constellations of practices that have significantly transformed higher education institutions over the past two decades or more. See Newson, 1992, 1994; Newson and Buchbinder, 1988.

7. The three include the Natural Sciences and Engineering Research Council (NSERC), the Social Sciences and Humanities Research Council (SSHRC), and the Medical and Health Studies Research Council (MHSRC).

8. As announced by Dr. Lyn Penrod, president of the SSHRC, and other staff members of the SSHRC in meetings with the Social Sciences Federation of Canada in the fall of 1994 and 1995.

9. It should be noted that performance indicators facilitate as well as arise out of managerialism, and in this sense, they are one element—albeit a significant one—of a larger constellation of changes that can be related to restricted autonomy and diminished self-governance in universities (Newson, 1992; Newson & Buchbinder, 1988).

10. We can only mention here the recent application of market-oriented regulating concepts to issues such as tuition fees, the funding of new teaching and research programs, interinstitutional competition, and so on.

11. In Alberta, Canada, for example.

12. We use the word *perceived* here because we do not want to assert that knowledge workers will be important in the kind of economies and polities that much of the policy literature envisions. In fact, some scholars challenge this anticipated need for a large supply of knowledge workers in the kind of futures to which current trends may be leading. See Henwood, 1995.

13. This is well displayed in patent and licensing conflicts where those who seek to "own" the use of intellectual ideas must be able to demonstrate their proprietary claims to original discovery.

14. For example, a long-term NRC researcher recently informed Newson that the time sheet was no longer being employed by NRC because it failed to secure credibility with NRC workers.

15. In fact, we think it may be important to distinguish at least two forms of corporatism emerging within corporate-linked universities: managerial corporatism and entrepreneurial corporatism. An illustration of the potential conflict between these occurred at a university in California in which the central administration proposed to establish an "arms-length" corporation through which all research involving links with corporate sponsors and clients would be coordinated. The proposal was brought to the faculty for approval, and it was rejected. Many argued that they were entitled to be the primary financial beneficiaries of their research, not the university.

16. Generally speaking, these dangers involve the reconceptualization of the purposes served by institutions of higher education. See Polster (1994, 1996a), Newson (1992, 1994), and Buchbinder and Newson (1990). Our work has contributed to a growing critique of various aspects of managerialism, corporatism, and associated trends.

REFERENCES

Bowen, H. (Ed.). (1974). *Evaluating institutions for accountability* (New Directions for Institutional Research, No. 1). San Fransciso: Jossey-Bass.

Bruneau, W. (1994, November). *The perils of performance indicators.* Working Paper of the Committee on Performance Indicators and Accountability of the Canadian Association of University Teachers.

Buchbinder, H., & Newson, J. (1988). Managerial consequences of recent changes in university funding policies: A preliminary view. *The European Journal of Higher Education, 23,* 151-165.

Buchbinder, H., & Newson, J. (1990). Corporate-university links in Canada: Transforming a public institution. *Higher Education, 20,* 355-379.

Cassin, M., & Morgan, J. G. (1992). The professoriate and the market-driven university: Transforming the control of work in the academy. In W. Carroll, L. Christiansen-Ruffman, R. Currie, & D. Harrison (Eds.), *Fragile truths: Twenty-five years of sociology and anthropology in Canada* (pp. 247-260). Ottawa: Carleton University Press.

Currie, J. (1996). The effects of globalisation on 1990s academics in greedy institutions: Over-worked, stressed-out, and demoralised. *Melbourne Studies of Education, 37*(2), 101-128.

Henwood, D. (1995). Info fetishism. In J. Brooks & I. Boal (Eds.), *Resisting the virtual life* (pp. 163-172). San Fransciso: City LightsBooks.

Johnes, J., & Taylor, J. (1990). *Performance indicators in higher education: UK universities.* Buckingham, UK: Open University Press.

Kogan, M. (1986). *Education accountability: An analytic overview.* London: Hutchinson.

McNeil, M. (1995, May). U.K. is no nirvana for academics. *The Caut Bulletin,* p. 9.

Newson, J. (1992). The decline of faculty influence: Confronting the corporate agenda. In W. Carroll, L. Christiansen-Ruffman, R. Currie, & D. Harrison (Eds.), *Fragile truths: Twenty five years of sociology and anthropology in Canada* (pp. 247-260). Ottawa: Carleton University Press.

Newson, J. (1994). Subordinating democracy: The effects of fiscal retrenchment and university-business partnerships on knowledge creation and knowledge dissemination in universities. *Higher Education, 27,* 141-161.

Newson, J., & Buchbinder, H. (1988). *The university means business: Universities, corporations, and academic work.* Toronto: Garamond.

Noble, D. (1989, October 8). Higher education takes the low road. *Newsday,* Ideas Section, p. 7.

Orzach, L. H. (1992). *International authority and professions: The state beyond the nation-state.* John Monnet Chair Papers, The European Policy Unit at the European University Institute.

Performance indicators: Accountability or bean-counting? (1996, May/June). *The OCUFA Forum,* Special Supplement, pp. 1-2.

Polster, C. (1994). *Compromising positions: The federal government and the reorganisation of the social relations of Canadian academic research.* Unpublished doctoral dissertation, York University.

Polster, C. (1996a). Dismantling the liberal university: The state's new approach to academic research. In R. Brecher, O. Fleischman, & J. Halliday (Eds.), *University in a liberal state* (pp. 106-121). Aldershot: Avebury.

Polster, C. (1996b, May). *Re-adjusting ourselves to death: Assessing and transcending academics' response to the dismantling of the liberal university.* Presented at the Conference on Liberal Arts and the Future of Higher Education, Banff Conference Centre, Alberta, Canada.

Reich, R. (1992). *The work of nations.* New York: Vintage.

Smith, D. (1990). *Conceptual practices of power.* Toronto: University of Toronto Press.

Strauss, S. (1993, January 18). Research Council tries to mix oil and water. *The Globe and Mail,* p. A11.

Trow, M. (1994). Managerialism and the academic profession: The case of England. *Higher Education Policy, 7*(2), 11-18.

CHAPTER 9

Changing Accountability and Autonomy at the "Coalface" of Academic Work in Australia

Lesley Vidovich
Jan Currie

On accountability:

We now spend more time giving an account of
what we are doing than we spend actually doing it.

On autonomy:

Just this loss of sense of agency, of autonomy,
and a feeling that things have been done to
you. So it is really a sense of a loss of
professional decision-making capacity.

> *—Responses from two academics in a 1994-1995*
> *interview study of the changing nature of*
> *academic work in Australia*

DEFINITIONS OF ACCOUNTABILITY AND AUTONOMY

It is not the intention here to provide an extensive overview of the nature of these concepts; however, some brief definitions

AUTHORS' NOTE: This chapter is based on a research study that has been funded by grants from the Australian Research Council and Murdoch University. We thank them and the 115 respondents who were interviewed. Special thanks to Harriett Pears for contributing her extensive skills with NUD•IST and to the other interviewers, James Bell, Jim Breadmore, and Margaret Crowley.

are required to set parameters for the subsequent discussions. Accountability is described by Berdahl and McConnell (1994) as being answerable to various constituencies for responsible performance. They cite Paul Dressel's definition, which will be employed in this chapter:

> Responsible performance, then, involves using allocated resources legally and wisely to attain those purposes for which they were made available. Responsible performance requires continual accumulation of evidence of the extent to which purposes are achieved; reviewing the evaluation evidence to clarify the avowed goals and their interpretation; consideration of the relevance, effectiveness, and costs of the processes used to achieve the goals; and continuing effort directed at improving the educational processes used or finding more effective processes. (Berdahl & McConnell, 1994, p. 58)

Definitions of autonomy are more diffuse than those of accountability. In relation to universities, two levels of autonomy are often distinguished: institutional and individual. Individual autonomy is usually associated with the notion of academic freedom. However, Slaughter (1994) employs a broader construction of academic freedom (based on that used by the American Association of University Professors) to encompass a collective right to self-governance, suggesting a confluence of individual and institutional autonomy. In Australia, Linke (1990), the chair of a project on academic freedom and institutional autonomy, defined the former as the exercise of professional judgments without fear of retribution and the latter as the right of institutions to be self-determining. Berdahl and McConnell (1994) emphasize that although they are closely related, these terms are not synonymous. That is, academic freedom is not guaranteed by institutional autonomy, although the authors believe that a high degree of autonomy fortifies academic freedom. Bartos (1990), however, drives a deeper wedge between these two notions by pointing out that a university's autonomy may be actively exploited to restrict the freedom of its academic staff, especially in situations where the interests of management and staff are different. This scenario is increasingly the case, according to commentators like Bessant (1995), who argue that there is a growing gap between senior executive groups and academic workers as a result of adopting corporate management practices in universities. Meek (1995) believes that autonomy can be viewed as a relational issue that involves balancing power between government and institutions at one level, then between institutional management and academics at the "coalface" at another level. This chapter uses two distinct notions of autonomy: autonomy for the institution to act independently of government (be self-determining) and autonomy of individuals within institutions to act as professionals to govern themselves and be free to speak out on any issue.

THE POLICY CONTEXT

By the 1980s, a major feature of the global context of higher education was the transition from elite to mass systems, on the assumption that if a larger proportion of the population was university educated, the skills base of a country's workforce, and hence its position in the global marketplace, would be enhanced (Dudley & Vidovich, 1995; Marginson, 1993). However, this rapid expansion of higher education systems was occurring at a time of global economic constraint, and thus governments were under pressure to limit public expenditure and obtain "value for money" from their systems of higher education. Governments were no longer simply prepared to provide the funds (inputs) but began to turn their attention to outcomes—hence their concerns with accountability (Van Vught & Westerheijden, 1994).

Within this global context, Australia's Hawke Labor government, reelected for a third term in 1987, immediately initiated reforms in higher education as a key element in its micro-economic reform agenda. Minister John Dawkins's Green (discussion) Paper of 1987 and the White (policy) Paper of 1988 triggered a "revolution" in Australian higher education (Karmel, 1990), especially in relation to increasing accountability. In particular, the institutional profile that was to be negotiated with the Commonwealth Government, and would then form the basis for funding, would become the main mechanism used to hold institutions to account. Furthermore, in a major departure from long-standing funding principles, the White Paper foreshadowed the use of performance indicators as a basis for allocation of funds (Dawkins, 1988). It identified a preliminary range of indicators, including student satisfaction, completion rates, relative staffing levels, research publications, and consultancy rates.

The subsequent and ongoing momentum of the Dawkins reforms in relation to accountability was demonstrated by the rapid succession of groups reporting on the further development of performance indicators. By December 1988, a working party of the Australian Vice Chancellor's Committee, in association with the directors and principals in advanced education, had identified thirty performance indicators, and its recommendation for further development of the indicators was accepted by the government. Consequently, a Performance Indicators Research Group chaired by Russell Linke was established in February 1989. This group reported in September of that year, although it presented its performance indicators with cautions about the validity and reliability of available data and the need to use multiple indicators to avoid promoting uniformity. Furthermore, the report emphasized that quantitative indicators should be only an adjunct to qualitative judgments (Linke, 1991).

Meanwhile, the notion of quality, which had been percolating into Australian education since the mid 1980s, moved to center stage in October 1991, with Minister Peter Baldwin's policy statement, *Higher Education: Quality and Diversity in the 1990s*. Despite the many different definitions of quality (Harvey & Green, 1993), it was clearly quality as accountability to stakeholders that was the basis of this ministerial policy (Baldwin, 1991), rather than quality as excellence, which has a more traditional presence in universities. Although Minister Baldwin supported the use of quantitative performance indicators, he acknowledged their limitations, in a reiteration of the Linke Performance Indicator Group cautions. Furthermore, in a reversal from Minister Dawkins's White Paper stance, Minister Baldwin emphasized that the government had no intention of prescribing performance indicators as a basis for redistributing operating grants to universities. Rewards for demonstrating quality would be separate from and additional to operating grants ($76 million indexed annually for three years)—a carrot rather than a stick!

After Higher Education Council (HEC) discussion papers and a report on the more specific parameters of quality in Australian higher education during 1992, Baldwin appointed a Committee for Quality Assurance in Higher Education (CQAHE) to conduct a three-year cycle of quality audits between 1993 and 1995. The Australian Vice Chancellor's Committee had wanted quality assessments based on a national set of performance indicators, but the HEC decided to leave the matter to CQAHE, given the complexity of the issues, thus diverting controversy (Department of Employment Education and Training, 1993). However, during this time the Department of Employment, Education, and Training (DEET) was continuing work on refining performance indicators, as detailed in its report of 1994 entitled *Diversity and Performance of Australian Universities*. Interviews conducted by Vidovich during 1995 with CQAHE members revealed that they had used some of these quantitative indicators in their quality assessments, but only to inform their more qualitative value judgments.

Arguably then, by the end of 1995, accountability construed as quality was still in the ascendancy, compared to accountability through quantitative performance indicators. Quality was the more publicly visible form of government-directed accountability. The change in emphasis from coercion (White Paper) to incentive ($76 million annually), from performance indicators to quality, and thus from quantitative to more qualitative assessments, we believe, represented a clever transformation of the accountability agenda to make it more acceptable to academics and more consistent with university culture.

Within this climate of enhanced accountability, concerns about autonomy (both institutional and individual) were increasingly emerging from within the higher education sector. Fears about a threat to autonomy were voiced as early as the Dawkins 1987 Green Paper (Karmel, 1988). Then, in 1989, in response to growing criticisms, Minister Dawkins released a media statement that he intended to legislate to protect institutional autonomy and academic freedom. As an interim measure, he commissioned the Project on Academic Freedom and Institutional Autonomy to be conducted by Russell Linke (also of the Performance Indicators Research Group). It is interesting to note that Brian Wilson, the vice chancellor of the University of Queensland, was on the reference group for autonomy, and he later went on to chair CQAHE. Thus, with Linke and Wilson, it could be said that there was a strong cross-fertilization of thinking about the twin issues of accountability and autonomy, or even that autonomy was being reconstructed within limits set by new accountability requirements.

In his subsequent report on autonomy, Linke acknowledged that developments such as the use of institutional profiles as a basis of funding; the transfer of research funds to the Australian Research Council ("clawback") and the establishment of the National Priority

(Reserve) Fund, both from university operating grants; the restructuring of management; and the increasing Commonwealth statistical requirements had all contributed to anxiety over autonomy (Linke, 1990). The report recommended against legislation to protect academic freedom and institutional autonomy, as had been mooted by the Minister, largely, it was claimed, because it had not been particularly successful overseas. Instead, the Linke report proposed guidelines on both accountability and autonomy. The government, however, did not consider either legislation or guidelines to be satisfactory (Baldwin, 1991). In rejecting these alternatives in his 1991 policy statement on quality, the new minister, Peter Baldwin, acknowledged concerns over autonomy by asking the HEC to adopt a watching brief on the matter (Baldwin, 1991), seemingly a very "soft" option. However, this did not deflect mounting tensions. The prominence of both accountability and autonomy as key issues in higher education at that time was reflected by the special issue of the *Australian Universities' Review* devoted entirely to these themes and overviewed in the introductory paper (Hindness & Hunter, 1991).

In 1993, the government's first national report on higher education again raised the issue of anxiety about academic freedom and institutional autonomy since the White Paper and the abolition of the Commonwealth Tertiary Education Commission (a more independent advisory body than the HEC). However, it simply reiterated the minister's commitment to achieving a balance between accountability and autonomy (DEET, 1993). Thus, specific measures to protect autonomy, such as legislation and guidelines, were rejected and replaced with reassurances—in the end, not very comforting to most academics. In fact, since the 1987 Green Paper, the official government rhetoric has repeatedly emphasized that there need not be conflict between accountability and autonomy (Baldwin, 1991; DEET, 1993; HEC, 1992), but more specific mechanisms for addressing the tensions do not seem to have emerged.

It is within this policy context that academics at the "chalkface" were interviewed for this study. To what extent has government policy in relation to accountability and autonomy translated into changes in the nature of academic work? What are some specific examples of changes in daily working practices? Do academics perceive accountability and autonomy to be in a state of balance, as the government continues to assert?

THE INTERVIEW FINDINGS

Interviews on the changing nature of academic work were conducted during 1994 and 1995 with respondents at three Australian universities: Sydney, Murdoch, and Edith Cowan. These institutions were chosen to represent different contexts in Australian higher education, especially in terms of age, status, and size. Sydney University is the oldest in Australia (established in the 1850s) with a current student population of approximately 30,000, and it has traditionally enjoyed a high-status reputation. Murdoch University was established in the 1970s as an alternative or boutique university, and it has a current student enrollment of about 8,000. Edith Cowan University was a college of advanced education (focusing almost exclusively on teaching rather than research) prior to the 1988 reforms by Minister Dawkins, and it has a current student enrollment of 17,000.

One section of the interview schedule asked academics whether they had perceived changes in accountability requirements and/or changes in their sense of individual autonomy over the previous five years. The NUD.IST software program was used as a tool for analysis. Although tables are used here to display numbers and percentages of respondents and responses in the various categories that emerged from the data, the aim is not to make strict quantitative comparisons but to describe general patterns.

Accountability Results

Table 9.1 shows that a large majority of respondents at each university had experienced increased accountability in the previous five years. No respondents at any of the three universities reported feeling less accountable over that time. It seems, however, that the increased accountability was experienced by a larger percentage of the sample at the pre-Dawkins universities (92% at Sydney and 88% at Murdoch) than at Edith Cowan (75%). This finding possibly reflects the more bureaucratic structure Edith Cowan had historically inherited, where accountability was already a major feature, so that the effect of the changing accountability climate was less marked.

TABLE 9.1   Accountability by Respondents: Sydney, Murdoch, and
Edith Cowan Universities, Frequencies (and Percentages)

Institution	Increased	Same	Total
Sydney	26 (92%)	2 (7%)	28 (100%)
Murdoch	53 (88%)	7 (12%)	60 (100%)
Edith Cowan	27 (75%)	9 (25%)	36 (100%)

Responses indicating increased accountability were further subdivided to identify the perceived source of the growing demands as either internal or external to the university. Those responses coded as *external* were further subdivided depending on whether government or some other body (such as a professional association or employer group) was perceived to be making the demands. Of course, it is not a clear-cut exercise to separate internal and external demands for accountability; these are often closely interrelated and difficult to distinguish. As one respondent put it, "Many of the demands come from Canberra, DEET. They ask for information about research, they ask for information about all kinds of things, and then they go to the administration and the administration passes them to individual academics."

However, given the distinction in the literature about an internal focus of accountability related to professional development and improvement, compared to an external focus related to tightening government control, it was considered appropriate to begin to tease out these dimensions.

The predominant perception at all three universities was of internally generated accountability mechanisms (44% to 52% of responses), followed by a significant percentage (36% to 40% of responses) at each of the institutions of external accountability to governments. Senior staff were more likely than junior staff to identify government as the source of demands for accountability. This pattern might suggest that senior staff are taking a greater share of the responsibility for increased accountability, a point made in several interviews. Junior staff may simply note the increasing accountability to "higher authorities" without being able to differentiate the source.

As increased accountability was the predominant response at each university, quotes have been selected and presented below to provide more detailed insights into examples of accountability mechanisms foremost in the minds of respondents, in the core university activities of teaching and research.

1. Accountability in teaching. In teaching, it was the compulsory course evaluations by students that featured in interviews. There was widespread concern about the weaknesses in current systems of course evaluations, especially in relation to the validity and reliability of the surveys, as well as the potential impact of always giving students what they want in order to avoid adverse evaluations. Furthermore, the reporting of course evaluation results to superiors was noted as a new phenomenon.

> Three years ago, it would have been unheard of at the University of Sydney that somebody would say: "we'll put a set of questions across everybody in your group, you won't be there when we do it, we'll send them back to the person responsible for your course, you'll then write up what you thought about it, and we'll then have a talk to you about it." That really is something quite different. (Sydney)

> We have surveys on the courses. This has only recently started. . . . You can't afford to have a bad day in any way. . . . Previously it was a voluntary thing where you went and got a survey, basically for your own feedback. Now it is presented to the rest of the Department so it opens up a whole area of being scrutinized by peers. (Murdoch)

> There is obviously a greater trend toward students evaluating, . . . Compulsory student evaluations were part of the university restructuring and the first time I had that in a formal way was first semester 1992. (Edith Cowan)

2. Accountability in research. In research, reporting on the number of publications as well as the documentation associated with grants (endless form-filling) appeared to have increased significantly. Refusal to complete forms was perhaps the most frequently cited example of resistance to increased accountability, but then some respondents who were angry and wanted to resist had found the threat of funding withdrawal sufficient sanction to force compliance.

> There are a lot more forms to fill out. It used to be that you appointed someone and left them to get on with the job in their own way. . . . Now there is much more monitoring. Research is monitored through a

system in which points are awarded to publications, and research funding which comes into the department is determined by the number of points scored. In every way, there is more monitoring. (Sydney)

The need to be constantly responding to directives from Canberra which intrude into everybody's lives, I suppose more particularly the lives of those in administrative positions. . . . Constant requests for research information about both publications and research grants, requested in every conceivable format. So you no sooner seem to have finished one set of such information than they want pretty much the same thing but in a different format, which people find very frustrating. (Murdoch)

There's definitely more directives from DEET, filling in forms. I'm actually rather resistant in this regard. Probably doesn't do me too much good. Just endless forms about your research activity, this, that, and the other thing, and half the time, I don't fill in the forms. They've clawed back the base grants—so in a sense what it will do is force individuals into some reporting mechanisms if they want to get the loading. If you want to resist the system you lose the money. (Edith Cowan)

AUTONOMY FINDINGS

Table 9.2 reveals some significant differences between universities in respondents' sense of individual autonomy in defining their own work directions. At the pre-Dawkins universities, about two thirds of respondents (70% at Sydney, and 65% at Murdoch) identified a decreased sense of autonomy, and very few, if any, experienced an increased sense of autonomy. By contrast at Edith Cowan, only half of the respondents (50%) felt less autonomous, and almost one quarter (22%) experienced an increased sense of autonomy. This finding is also likely to reflect Edith Cowan's history as a more bureaucratically structured former college, where some staff experienced increased autonomy with the change to university status in the late 1980s.

The decreased category was subdivided into a general sense of loss of autonomy (between 38% and 47% of responses at the three universities), direct interference with teaching (6% to 15%), a lack of time creating the de facto effect of reducing autonomy (0% to 5%), and

TABLE 9.2 Autonomy by Respondents: Sydney, Murdoch, and Edith Cowan Universities, Frequencies (and Percentages)

Institution	Same	Decreased	Increased	Total
Sydney	3 (17%)	12 (70%)	2 (11%)	17 (100%)
Murdoch	18 (35%)	33 (65%)	0 (0%)	51 (100%)
Edith Cowan	9 (28%)	16 (50%)	7 (22%)	32 (100%)

direct interference with research (3% to 19%). The interference with research category showed the biggest difference between universities, with Edith Cowan respondents reporting that form of reduced autonomy least often, probably reflecting the nascent character of research at that institution.

Senior staff were more concerned about reduced autonomy over the previous five years than junior staff, and senior staff were more likely to identify interference with research. This pattern may well suggest that junior academics have never enjoyed a high degree of autonomy, in either teaching or research, as suggested in one of the interviews. By contrast, the senior staff, who are more often involved in large-scale research grants that now require considerable accountability, are experiencing a significant decline in their ability to set their own directions and priorities. They may also be in a better position to identify pressures from both the administration within the university and outside influences.

As decreased autonomy was the predominant response at each university, quotes have been selected and presented below to provide more detailed examples of the ways in which academics felt that their sense of autonomy had been eroded in the previous five years.

1. General sense of decreased autonomy. Reference to threats to professionalism and lack of trust were frequent responses. Although a number of respondents referred to the increased autonomy with devolution, most of these respondents then went on to contrast the reality of increasing constraints on academic work.

We have lost autonomy. My day is driven by what I have to do, and not choosing what I want to do. Personal choice is gone. (Sydney)

In the past, you were trusted to be professional. . . . I am so angry about it (loss of autonomy) that I am quite prepared to get away with anything. Now I feel that I am not being treated as a professional, so I don't have to behave like one. I am just going to send the pieces of paper up and down and get on with what really interests me. . . . I feel that I have been pushed from working from normative rules right down to coercion and so that entitles me to get away with whatever I feel like. (Murdoch)

It's a double-edged one, that one. The autonomy that's increasing is in a bigger frame that is more constrained. . . . There's been an increasing devolution and responsibility and budget accounting, through the organization. So you get a greater sense of autonomy, but it's in an economy that's restrictive, so it's a fool's paradise. (Edith Cowan)

2. *Interference with teaching.* A vocational emphasis in teaching at the expense of broader social goals was of concern, as was a more centrally mandated curriculum that did not allow academics to modify content.

Absolutely. Autonomy has been lost. I don't perform best when someone is looking over my shoulder. If staff members come to my lectures, I can't just ignore that person. I'm aware that I'm changing my teaching. I shift attention. The notion of feeling accountable all the time is like a Big Brother. It's not supportive. (Sydney)

To give you an example, we currently are putting in place employer panels to act as advisory panels for programs about academic content. We are having it explained to us that the Quality Assurance Program didn't quite meet the expectations or standards that DEET had in mind for us, and these are the sorts of things we need to do. The employability of our graduates is also going to be enhanced by having greater employer contact. Well, that may all be important, but I would have thought that there were other arguments that should be getting a hearing too, such as the social role of the university is more than just providing employment and skills for employers. Employers are but one interest group in the community, and there are many other people. If these panels have a great degree of power to start prescribing the content of courses, well, it means that critical analysis over the role of employer groups, in certain cases, may be a touchy subject. (Murdoch)

The first thing that came to mind was reduced autonomy or reduced sense of ownership of what I am teaching. . . . I am faced with courses at relatively short notice and a lot of the courses I am involved in are pretty much cut and dried, and I could see that it is very, very difficult to really make much of a change. . . . Another perception of the whole thing may be that the program has become better organized and the persons in those positions of responsibility feel that they have it more under control. (Edith Cowan)

3. Interference with research. A shift from pure to applied research within government-designated priorities was seen by some as a short-sighted approach.

In Cooperative Research Centres, we are being directed into the areas for research; that channels into the students working in my group. That is where the dollars are coming from so we have less autonomy in terms of the programs that we can get involved in. (Sydney)

I think that we have lost autonomy in research. . . . If you look at the way DEET clawed back money from the universities and redistributed it according to government priorities. So if you put in for an ARC [Australian Research Council] research grant, you have about [a] one in four chance of getting it. You have almost no chance of getting it if you are not in one of the priority government areas. (Murdoch)

Put it this way, I am wondering how much longer I can hold on to my autonomy. I'm getting these messages which come from our own management which obviously in turn come from Canberra and I find it increasingly unattractive. . . . One is being told for example that one must—apart from going out grubbing around for research money— try to get contracts through business. We must be involved in much more team research; we must use more and more research students. (Edith Cowan)

CONCLUSION

To reiterate the "big picture" findings of this study, the predominant response in the samples interviewed at Sydney, Murdoch, and Edith Cowan universities was a change in the nature of academic work toward greater accountability and reduced autonomy. The pre-Dawkins universities revealed similar response patterns, but Edith Cowan respondents did not experience these trends to the same degree.

Arguably, its historical context as a former college meant that it was undergoing changes from a different baseline position.

There appears to be a complex interrelationship between the issues of accountability and autonomy. For many respondents in this study, the increased accountability translated directly into reduced autonomy. However, it should also be noted that among the respondents from all three universities, increased accountability (75% to 92%) was experienced more often than reduced autonomy (50% to 70%), suggesting that not all academics perceive a direct relationship between the two. Overall, however, the data from this study provide sufficient evidence to question the government's repeated assertion that accountability measures should not threaten autonomy (Baldwin, 1991; DEET, 1993).

Although the government's policy documents were strong on rhetoric about there being a range of stakeholders in higher education, many respondents in this study were negative about the extent to which government was "calling the shots." Although accountability per se was seen as legitimate, it was the specific nature of accountability requirements (especially repetitive form-filling) that was brought into question by the critics. Current mechanisms were often seen to be irrelevant extra burdens that shifted the emphasis of academic work away from more productive activities in teaching and research: They were distractions from the "main game." In follow-up interviews, many respondents contrasted an ideal of a community of professional scholars who were capable of self-regulation in the interests of students and the wider community with the current reality of government intervening to construct its own version of accountability. Such reactions from academics at the chalkface are consistent with Buchbinder and Rajagopal's (1996) assertion that budgetary requirements for accountability have become an end in themselves, substituting as the valued criteria for making professional academic judgments.

It is not only the direct government[1] intervention, particularly in the form of tying funding to performance, but also the subsequent (often knee-jerk) reactions from universities that augment the climate of accountability. Many universities have tried to anticipate government policy directions and initiated a further set of accountability mechanisms, in attempting to position themselves favorably in the funding stakes. For instance, some universities are actively developing teaching performance indicators that would sit in parallel with existing research performance indicators, even though the government has only tentatively foreshadowed possible moves in that direction. The argument has been put by some university managers that the proactive development of accountability measures within universities is likely to protect them against the imposition of external accountability. As an example, the former vice chancellor of the University of Melbourne, David Penington (1990), in trying to forge the notion of performance appraisal for staff in 1992, emphasized that if a university has appropriate internal processes in place, it reduces the chance of intervention by external processes "foreign" to universities. This proactivity suggests that universities have begun to internalize or normalize the culture of accountability set in motion by the government.

Government is thus able to use accountability mechanisms to maintain central control over the "products" of universities while leaving details of the "processes" to individual institutions. This strategy is referred to as self-regulation (Neave & Van Vught, 1991) and also "steering at a distance" (Kickert, 1991), where the steering is achieved by setting performance indicators and offering performance-related rewards—Lyotard's (1984) notion of legitimation of education through "performativity." Performativity was certainly a feature of Australia's quality policy, where the biggest rewards of money (above operating grants) and status went to those universities ranked highest on their performance. The 1996 HEC-commissioned report, which proposed linking general university funding to performance indicators across a range of university activities, would extend performativity from the margins, as was the case with the quality reviews, to the core of university functioning.

Stephen Ball's (1994) thesis is that government control through a discourse of self-management, in conjunction with a discourse of competitive markets, is legitimized through a discourse of autonomy. However, he believes that this autonomy is less real than apparent and points out that the manager's autonomy becomes the teacher's (or academic's) constraint, widening the cultural gap between the two. Nixon (1996) points to further status and autonomy differentials between top-level academics (with a high profile in research and marketing) on the one hand and a "new proletariat" (with little opportunity to exercise independent judgments and self-regulation) on the other. Drawing on Foucault, Ball (1994) identifies self-management and the market as disciplinary systems or micro-technologies of power, consistent with observations made by commentators such as Meek (1995), who argues that institutional managements now serve the role of government proxy. The end result, according to Ball, is that professionality is replaced by accountability, and collegiality by costing and surveillance.

It is our opinion that Australian policy and practice has moved too far toward bureaucratically defined and economically oriented accountability, which is driven from outside universities. There is a need to tip the balance further in favor of an internal impetus with professional accountability, and hence autonomy of academics, as a basis. Furthermore, it concerns us that the scope for more broad, qualitative indicators of performance may have been only tolerated, while work was being done to refine more specific quantitative performance indicators. With the end of Australia's three-year cycle of quality reviews in 1995 and the change of government in 1996 (from Labor to Conservative Coalition), the accountability agenda has been refocused toward the use of performance indicators. The report commissioned by the HEC (1996), which proposes performance-based funding of universities, strongly recommends that academics be incorporated into the process of defining the performance indicators to be used, so that there is a sense of ownership by the sector, thus straddling the external/internal divide. Although this might seem to be a laudable move, we contend that consultation with academics will not mitigate the fact that quantitative performance indicators are still crude instruments for measuring the attainment of even instrumental, short-term goals, let alone the broader, long-term goals of education. We argue that the widespread use of such instruments to determine funding levels for universities will distort the process of education in ways that will not serve the interests of stakeholders.

Tapper and Salter (1995) emphasize that autonomy has always been exercised within political constraints and, along with other commentators, they draw attention to the fact that as overall government funding increases, with the expansion from elite to mass higher education (although funding per student actually declined with this expansion), so will the pressure for political control (Mahony, 1991; McGregor, 1993; Tapper & Salter, 1995). With the recent trend to reconstruct universities as an economic resource, governments are claiming the right to expect universities to fulfill national needs.

Furthermore, they are refining the mechanisms at their disposal to ensure compliance with their expectations (Tapper & Salter, 1995). Funding is increasingly being used as the carrot (or is it a stick?) to force universities and academics to tow the government line. We would make the point that even given government demands for universities to contribute to fulfilling national needs, those needs should be defined broadly to include long-term social and cultural dimensions and not simply the economic requirements of the workforce at that moment. Universities have traditionally occupied a unique social position in terms of both enrichment and a critical voice in society, but the current instrumental emphasis, if it continues, will put that in jeopardy.

Both Tapper and Salter (1995) and Mahony (1991) claim that autonomy is not a passive but a dynamic concept, and thus it will change with time and it will require continual negotiation. Therefore, on this basis, academics need to continue the process of negotiation over the balance between accountability and autonomy, at both institutional and individual levels, if they are to preserve the unique (and not exclusively economic) contributions that universities make to society.

NOTE

1. In Australia, there has been a growing trend toward ministerialization of education policy, with ministers acting proactively to set policy directions, which are then implemented (to the extent that any policy is actually implemented) through the government department responsible for education (now called DEETYA—Department of Employment, Education Training and Youth Affairs—at the federal level).

REFERENCES

Baldwin, P. (1991). *Higher education: Quality and diversity.* Canberra: Australian Government Publishing Service.

Ball, S. J. (1994). *Education reform: A critical and post-structural approach.* Buckingham and Philadelphia: Open University Press.

Bartos, M. (1990). The academic freedom charter experience. *Australian Universities' Review, 33*(1/2), 23-37.

Berdahl, R. O., & McConnell, T. R. (1994). Autonomy and accountability: Some fundamental issues. In P. G. Altbach, R. O. Berdahl, & P. J. Gumport (Eds.), *Higher education in American society* (pp. 55-72). Amherst, NY: Prometheus.

Bessant, B. (1995). Corporate management and its penetration of the university administration and government. *Australian Universities' Review, 38*(1), 59-62.

Buchbinder, H., & Rajagopal, P. (1996). Canadian universities: The impact of free trade and globalization. *Higher Education, 31*, 283-299.

Dawkins, J. (1988). *Higher education: A policy statement.* Canberra: Australian Government Publishing Service.

Department of Employment Education and Training. (1993). *National report on Australia's higher education sector.* Canberra: Australian Government Publishing Service.

Dudley, J., & Vidovich, L. (1995). *The politics of education: Commonwealth schools policy 1973-1995.* Melbourne: Australian Council for Educational Research.

Harvey, L., & Green, D. (1993). Defining quality. *Assessment and Evaluation in Higher Education, 18*(1), 9-34.

Higher Education Council. (1992). *Achieving quality.* Canberra: Australian Government Publishing Service.

Higher Education Council. (1996). *Performance-based funding of universities.* Canberra: Australian Government Publishing Service.

Hindness, B., & Hunter, I. (1991). Introduction. *Australian Universities' Review, 34*(1), 2-3.

Karmel, P. (1988). Analysis of specific and resource allocation proposals. In G. Harman & V. L. Meek (Eds.), *Australian higher education restructured?* (pp. 53-64). Armidale, NSW: University of New England.

Karmel, P. (1990). Reflections on a revolution: Australian higher education in 1989. In I. Moses (Ed.), *Higher education in the late twentieth century* (pp. 24-47). St. Lucia: University of Queensland.

Kickert, W. J. M. (1991, March). *Steering at a distance: A new paradigm of public governance in Dutch higher education.* Paper presented at the European Consortium for Political Research, University of Essex.

Linke, R. (1990). *Academic freedom, institutional autonomy, and accountability in higher education.* Canberra: Australian Government Publishing Service.

Linke, R. (1991). *Performance indicators in higher education.* Canberra: Australian Government Publishing Service.

Lyotard, J.-F. (1984). *The postmodern condition: A report on knowledge.* Minneapolis: University of Minnesota Press.

Mahony, D. (1991). Autonomy and the post-Dawkins universities. *Education Research and Perspectives, 18*(1), 14-24.

Marginson, S. (1993). *Education and public policy in Australia.* Melbourne: Cambridge University Press.

McGregor, G. (1993). On the nature and scope of university autonomy: Minimal, precarious, and vital. *British Journal of Educational Studies, 41*(1), 46-51.

Meek, V. L. (1995). Introduction: Regulatory frameworks, market competition, and the governance and management of higher education. *Australian Universities' Review, 38*(1), 3-10.

Neave, G., & Van Vught, F. A. (1991). Conclusion. In G. Neave & F. A. Van Vught (Eds.), *Prometheus bound: The changing relationship between government and higher education in Western Europe* (pp. 239-255). Oxford: Pergamon.

Nixon, J. (1996). Professional identity and the restructuring of higher education. *Studies in Higher Education, 21*(1), 5-16.

Penington, D. (1990). Can real universities survive the Unified National System? In J. Anwyl (Ed.), *1989 Spring lectures on higher education.* Melbourne: University of Melbourne.

Slaughter, S. (1994). Academic freedom at the end of the century: Professional labour, gender, and professionalization. In P. G. Altbach, R. O. Berdahl, & P. J. Gumport (Eds.), *Higher education in American society* (pp. 73-100). Amherst, NY: Prometheus.

Tapper, E., & Salter, B. (1995). The changing idea of university autonomy. *Studies in Higher Education, 20*(1), 59-71.

Van Vught, F., & Westerheijden, D. (1994). Towards a general model of quality assessment in higher education. *Higher Education, 28,* 355-371.

CHAPTER 10

The Entrepreneurial University

Macro and Micro Perspectives From the United States

Edward H. Berman

In 1987, John Best sketched a framework to facilitate our understanding of the transformation of American higher education since 1945. This "revolution of markets and management," as he characterized these changes, located the contemporary college and university system within the context of the managerial and bureaucratic changes that have characterized the American economy and corporate structure in the past two generations. Today's higher education system operates within a market economy distinguished by fierce competition among many purveyors (colleges and universities) of similar products (singly, a course; collectively, an education), which vie with one another for increasingly fickle and demographically changing consumers (students) (Best, 1988).

Numerous commentators have, of course, noted the significant changes that have transpired in American higher education during the last generation. Some of these, for example, Bowen and Schuster's (1985) *American Professors*, focus on the state of the professoriate and its importance to national life; others, for example, Karabel and Brint (1989), reexamine the stratification issue through their study of the contemporary junior/community college; and still others, for example, Thelin and Wiseman (1989), concentrate on the role of intercollegiate athletics in the academy. The issue of corporate influence on the direction of higher education has been examined by others in addition to Best, for example, Slaughter's (1990) *The Higher Learning and High Technology* and Slaughter and Leslie's (1997) more recent *Academic Capitalism*, to mention only two among many studies.

These changes have coincided with additional pressures confronting American higher education. Over the past decade, and particularly during the past five years, many public universities in the United States have had to contend with a combination of severely reduced budgets, demands for greater accountability, and calls for enhanced productivity. The particulars differ from state to state and region to region, but similar trends manifest themselves nationally despite the markedly decentralized nature of American higher education. Indeed, a 1995 *New York Times* article noted New York Governor George Pataki's proposal to reduce the budget of the state's public colleges and universities by some 12.6%, whereas the University of California has seen its appropriations reduced by over one quarter during the past five years (Honan, 1995b).

It is, of course, no less true for being trite to note that the fiscal crisis of the state is causing severe problems for many public (and not a few private) universities in the United States. Tax revenues have failed to keep pace with demand for more support for such state priorities as prisons, health care, and primary and secondary schooling. The dramatic Republican Party sweep of the U.S. Congress in 1994, and many state legislatures as well, gave added impetus to the tax-reduction/anti-government frenzy that has long been integral to American political life. Accordingly, the percentage of state revenues appropriated for higher education has decreased in many locales; for example, in Florida, the figure has dropped to 7.6% from 10% several years ago; in Massachusetts, the decrease has been from 7.8% to 4.7% (Adler, 1996; Breneman, 1995). Indeed, if present trends continue, it is estimated that by the year 2000, California will spend 18% of its state budget on prisons and only 1% on its university system (Katz, 1996).

Some states have responded by raising tuition (increased by 125% at the University of California system) and/or by reducing university programs and staff positions while simultaneously encouraging early faculty retirements. Others, notably the state of Maine, are putting greater resources into distance learning and the accompanying technological hardware, arguing that permanently reduced appropriations for higher education dictate a more cost-effective instructional "delivery system" than the usual teacher-student classroom setting. Increasing faculty teaching loads has been a common administrative reaction to reduced appropriations across the country. The steady growth in the number of part-time faculty—who according to generally accepted estimates now account for about 30% of all classes taught nationally—is yet another way to reduce costs while simultaneously enhancing tuition revenue (Breneman, 1995; Honan, 1995a).

Concomitant with the steady downward pressure on higher education budgets has been the equally steady pressure for greater institutional and professorial accountability. Demands for this accountability come from a variety of sources, but the most marked are agencies of both the federal and state governments. A particularly egregious example of this accountability mania at the institutional level takes the form of the newly created State Postsecondary Review Entities, which grew out of the 1992 reauthorization of the federal Higher Education Act. The particulars are of no import at this juncture. Suffice it to say that the creation of such entities poses serious threats to the traditional methods of institutional assessment, as it has long been practiced through regional accrediting agencies, which as a matter of course involved considerable faculty voice in the accrediting/assessment procedures (Benjamin, 1994; Cage, 1995). Faculty increasingly are being subjected to pressures to "account" for their time, as state agencies insist on the submission of regular worksheets documenting time spent "on task."

Reduced appropriations for higher education and the increased calls for accountability cannot be separated from the theme highlighted by John Best and noted above. A former president of the American Association of University Professors has characterized the trend so pervasive in contemporary public colleges and universities as "this market-driven debasement of higher education" (Pratt, 1994). The effort to commodify higher education even further continues apace. Both state politicians and too many university presidents insist that higher education increase its productivity while reducing costs. One way to achieve this, it is widely held, is to follow the corporate sector's lead by downsizing and, particularly, restructuring the nation's higher education system.

The influence of the marketplace on the direction of American higher education is perhaps most obvious in the numerous commercial ventures that increasingly link colleges and universities to for-profit ventures. Many of these, particularly those involving prestigious institutions, have by now been well documented; I shall briefly return to this theme below. To demonstrate that the reach of the marketplace extends far beyond the nation's most influential public universities, I shall note as well the degree to which this revolution of markets and management has penetrated one regional public university. It is clear that the issues raised at this institution are not singular to this campus; rather, they reflect similar trends at comparable universities across the country. Before explicating this issue, however, it is worth mentioning other less obvious manifestations of capital's penetration of the network of higher education.

TOWARD THE COMMODIFICATION OF UNIVERSITY LIFE

In an insightful—and largely overlooked—study, Clyde Barrow (1990) documents the degree to which, and the methods whereby, capital helped to shape American higher education in the period from 1894 to 1928. The theory of scientific management espoused by F. W. Taylor and his acolytes, which so grasped the imagination of the nation's industrial and manufacturing sectors, also found a receptive audience among American educators. Raymond Callahan's (1962) *Education and the Cult of Efficiency* succinctly summarizes how the principles of Taylorism designed for the factory floor were adapted and applied to the rapidly expanding primary and secondary system during the early decades of the twentieth century. In a less familiar story, Barrow documents how Taylor's principles were incorporated into university practice as well.

In a move reminiscent of these earlier efforts to Taylorize American higher education and make it more efficient, today's university administrators have turned to two of the latest corporate-generated guarantees of product enhancement, strategic planning and total quality management (TQM). There is a certain irony in these attempts once again to structure higher education along corporate lines. And a strong sense of *déjà vu* as well. At my own university, for example, the recently retired president—who incidentally referred to himself as the chief executive officer (CEO)—invested considerable energy and resources in an effort to institutionalize the major tenets of TQM. This was accomplished over regular opposition of faculty, who argued for additional resources for instructional purposes or library materials. The president mouthed the platitudes of TQM—which emphasizes teamwork, shared decision making, and employee empowerment—while simultaneously strengthening the hierarchical-bureaucratic managerial model and systematically excluding meaningful faculty involvement from the university governance process. The contradictions were blatant; more worrisome, perhaps, was the fact that he and his supporters either were oblivious to these contradictions or simply did not care (Mangan, 1992).

By the 1980s, strategic planning had become fashionable on many American campuses. And so it was at my institution, the University of Louisville. The enthusiasm for planning coincided with the arrival of a new president in 1981 and with greater efforts to better coordinate the state's public institutions by a nonpolitical Council on Higher Education. One of the president's early efforts was the development of a strategic plan to better position the university for its redefined mission within the state system.

This plan led to a significant institutional reorganization, accomplished amid the predictable protestations and cautionary pleas from faculty and other constituencies, pleas rejected by the president, who harshly criticized the faculty's failure to recognize the university's long-term interests while protecting its own through its collective obstructionist behavior. This reorganizational phase was marked by presidential demands for greater accountability, especially from the faculty; an emphasis on increased faculty productivity; new budgeting techniques and lines of reporting; and the addition of numerous well-compensated administrators. Faculty and staff salaries and increments would reflect performance-based measures, standards from which high-ranking administrators and the president himself were exempted.

In the early 1990s, the University of Louisville embarked on its second strategic plan under this president. The process leading up to the presentation of the master plan was in keeping with the principles of George Keller's (1983) *Academic Strategy*, the bible of the current crop of university administrators who draw on the corporate model for guidance. The particulars of the process need not concern us here, nor can we give attention to the specific changes advocated. However, brief mention should be made of one element of the new plan for what it suggests about the efficacy of strategic planning.

The initial strategic plan in the early 1980s called for the creation of a new college in keeping with the university's redefined mission as mandated by the state coordinating council. The new college would incorporate several existing programs and departments. Numerous faculty voices were raised against this proposal, most arguing that such reorganization for the sake of administrative convenience could not be justified programmatically. Discussions between faculty and administration over this issue were heated, frequently turning rancorous. The president prevailed, the new college was created, and a dean was appointed over the express and unanimous objections of the faculty search committee.

By the decade of the 1990s, the president had altered his priorities. Accordingly, a new strategic plan was launched. This plan, implemented in 1992 and entitled *A Strategy for the 1990s*, called for the dissolution of the same college that had been created only a few years earlier. The president's explanation for this flip-flop? The structure of the college was now inappropriate for the mission ahead. Little else in the way of explanation was offered about this issue that had caused widespread dissension on campus.

For at least the past 15 years, commentators have warned about the corrosive effects on American university life of a growing corporatist perspective, whether this involves internal management practices or relationships linking universities to for-profit corporations. The list of university-corporate affiliations negotiated since then reads like a *Who's Who* tying the most influential academic institutions to powerful corporate bodies. Harvard, for example, cooperates with Monsanto Chemical and DuPont in the field of genetic research, Carnegie Mellon is paired with Westinghouse in robotics research, and Stanford has affiliations with too many corporations to be enumerated, although some of the more visible include IBM, Texas Instruments, and General Electric. The Massachusetts Institute of Technology recently established its New Products Program, under terms of which corporations pay a specified fee in exchange for new products to be developed within two years (Bilik & Blum, 1989; Minsky & Noble, 1989; Noble, 1982; Soley, 1996; Stark, 1983).

By the mid-1990s, some of these relationships led to scandals that called into question the autonomy as well as the integrity of several universities. In 1995, administrators at the University of California at Irvine sought to cover up unprofessional, and probably criminal, activities by several faculty members affiliated with the university's Center for Reproductive Health. The particulars read like material drawn from a Grade B daytime soap opera, involving hush money, retaliation against whistle blowers, and the theft of patients' fetal eggs and subsequent implantation into infertile women. As distressing as these particulars might be, they should not obscure the larger message. In this era of shrinking revenue for higher education, "universities everywhere want faculty members who can bring in money, not only through research grants and contracts, but through clinics, patents, licensing agreements, and any other product of their intellectual activity from which administrators can take a cut." We should not lose sight of the fact, this observer notes, that "the fertility-clinic scandal illustrates the dangers posed by a private, profit-making, faculty venture inside a university—and a publicly supported one at that" (Wiener, 1995, pp. B1-B2).

The University of Arizona may now be more mindful than earlier of the dangers represented by involvement in many for-profit ventures. The university has recently paid a $4 million settlement to a university-affiliated spinoff company that sued, claiming that the university had sold the company's patented inventions to other companies. The Arizona story is replete with the usual conflict-of-interest charges, claims of unprofessional conduct by one faculty colleague against another, and recriminations among faculty and administrators. Although the particulars may vary, the larger message is similar to the one growing out of the Irvine imbroglio: University involvement in profit-making ventures is replete with dangers to the institution's traditional role as well as to its reputation (Blumenstyk, 1995).

The establishment of endowed professorships has provided increasing numbers of American universities another way to generate revenue of late. Valuable though these gifts may be, however, they usually involve only one-time money rather than the possibility of continuing capital generation that might flow from a patented product. Many of these newly endowed chairs have been created to honor prominent corporate executives or, more generally, the free enterprise system. The Reliance Professorship of Private Enterprise at the University of Pennsylvania, for example, initially stipulated that the chair holder "be a spokesperson for the free enterprise system"

(Soley, 1996, p. 126). Similar examples can be found across the country, at campuses large and small. These include the Ronald Reagan Chair of Broadcasting at the University of Alabama and the John G. McCoy-Bank One Corporation Professorship of Creativity and Innovation at Stanford. As significant as these proliferating ventures may be, they continue to be overshadowed by a more public display of the university's relationship with the corporate sector.

Perhaps the most visible manifestation of today's entrepreneurial university, at least to the general public, are the revenue-generating athletic programs, that is, football and basketball. Games between major institutional rivals are now an integral part of the American entertainment and media industry. The sums involved are considerable and can be counted in the millions of dollars, sometimes in the hundreds of millions. These programs frequently determine the priorities established by colleges and universities and, at the same time, they have played crucial roles in shaping campus culture over the past twenty-five years.

There is a growing professional literature examining the influence of athletic programs on institutional decision making. The popular press has also had more than enough copy in the past decade to fill its pages with scandalous stories detailing payments and privileges accorded to "student-athletes," the exploitative nature of the relationships between the colleges and their (particularly African American) athletic recruits, the abysmally low graduation rates achieved by football and basketball players, the consistency with which university administrators ignore their players' abusive (and not infrequently criminal) sexual behavior, and the hot-tub adventures of star hoopsters and high-rolling (and sometimes felonious) Las Vegas gambling figures (Benedict, 1996; Blum, 1996; Sperber, 1990; Thelin, 1994; Trani, 1995).

More recently, attention has turned to the growing number of arrangements whereby universities agree to outfit their players in major revenue-producing sports with equipment displaying the logo of the sponsoring company, for example, Reebok, the footgear manufacturer. A recent article summarized the particulars of Reebok's new contract with the University of Wisconsin as follows:

> Reebok . . . has agreed to furnish the university's 22 varsity sports teams with footwear, uniforms, and warm-up clothing. The company will also contribute $2.3 million for scholarships, payments to coaches,

sports programs, and community-service projects. In return, every Badger [University of Wisconsin] athlete will wear Reebok's shoes and display the company's insignia on his or her uniform. More to the financial point, Reebok will enjoy exclusive rights to market clothing modeled on the university's athletic wear. (Naughton, 1996b, p. A65)

But lest the impression be given that these problems are peculiar only to America's high-profile "name" universities, let me mention a few examples of how the same entrepreneurial mentality shapes events at a less prestigious institution.

Although the University of Louisville has until recently been credited with running a "clean" program, it has of late been subjected to increased public scrutiny and a rising level of criticism on several levels. The emerging pattern bears a striking resemblance to other programs that have been unfavorably compared to Louisville's heretofore "clean" program. Several specifics will suggest the dimension of the issue.

Twenty years ago, the faculty, through its elected senate, exercised at least nominal control over the university's athletic program. At that time, the men's basketball team was enjoying considerable success on the court, which was reflected in the revenue generated for the athletic program and the university at large. The football program, however, was another story. Seasons of poor performance, coupled with the very large expenditures required to mount the program, resulted in a regular deficit that drained not only the other athletic programs but the university's meager general fund as well. On a regular basis, the football program dipped into the general fund to pull itself out of red ink. In the early 1980s, as the university's financial situation deteriorated, the faculty senate voted to discontinue funding the athletic program from the general account, arguing that the existing practice drained money from the university's already underfunded academic programs. The athletic programs accordingly were freed from direct faculty oversight and were reorganized under an independent athletic council.

The new arrangement has been marked by several internal miniscandals (e.g., the athletic director paying bonuses to his staff from funds derived from a basketball tournament), which led the president to appoint his personal representative to oversee the program. The current council is composed of the president and his representative, members of the athletic department, outside lay members drawn from an elected Athletic Association, and a faculty representative. Decisions on the disposition of revenues generated from the football and basketball teams are made by the council. Several members have reported that the meetings are pro forma, the significant decisions having been made in advance by the president and his supporters on the council (personal communication, January 12, 1992). It is important to note that revenues generated from the athletic program have been retained by the Athletic Association and that none have been returned to the university to fund its academic programs.

The university's athletic program suffered a major embarrassment in 1996, when the national body charged with regulatory oversight of Division I teams found the basketball program guilty of providing illegal subsidies to one of the team's stars. After lengthy hearings and considerable expense in the form of a legal defense team, the basketball program was placed on probation for several years, a penalty with little meaning save the inability in the future to claim that the university's athletic program has never been placed under sanctions (McGeachy, 1996). Apparently, however, athletic program officials decided this reprimand did not have to be taken seriously. The next year, the assistant basketball coach illegally paid hotel expenses for the father of one of the team's players. The head coach dismissed the adverse publicity as little more than a nuisance ("Lack of Control," 1997).

Within the past decade, the fortunes of the football team have improved to the point that it has begun to attract national attention, with revenues to match. This increased visibility has been accompanied by calls for the construction of a new on-campus football complex to replace the existing 37,000 seat stadium, considered too small to accommodate all the fans and too antiquated to impress the high school recruits whom the coach hopes to enroll at the University of Louisville as student-athletes. Prominent community boosters organized a campaign over several years to raise revenue to fund this new football complex. This campaign was declared successful in 1996, and the university's board of trustees authorized construction to proceed.

The total cost for the football complex is estimated to be $60 million. Of this amount, $18 million will be raised from a planned local bond issue. The remainder will come from ticket sales and, most important, corporate donors. The edifice will officially be named the

Papa John Cardinal Stadium in recognition of a $5 million grant from the owner of the Papa John's pizza chain (Shafer, 1996).

It was perhaps a cruel coincidence that the football team's fortunes descended to a low point during 1997, just as concrete was being poured for the new stadium. That season, the team won only one game while losing ten. Fewer than 10,000 fans attended the last home game, down from 35,000 at the season opener. Public criticism of the coach and calls for his dismissal were turned aside by the university president, who voiced his support for coach Ron Cooper on several occasions. By season's end, however, President Shumaker reversed fields, and Cooper was fired—but not before being rewarded with a most generous severance package (McGeachy, 1997). The rationale for paying someone $1 million (after taxes) not to work at the university was noted succinctly by the president, who wrote that "we gathered as much information as possible about the situation, weighed all the options, and made a business decision that was best for U of L" (Shumaker, personal communication, December 18, 1997).

Two issues, quite aside from the ethical ones, seem worth mentioning here in passing. First, some argue that the emphasis on generating funding for the football program has come at the expense of comparable efforts to raise revenue for the university's chronically underfunded academic mission. The president regularly dismissed this argument, countering that those who donate to the university's athletic endeavors would not provide funding for its academic mission. To this, the critics have responded: Certainly they won't if the president doesn't indicate to the community at large that the university's academic mission must take precedence over its athletic programs. Second, quite aside from the issue of the appropriateness of a public university accepting funds that will facilitate extensive free marketing for a pizza mogul (how else can we characterize such transactions?), how sensible is it, measured exclusively in economic terms, to spend $60 million on a stadium that, by the most generous estimates, will be in use no more than a dozen days annually? The university's football team will play a maximum of eight games in the stadium during any one season; there are too many other stadia in Louisville to expect that the new complex can be rented to other teams (high schools) or for other events (e.g., rock concerts, gospel meetings) on more than a handful of occasions.

The opening of the 1995-1996 academic year at the University of Louisville was marked by the inauguration of its sixteenth president.

The search for this new president was conducted in almost total secrecy by the Board of Trustees and a consulting firm, faculty involvement was minimal, visits to and around campus were carefully stage-managed, and the four finalists had limited opportunities to discuss substantive issues with faculty. One of the unsuccessful candidates remarked in several campus settings that he was attracted to the position because of the opportunity to forge stronger relationships with the business community and the university's high-profile sports program (Hershberg, 1995b).

In his inaugural address, the new president noted the importance of facing the many challenges ahead with an entrepreneurial spirit. He also mentioned how the university must become "a catalyst for the international development of our region's economy, educational institutions, and cultural life" (Shumaker, 1995). In keeping with these dual emphases, he brought with him from his previous position a coordinator for a newly launched Institute for International Development. Funded with start-up monies from the president's contingency fund and full support of the trustees, the institute seeks to secure grants and contracts from a variety of foreign concerns. According to an official university press release, the institute to date has "reached an agreement with China's State Information Center to help Kentucky businesses and industries explore commercial possibilities in that nation, and also has teamed up with ITT Federal Services International Corporation to offer technical training in Saudi Arabia" (*University of Louisville News Digest*, May 2, 1996). President Shumaker reported that the initial $250,000 investment in the institute has already paid dividends, citing grants and contracts worth more than $1 million.

The most visible manifestation of this new international development thrust is the opening in Hong Kong and Athens of programs to offer master's degrees in business administration. Students enrolled in the program must complete thirty-six hours worth of credits in classes taught by an itinerant band of University of Louisville Business School faculty who will offer courses on an accelerated basis, including intensive study on evenings and weekends. These programs are offered in hopes of generating revenue for the university, while simultaneously affording some faculty the opportunity to teach in another setting. But it is unclear exactly how this effort will do more than break even financially. Students in overseas locales will pay in tuition approximately what is charged out-of-state students on the home campus, but it is not apparent how these fees can do more than just offset program expenses (personal communication, June 11, 1996). The institute is exploring several other new projects as well, including offering a degree in computer science in Cairo and a nursing degree in Abu Dhabi.

A series of events toward the end of 1996 raised questions about the relationship between such entrepreneurial activities and the direction of the American university at the close of the twentieth century. The announcement by University of Louisville President Shumaker that he proposed to privatize the Institute for International Development while transforming it into a for-profit corporation with himself at its head led to a public outcry. One member of the university's Board of Trustees resigned his position, criticizing the plan as "so ill-conceived and misguided that my time could be better spent elsewhere" (Jennings, 1996). The local newspaper editorialized that "his [Shumaker's] grandiose plan to turn the nascent overseas venture into a for-profit corporation with himself at the helm was too much, too fast, too soon" ("Tending to Business," 1996, p. A16). The next day a newspaper commentator wondered "what we're dealing with here. The possibilities range from academic megalomania to the best business deal east of East Timor" (Hawpe, 1996, p. D3).

The practice of American universities establishing overseas programs is hardly new. Boston University, the universities of Maryland and Southern California, and Johns Hopkins University have had such programs for at least 30 years now. In the past 15 years or so, many other American universities have opened overseas branches. But difficult times have set in. A number of these closed within the past several years, as tuition revenues have failed to keep pace with operating expenses (Rubin, 1996).

Initiatives intended to expose provincial American university students to international issues and concerns are obviously to be applauded. Too frequently, however, such efforts get conflated with unrealistic institutional aspirations, and the result is that the students' legitimate interests are subordinated to new institutional requisites. Once again, events at one university provide a representative account of a common trend in American higher education.

Toward the end of 1997, University of Louisville personnel commenced negotiations to purchase a fourteenth-century, ninety-nine-room Tuscan villa once owned by the Medici family. Several faculty and administrators toured the property, and the current owner, Contessa Marcella Amati-Cellesi, visited Louisville to confer with university officials. According to an internal university document, ownership of the villa, La Magia, "will become part of the blueprint that will lead our institution to national preeminence, recognized for success in creating a culture of unassailable quality, intellectual vigor, innovation, and entrepreneurship" (The University of Louisville at La Magia, 1997, p. 2). Many specifics concerning the financial aspects of the negotiations have not been shared by university administrators. Even in the absence of such information, it is possible to estimate that the cost to the university will be not less than $10 million. Included in this figure is an assumable $4 million mortgage, at least the same amount for renovations, a guaranteed annual annuity to the Contessa and her family, and ongoing maintenance expenses.

Several comments are warranted before moving to other issues. At least one prominent American university with extensive experience in international programs has turned down the opportunity to purchase La Magia. The University of Louisville, on the other hand, has relatively few faculty with experience in mounting overseas programs, and the curriculum has long been marked by a paucity of offerings that focus on international issues. In fact, as recently as December 1997, the College of Arts and Sciences had to cancel a proposed two-week study trip to Venice because only four students enrolled. Despite this, university personnel claim they can guarantee at least fifty students will reside at La Magia for an academic year and pay an $8,000 fee. Some on campus have begun to question how the purchase of this villa can be justified in view of the increasing number of part-time instructors the university uses to reduce costs, the inadequacy of classroom technology, the lamentable state of the main library, and the generally low salary schedule for faculty and staff, save ranking administrators (personal communication, January 7, 1998).

CONCLUSION

It is perhaps a sign of the times that the few episodes noted above will surprise few who have read this far. There is also the danger that such recitation can sound almost querulous, which obviously is not the intention. Although the particulars vary from one institution to another, it is patently clear that the events recounted here are more representative than not of directions taken on many college and university campuses over the past decade. It would be easy to summarize this under the heading of "University as Whore," or some such catchy title. And, of course, such a characterization would not be completely inaccurate. To leave it at that, however, may give some psychic satisfaction, but it misses the larger point, which is the manner in which the modern university is being shaped by external pressures, particularly those of the marketplace. The effort to further integrate the American university into the marketplace could not be accomplished without an alliance linking representatives of capital with higher education governing bodies (boards of trustees or regents) and administrators who serve to make acceptable to faculty the new institutional priorities. American universities and their students increasingly are viewed as an important source of revenue for the corporate sector, and many members of governing boards hope to facilitate corporate access to the campuses that they govern (Mercer, 1996).

A program in the planning stages at the University of Louisville illustrates just how tight these linkages are. For a number of years, the package delivery company United Parcel Service (UPS) has maintained a regional distribution hub at the Louisville airport. In December 1997, UPS officials announced a planned expansion at one of its regional centers, Louisville being among the sites under consideration. Local Chamber of Commerce officials estimated that some 6,000 jobs could be created over the next seven years if the city was the selected site (McGinty & Ward, 1997). The majority of UPS's current employees work part-time, and many of these are college-age students who work at night. To make the Louisville site more attractive to UPS officials, the University of Louisville and two other postsecondary institutions have put together a plan to attract to Louisville students who would be willing to work part-time at UPS. According to one report, this program "would include early-morning or evening classes; special hours for counseling and registration; study spaces and remote computer connections at UPS; transportation between work and school; and even separate dormitories with quiet hours for daytime sleepers" (Goetz, 1997, p. A17). University President Shumaker cited this as "an example of three institutions responding very quickly to a pressing economic need" (Goetz, 1997, p. A17). This effort to create, in Shumaker's words, a "college within the university" that would serve local corporate interests while favoring one group of students has engendered considerable opposition across campus (personal communication, January 10, 1998). On March 4, 1998, UPS announced an $860 million project in Louisville, tied to the university offer.

The restructuring under way at many American universities exposes numerous political conflicts. The most obvious pits governing boards and university administrators against the faculty, as the latter attempt to maintain their traditional prerogatives in the face of administrative/political fiats that some of these be weakened or abrogated. The nationwide assault on faculty tenure mounted by trustees and state legislators is one manifestation of this trend. Nor can the increased institutionalization of posttenure review practices mask the real intent to abolish tenure completely (Magner, 1996a, 1996b). A struggle has also emerged between activist members of governing boards, who insist that their universities be managed along corporatist lines, and noncompliant university presidents, who argue for continuing faculty involvement in university governance and decision making. When presidents resist such pressures, governing boards remove them or force their resignations. Such was the fate during 1996 of the presidents/chancellors of such major public universities as the University of Minnesota, the State University of New York, and, most prominently, the Berkeley campus of the University of California (Healy, 1996; Wong, 1996).

Two additional points need mentioning in closing, one drawn directly from the material above, the other more tangential, but equally important. The issue of revenue-generating athletic programs on campus casts a long shadow over that of gender equity—or more specifically its lack—in university athletic programs. The American judicial system has made abundantly clear over the past decade that any institution of higher education receiving federal funds must expend these in a manner that promotes gender equity. It is stating the obvious to note that sports programs regularly do not comply with this mandate, a generalization that applies to small institutions that do not generate revenue from their athletics programs as well as to those that bring in considerable monies (Naughton, 1996a).

The second issue is even more contentious, and perhaps for that reason, it is not one regularly mooted. But it certainly is one that needs considering, especially in any discussion of the changing nature of university work. Put simply, the question is, Should institutions like the University of Louisville attempt to transform themselves into research universities, or should they be content to function primarily as teaching and service institutions? The path to prestige, if not fame, in today's American university system demands recognition as a Level I research institution. But, in a nutshell, the issue is quickly translated into one of resources, in terms of both personnel and finances. Several interrelated examples will illustrate the conundrum.

The College of Arts and Sciences, the university's largest division, needs to offer incentive packages to attract qualified faculty, particularly in the sciences, where institutional competition is very keen. Research programs are always expensive, but this is especially true in the sciences, where faculty require updated facilities and equipment, as well as start-up costs, to run laboratories. It is estimated that laboratory renovation (long overdue) for one new hire in biology, coupled with start-up funds to get that laboratory operating, will cost $375,000. The college has allocated $750,000 over a three-year period to cover the start-up costs for new faculty in the sciences. The college has inadequate funds in its own budget to support these efforts, and is consequently importuning the Office of the Provost and the Graduate School to secure the additional funding (personal communication, June 12, 1996).

At the same time, the Chemistry Department is demanding additional funds to hire faculty, particularly to staff its growing Ph.D. program, which is generally considered by insiders to be among the university's strongest doctoral programs. Outside evaluations are less enthusiastic; a recent study ranked the program 136th in a national sample of 178 programs. And so it is with other programs; the MBA program was ranked 235th out of 281 programs surveyed, whereas the Law School was ranked 118th in a pool of 178 (Hershberg, 1995a). And all of this in a state that is the sixth-poorest in the country, has one of the lowest rates of secondary school graduation in the nation, and which is always woefully short of funding for education at all levels.

The University of Louisville is currently categorized as a Level II research university, according to the Carnegie Foundation's accreditation standards. The president recently announced an ambitious plan to move the institution to Level I by the year 2008. This would entail, among other things, doubling the number of doctoral graduates, increasing the amount of sponsored funding (external grants) dramatically, and raising the university's endowment to a minimum of $500 million from its current level of half that amount. In making this announcement, President Shumaker emphasized that "raising the university to a higher educational plateau could result in a significant economic impact on the [local] area." He continued by noting that "employers, like United Parcel Service and numerous health care companies in Louisville, will benefit from a more recognized university." And, he concluded, "there is a lot of money at stake" (Begley, 1997, p. 1).

The contradictions that inhere in the current situation are patent. The University of Louisville's research capacity is inadequate in the extreme, as measured by various indices. At the same time, the president hopes to overhaul the university within a decade, to refocus its efforts and enhance its programs so that it can better contribute to local economic growth. Two questions arise from this effort. First, can the goals be attained? An understanding of the long-term investment and time required to transform other third-rate public universities—for example, the State University of New York at Buffalo and Indiana University—into the respectable research institutions that they are today suggests the difficulty of doing so. Second, if the university is to be transformed, should the major reason for doing this be a form of narrowly focused economic instrumentalism?

Perhaps it is indeed time for an institution like the University of Louisville—and the many comparable ones across the United States—to reconceptualize its mission, and for the faculty to do likewise. But many faculty are socialized into the profession in a manner that places a premium on research. And all the rhetoric to the contrary notwithstanding, prestige within the academy continues to flow to those with significant research achievements. On the other hand, should the faculty agree to deemphasize its traditional research function, would the public and the state be better served by a University of Louisville that did the bidding of a corporate sector that views knowledge merely as another commodity to be bartered in the marketplace?

REFERENCES

Adler, M. N. (1996, November-December). Higher education squeezed by state funding pressures. *ACADEME*, p. 103.

Barrow, C. W. (1990). *Universities and the capitalist state: Corporate liberalism and the reconstruction of American higher education, 1894-1928.* Madison: University of Wisconsin Press.

Begley, D. (1997, January 30). Shumaker looks to 2008. *The Louisville Cardinal,* p. A12.

Benedict, J. R. (1996, December 27). Colleges protect athletes, not students. *The New York Times,* p. A12.

Benjamin, E. (1994, July-August). From accreditation to regulation: The decline of academic autonomy in higher education. *ACADEME,* pp. 34-36.

Best, J. H. (1988). The revolution of markets and management: Toward a history of American higher education since 1945. *History of Education Quarterly, 28,* 177-189.

Bilik, L. J., & Blum, M. C. (1989, January-February). Deja vu all over again: Initiatives in academic management. *ACADEME,* pp. 10-13.

Blum, D. E. (1996, April 26). Trying to reconcile academics and athletics. *The Chronicle of Higher Education,* pp. A51-A52.

Blumenstyk, G. (1995, July 21). Turning off spinoffs. *The Chronicle of Higher Education,* pp. A33, A35.

Bowen, H. R., & Schuster, J. H. (1985). *American professors: A national resource imperiled.* New York: Oxford University Press.

Breneman, D. W. (1995, September 8). Sweeping, painful changes. *The Chronicle of Higher Education,* pp. B1-B2.

Cage, M. C. (1995, January 20). Regulating faculty workloads. *The Chronicle of Higher Education,* pp. A30, A33.

Callahan, R. (1962). *Education and the cult of efficiency.* Chicago: University of Chicago Press.

Goetz, D. (1997, December 12). Program would cater to student-workers. *The Courier-Journal,* p. A17.

Hawpe, D. (1996, November 10). The empty chair. *The Courier-Journal,* p. D3.

Healy, P. (1996, August 9). Activist Republican trustees change the way public universities seek presidents. *The Chronicle of Higher Education,* pp. A19-A20.

Hershberg, B. Z. (1995a, March 13). First U of L finalist arrives for interviews. *The Courier-Journal,* pp. A1, A19.

Hershberg, B. Z. (1995b, July 9). Challenges confront an urban school. *The Courier-Journal,* pp. A1, A19.

Honan, W. H. (1995a, April 4). Professors battling television technology. *The New York Times,* p. A8.

Honan, W. H. (1995b, February 22). State universities reshaped in the era of budget cutting. *The New York Times,* pp. A1, A13.

Jennings, M. (1996, November 5). Mulloy left U of L in policy dispute with Shumaker. *The Courier-Journal,* pp. A1, A10.

Karabel, J., & Brint, S. (1989). *The diverted dream: Community colleges and the promise of educational opportunity in America, 1900-1985.* New York: Oxford University Press.

Katz, I. (1996, June 2). America offers a bull market in jails. *Manchester Guardian Weekly,* p. 13.

Keller, G. (1983). *Academic strategy: The management revolution in American higher education.* Baltimore, MD: Johns Hopkins University Press.

Lack of control [Editorial]. (1997, June 27). *The Courier-Journal,* p. A16.

Magner, D. K. (1996a, September 20). Minnesota Regents' proposals would effectively abolish tenure, faculty leaders say. *The Chronicle of Higher Education,* pp. A11-A12G.

Magner, D. K. (1996b, December 20). U. of Texas, with an eye on the legislature, starts a system of post-tenure reviews. *The Chronicle of Higher Education*, pp. A11-A12.

Mangan, K. S. (1992, August 12). TQM: Colleges embrace the concept of "total quality management." *The Chronicle of Higher Education*, pp. A25-A26.

McGeachy, A. (1996, September 13). Records cast doubt on Samaki Walker's summer job. *The Courier-Journal*, pp. A1, A5.

McGeachy, A. (1997, November 21). Cooper gets $1 million—tax free. *The Courier-Journal*, p. A1.

McGinty, D., & Ward, J. (1997, December 12). UPS plans major expansion. *The Courier-Journal*, p. A1.

Mercer, J. (1996, September 27). Companies seek economic gain from their gifts to colleges. *The Chronicle of Higher Education*, pp. A37-A38.

Minsky, L., & Noble, D. (1989, October 30). Corporate takeover on campus. *The Nation*, pp. 491, 494.

Naughton, J. (1996a, November 29). Appeals court affirms that Brown U. discriminated against female athletes. *The Chronicle of Higher Education*, pp. A41-A44.

Naughton, J. (1996b, September 6). Exclusive deal with Reebok brings U. of Wisconsin millions of dollars and unexpected criticism. *The Chronicle of Higher Education*, pp. A65-A66.

Noble, D. F. (1982, February 6). The selling of the university. *The Nation*, pp. 129, 143-148.

Pratt, L. R. (1994, September-October). A new face for the profession. *ACADEME*, p. 39.

Rubin, A. M. (1996, March 22). Declining enrollment and economic woes force U.S. universities to close campus in Japan. *The Chronicle of Higher Education*, p. A41.

Shafer, S. S. (1996, May 17). Papa John's founder fills deluxe order: $5 million. *The Courier-Journal*, p. A1.

Shumaker, J. (1995, September 28). *Continuity, change, and community*. Presidential inaugural address, University of Louisville.

Slaughter, S. (1990). *The higher learning and high technology: Dynamics of higher education policy formation*. Albany: State University of New York Press.

Slaughter, S., & Leslie, L. L. (1997). *Academic capitalism: Politics, policies, and the entrepreneurial university*. Baltimore, MD: Johns Hopkins University Press.

Soley, L. C. (1996). *Leasing the ivory tower: The corporate takeover of academia*. Boston: South End Press.

Sperber, M. (1990). *College sports, inc.: The athletic department v. the university*. New York: Holt.

Stark, I. (1983, Spring). Industrializing our universities: Big business tests academic autonomy. *Dissent*, pp. 177-183.

Tending to business [Editorial]. (1996, November 9). *The Courier-Journal*, p. A16.

Thelin, J. R. (1994). *Games colleges play: Scandal and reform in intercollegiate athletics*. Baltimore, MD: Johns Hopkins University Press.

Thelin, J. R., & Wiseman, L. (1989). *The old college try: Balancing academics and athletics in higher education*. Washington, DC: School of Education, George Washington University.

Trani, E. P. (1995, March 17). The distorted landscape of intercollegiate sports. *The Chronicle of Higher Education*, pp. B1-B2.

The University at La Magia. (1997, November). Planning document, typescript.

Wiener, J. (1995, July 28). The perils of profit-making ventures. *The Chronicle of Higher Education*, pp. B1-B2.

University of Louisville News Digest. (1996, May 2). Daily e-mail bulletin.

Wong, S. (1996, July 12). Successor selection potentially difficult. *The Daily Californian*, pp. 1, 5.

PART IV

TRANSNATIONAL AND SUPRANATIONAL INSTITUTIONS AND MECHANISMS

Janice Newson

The chapters in Part III locate their analyses primarily within "pre-globalized" forms of organization, and from this vantage point, they explore how these forms are being drawn into, and transformed by, processes of change that can be attributed to globalization. By way of contrast, the three chapters of Part IV locate their analyses within institutions and mechanisms that potentially constitute the global sphere itself.[1]

Each chapter focuses on a body or mechanism operating from a transnational or supranational level that carries out activities and pursues objectives that contribute directly or indirectly to the global reordering of higher education. The Organization for Economic Co-operation and Development (OECD) conducts and disseminates research on social, economic, and political issues and promotes related policy changes in higher education among its member nations. The North American Free Trade Association (NAFTA) is a trade-regulating instrument (even though, ironically, it is conceived to be a "free" trade agreement) that places significant new demands on the higher education systems of partner nations. Mega-universities, with student bodies of over 100,000, deliver higher educational services via distance education technologies to geographically dispersed clientele. All chapters view these transnational and supranational bodies and instruments as powerful agents of converging globalizing forces and their policies and practices as potentially producing homogenizing effects on otherwise diverse sociocultural, economic, and political institutions. Also, each demonstrates how higher education policy at the national, subnational, and local institution levels is being absorbed into the agendas of these agents.

On the one hand, these chapters convey an impression of globalizing processes as difficult if not impossible to resist, being initiated and supported as they are by a powerful line-up of interventionist agents. As political leaders have been moved to admit in recent years, even governments find themselves "helpless" in the face of global pressures.[2] But if it is the case at all, this is only partly the case. The chapters also contain another equally if not more important and compelling story, which highlights the contingent, fluid, unpredictable, and indeterminate side of globalization. Nowhere is this more evident than in the workings of these transnational and supranational agents themselves.

In Chapter 11, Mick Campion and David Freeman examine megauniversities, showing the progressive possibilities that are inherent in being liberated from time and space—a characteristic that some believe is the distinctive feature of globalism. They try to expand the range of responses to this liberating moment in history. They imply that the mega-university can be seen as an organizational prototype of globalized higher educational institutions. To realize the promise—that globalism enhances the possibilities for increased democracy and empowerment—they argue that new global forms such as mega-universities will need to break from pre-global, modernist limitations in their social and production organization as much as they have in spatial and temporal organization.

According to Campion and Freeman's analysis, the existing megauniversities located in China, France, India, Indonesia, Korea, South Africa, Spain, Thailand, Turkey, and the United Kingdom—all essentially distance teaching universities—are hybrid institutions that combine the advantages of globalized communication systems and their supportive technologies with the deskilling and overly controlling aspects of modernist work organizations. They argue that more liberating alternatives could be developed under globalizing conditions. Such possibilities are contained in post-Fordism and post-bureaucracy, which adopt organizational strategies to production and social relations that are "more democratic, participatory, open, flexible, and perhaps even more efficient." Insofar as globalization tends to place knowledge creation and dissemination at the center of productive activity, Campion and Freeman's analysis provides a basis for proposing that the organizational strategies adopted in mega-universities could be adopted in other sectors that increasingly rely upon the skills and expertise of knowledge workers.

In Chapter 12, Robert Lingard and Fazal Rizvi adopt an unusual and fruitful strategy for untangling the role of the OECD in processes of globalization. They focus on a major activity of the OECD—organizing and sponsoring international conferences on key social, political, and economic issues—to display how the OECD serves as an "institutionalizing mechanism" of global ideologies specifically in the area of higher education policy reforms. They argue that organizations operating in an international context, like the OECD, are ideally equipped to mediate the social, political, and economic interactions between the emerging transnational and supranational level and the national level. In this regard, the OECD is a significant conduit of policies, ideas, and expert knowledge that subordinates the purposes of higher education to the requirements of international economic competitiveness and product innovation. In fact, as one of the bodies that is engaged in developing and promoting performance indicators and instruments of quality assessment, among other things, the OECD can be viewed as a key instrument at the international level of reordering the social relations of academic work (see Chapters 8 and 9 in Part III).

However, Lingard and Rizvi argue that the OECD's role in globalization is not accomplished simply or unproblematically. For example, they display the sociological and discursive complexity in the way that OECD-sponsored conferences advance the ideological tenets of neo-liberalism and globalism, securing member nations' commitments to higher education policy reforms. Also, Lingard and Rizvi demonstrate how the OECD, rather than simply being an initiator or promoter of globalism, is seeing its own methods and practices as an international organization reshaped by globalization. Globalizing influences flow in a two-way rather than one-way direction—from the OECD to member nations but also in reverse, from member nations to the OECD. The authors also outline some of the tensions and contradictions between the OECD's long-standing role as an international organization and its recent involvement in globalizing activities, including the possibility that it continues to function as a tool of U.S. hegemony, rather than as an organization that truly transcends particular national interests.

In Chapter 13, Heriberta Castaños-Lomnitz, Axel Didriksson, and Janice Newson provide a double-edged account of Mexico's inability, to date, to reap the anticipated benefits of its inclusion in NAFTA. Mexico's universities are at the center of the account. One edge of the account stresses the ways that Mexico's system of higher education is handicapped relative to its trading partners for taking up the new order of business required of it by NAFTA. Not only does it lack the capacity to adequately support the general literacy and educational advancement of Mexico's population, it also has not traditionally emphasized the kind of knowledge, skills, and expertise that is valued in the new NAFTA economic order. Moreover, since NAFTA was implemented on January 1, 1994, these disadvantages have been exacerbated by economic integration into the trade bloc itself. Not the least of the worsened situation is the serious fiscal crisis of 1995, which has crippled the actions of the state to provide sufficient funds to even maintain, let alone improve, public universities. NAFTA's effect here is much the same as the impact of World Bank policies, as viewed by Raj Pannu (1996) and others (George & Sibelli, 1994).[3]

On the other edge of the story, politics and history rather than economics assume primary roles. Using a case study of the major public university of Mexico—Universidad Autónoma Nacional de México (UNAM)—the chapter builds on historical documents and interviews with business leaders, academics, and government officials on the new requirements for universities to collaborate with industry to support economic integration. In spite of the public rhetoric, in private interviews, no member of the represented groups supported technology transfer and university-industry collaboration. To account for this contradiction, the authors reach back into the history of the university in Mexico, specifically UNAM's historic relation to the colonial, postcolonial, and postrevolutionary governments. They argue that in modern-day Mexico, two conflicting technological discourses are interwoven with the social, cultural, and political history of the university, and they now underlie a stalemate over the reforms and realignments required for successful economic integration. As is perhaps the case in other countries where universities have been deeply implicated in sociocultural projects, the Mexican public university is a significant site of politics. Thus, paradoxically, it is an important instrument of globalizing projects such as NAFTA and, at the same time, the place where resistance is most likely to take shape to the "re-mantled" (Pannu, 1996) Mexican state that has chosen to pursue this particular path of economic integration.

NOTES

1. The language here is somewhat awkward, but I am avoiding the reification of "the global" as though it already exists and trying not to assign to it a degree of coherence that is not empirically warranted. Thus I have avoided the use of such terms as *the global order*.

2. Sometimes this has happened in a moment of candor or desperation. Several years ago, a beleaguered Deputy Minister of Universities and Colleges in Ontario, Canada, representing the left-leaning social-democratic political party in governance, told an angry audience of university faculty members that it does not make any difference which political party is in power—the very same package of higher education policies will be adopted because of irresistible "international pressures." At other times, the "this-is-being-foisted-on-us-by-the-international-community" justification appears gratuitous and more a cover for politicians' own policy choices. The chapter by Lingard and Rizvi provides an example in Australia's Minister John Dawkins.

3. The World Bank is notably absent as the focus of a chapter in this section. Its higher education policies and their relation to globalization have been well documented elsewhere (Colclough, 1991; Pannu, 1996). We chose to emphasize here transnational institutions and mechanisms that have not received as much attention.

REFERENCES

Colclough, C. (1991). Who should learn to pay? An assessment of neo-liberal approaches to education policy. In C. Colclough & J. Manor (Eds.), *States or markets? Neo-liberalism and the development policy debate* (pp. 173-196). Oxford, UK: Clarendon Press.

George, S., & Sibelli, F. (1994). *Faith and credit: The World Bank's secular empire*. London: Penguin.

Pannu, R. (1996). Neoliberal project of globalization: Prospects for democratization of education. *The Alberta Journal of Educational Research, 42*(2), 87-101.

CHAPTER 11

Globalization and Distance Education Mega-Institutions

Mega-Ambivalence

Mick Campion
David Freeman

We begin this chapter by illustrating distance education's (DE's) relevance to processes of globalization. We then present a leading educationalist's view of DE's future. Next, by focusing on the implications of debates concerning Fordism and bureaucracy, we infer differing policy trajectories available for distance education in the context of globalization. In this way, we seek to ensure that a range of organizational possibilities continues to be considered.

Given changing technologies and market forces, DE is becoming an increasingly mainstream concern, and the relevance of debates about industrial practices to DE processes can be illustrated by the fact that until the late 1980s, DE policy formulation was overwhelmingly dominated by a claim made in the early 1970s by Otto Peters that DE was the most industrialized mode of educational provision (Keegan, 1986, p. 83). Consequently, we argue that current and related debates about Fordism and bureaucracy provide important conceptual tools for contemporary educationalists.

DISTANCE EDUCATION'S RELEVANCE
TO GLOBALIZATION

As Evans (1995) recently put it, open and distance education "represent a significant force in late modernity. Their means of disconnecting contiguity and proximateness from the educational process make them a potent globalizing force and means of accommodating to the demands of globalism" (p. 260). In other words, student and teacher no longer need to be in the same place at the same time for interaction to occur. Evans's statement, although short and economical, merits close reading by any who do not yet grasp the significance of DE to processes of globalization.

Earlier patterns of DE provision relied heavily on the postal service. Recent developments in computer communications indicate that we are moving into an era in which the possibilities for communication between those separated physically are of a different order. In such a context, the relevance of DE to the globalization debate should be beyond question. What remains and requires an urgent debate is whether the specific models of DE being promoted are more or less likely to empower those they are intended to serve. In other words, will these models make the emergence of a homogenized global economy and society more or less likely?

Evans (1995) concludes that the world generated by particular globalizing processes is uneven, but that it will not nurture many local cultures. He finds pessimistically that

> although there is a case for arguing . . . that there is a considerable diversity and diversification concomitant with globalisation, there is little likelihood of a myriad of small, local, traditional cultures being nurtured within globalisation. (Evans, 1995, p. 266)

The remarks of Evans and the illustrations that follow provide strong support for the more general thesis put forward by authors such as Beilharz (1997) and Hirst and Thompson (1996), who argue that the term *globalization* disguises a process more like previous periods of imperialism than it might be comfortable to remember. Furthermore, they argue that the common use of the term may help to generate a self-fulfilling prophecy by encouraging a sense of inevitability and powerlessness. By keeping open the space for alternative policy options, we seek to reduce that sense of inevitability and powerlessness.

GLOBALIZATION AND DISTANCE EDUCATION: THE CASE FOR AMBIVALENCE

It is now a truism that phenomena are often complex and riddled with contradictions. The relationship between DE and globalization is no exception. Hence, unlike Sir John Daniel (International Centre for Distance Learning [ICDL], 1995), who expresses confidence about a particular view of the future, we propose that ambivalence is warranted. The very nature of academic writing, debate, and critique—whether by Daniel, the authors of this chapter, or other writers—means that all too often we make things seem clearer and more one-sided than they really are. This is troublesome, for as the organizational theorist Mintzberg (1979) suggests, "power, is after all, gained at the locus of uncertainty" (p. 362). Hence, empowerment involves first acknowledging the uncertainties that surround us and only subsequently deciding upon a course of action. The chapter title's recommendation of "mega-ambivalence" signifies both that we believe any decision in favor of mega-universities is premature and that we consider the implications of such a decision to be of great educational significance.

We are not just saying that given contemporary interpretative frames (e.g., those influenced by postmodernism, poststructuralism, etc.), all empirical entities are nuanced and complex. Our case for ambivalence when examining globalization and DE derives from both the frames that we have been immersed in and what is happening on the ground.

Richard Guy's work on the problems and opportunities posed by DE in Papua New Guinea, a developing country, is useful here. Guy's (1991) observations from the field show that the deepest features of globalization—especially its almost fantastic potential to simultaneously and paradoxically open up and close down possibilities at the local level—are abundant in the "DE meets developing countries" nexus.

The mixed blessing nature of globalization is seen readily in DE. The central problem is that the developed world has supplied the models of DE for the developing world (Guy, 1991, p. 170). There are numerous additional flaws in the concept and practice of DE in developing countries (Guy, 1991, p. 159). On the other hand, not only does DE offer one of the routes into the world economy and its riches (and indeed into the world system), it also has potential for radical/ liberatory agendas (Guy, 1991, pp. 168-169). Guy's description of the experience of DE in Papua New Guinea illustrates the potential contribution of DE and simultaneously its capacity to threaten an indigenous culture at once rich and robust yet simultaneously in shock at the relentless assault upon it of the past half-century (pp. 158-160, 169-171). Not only stupidity or cultural imperialism but the very intractability of dilemmas can be the trigger that leads people, often reluctantly, to opt for technocratic models—precisely the ones capable of doing the most cultural damage (cf. Guy, 1991, p. 174). In that situation, people then opt to do what their resources allow because it is "better than nothing." That usually means using what resources already exist rather than customizing. This means using Western resources, often with their technocratic, instrumental rationality and culturally colonizing propensities. Ironically, even this type of resource-based justification for technocratic solutions does not always stand up, given that DE is not necessarily cheaper (Guy, 1991, p. 164).

THE MEGA-UNIVERSITIES

Where, then, does discussion of the mega-universities fit in this context and what are they? Sir John Daniel, vice chancellor of the United Kingdom's Open University, introduced the term in 1996 by defining a mega-university as a university possessing student enrollment of over 100,000 (ICDL, 1995, foreword). The ten mega-universities to which Daniel refers are located in China, France, India, Indonesia, Korea, South Africa, Spain, Thailand, Turkey, and the United Kingdom, and all are essentially distance teaching universities. Some have enrollments well in excess of 100,000; for example, Anadolu University in Turkey reportedly has 470,072 students, and CNED in France 350,000. Daniel's optimism about the role of such institutions is illustrated by his suggestion that "the story of the mega-universities is a clear pointer to how we can provide the next generation of humankind with education and training worthy of the twenty-first century" (ICDL, 1995, foreword).

His justification for this claim is that these universities have "broken out of the constraints of the eternal triangle of access, quality, and resources, which has traditionally limited the expansion of education" (ICDL, 1995, foreword). Our claim in this chapter is that Daniel's support for the mega-universities may well promote the emergence of a homogenized global economy and society, which increasingly threatens local cultural traditions and identities. The application of two frameworks from industrial/organizational sociology to DE policy provides us with a route into more substantive and specific issues, which, in turn, helps to concretize the hard choices posed when DE and globalization meet.

AN INTRODUCTION TO CONTEMPORARY DEBATES CONCERNING THE ORGANIZATION OF DISTANCE EDUCATION PROVISION

Fordism, Post-Fordism, and Neo-Fordism: Relevance to Distance Education

In the decades following World War II, Fordist methods, by which basic models with standardized parts were produced using standardized processes, flowed over from motor manufacturing to many other sectors of the economy, for example, to housing, schools, and hospitals. In this era, the principle of standard rights and services for all dominated (Murray, 1991, p. 22). Economists and managers subscribed to the view that large corporations operating with standardized production methods were necessary for efficient production (Hirst, 1994, pp. 112-113). Production processes of this kind required consumption patterns that valued uniformity and a functional aesthetic (Aglietta, 1976, p. 160). This was the era in which the planning and setting up of the UK Open University took place, an institution that has since been tremendously influential worldwide.

Fordism, then, evokes much more than the image of an assembly line. The manipulation of consumption patterns is as important as the manipulation of production processes. Roobeek (1987) argues that the postwar consensus that connected mass production, mass purchasing power, and social reproduction (social security) was supported by mass production industry, mass trade unions, and labor parties within democratic parliamentary systems (p. 133). However, this era has recently been seen by many as having ended:

> The intertwined development of mass production and mass consumption—the hallmark of the post-war economy—has broken down and alternative forms of industrial organization are emerging to replace it. The shift away from mass production industries to new information-intensive industries . . . is bringing about complementary transformations in industrial relations, economic institutions, and industrial organization. (Kenney & Florida, 1989, p. 136)

Badham and Mathews (1989) present this process of transition in a model that distinguishes between Fordism, post-Fordism, and neo-Fordism. In their model, the crucial distinguishing feature is the level of labor responsibility: low in Fordism and neo-Fordism and allegedly high in post-Fordism. The neo-Fordist strategy is seen to be exploitative, whereas post-Fordism is seen to have progressive potential.

Mathews (1989) reveals the potential radicalism of the post-Fordist agenda:

> The Post-Fordist perspective focuses on the need for flexibility and a capacity for innovation in an economy geared to dynamic structural adjustment. It is distinguished from competing neo-Fordist perspectives in its insistence that flexibility and skilled input are most efficiently based on the skilled input of workers taking increasing levels of responsibility for the design of their jobs, their workplaces, their products, and ultimately the management of their enterprises. (pp. 152-153)

A further facet of this model is revealed if differing accounts of the forces leading to these production strategies are outlined. One view would see changes in technology as the dominant force leading to changes in production strategy. Another would focus upon changes in the consumption market. Yet another would focus upon the more general sociopolitical environment, for example, general support for mass consumption and production (Elam, 1990). Mass production for mass consumption—the Fordist paradigm—has been brought into question in certain industries and more generally as a societal formation, as we have seen (cf. Roobeek, 1987).

Campion (1995) used the Fordism, neo-Fordism, and post-Fordism schema to categorize DE strategies in the following way:

> *The Fordist strategy* for distance education suggested a fully centralized single-mode national distance education provider gaining greater economies of scale by offering courses to a mass market, thereby justifying a greater investment in more expensive course materials. Rationalisation of this kind allows for increased administrative control and a more extreme division of labour as the production process is fragmented into an increasing number of component tasks.
>
> *The neo-Fordist strategy* extends the Fordist system by allowing much higher levels of flexibility and diversity and by combining low volumes with high levels of product and process innovation. However, neo-Fordist production retains a highly centralised Fordist approach to labour organisation and control. A neo-Fordist expression of distance education might well be represented by a centrally controlled, perhaps multinational, yet locally administered model of distance education. By also using self-instructional course materials for teaching on-campus students, it has the potential to massively reduce costs across the whole student population. However, and most importantly, a neo-Fordist manifestation of distance education bears a strong relationship to that of the Fordist route insomuch as it has an overall deskilling effect on academic staff.
>
> *The post-Fordist strategy* is characterised by high levels of all three variables; product innovation, process variability and labour responsibility. It is opposed to neo-Fordism and to Fordism, dispensing with a Taylorist division of labour and rigid managerial control and deliberately fostering a skilled and responsible workforce. A post-Fordist model of distance education would be decentralised and retain integration between the study modes. Academic staff would, however, retain autonomous control of their administered courses, and in so doing, would be able rapidly to adjust course curriculum and delivery to the changing needs of students. (p. 194)

We anticipate that analyses of mega-universities are likely to show them to be either Fordist or neo-Fordist and consequently as not opening up the progressive possibilities associated with post-Fordism.

Bureaucracy, Neo-Bureaucracy, Post-Bureaucracy: Relevance to Distance Education

The application of the Fordism schema to DE has been the subject of critique by Rumble (1995a, 1995b, 1995c). Rumble (1995b, p. 26) suggested that by reemphasizing the importance of student administration and student support—which he regarded as bureaucratic—he had displayed a major limitation of the Fordism schema's applicability to DE and open learning. However, Campion (1995, 1996) has subsequently argued the opposite by proposing, first, that bureaucracy grew within the Fordist era and, second, that the Fordist framework strengthens, and is in turn strengthened by, reconceptualizing the bureaucracy debates as a schema of bureaucracy, neo-bureaucracy, and post-bureaucracy.

We can start to grasp the overlap between bureaucracy and Fordism if we consider the following quotation from Clegg (1990):

> Modernist organisations may be thought of in terms of Weber's typification of bureaucratised, mechanistic structures of control, as these were subsequently erected upon a fully rationalised base of divided and deskilled labour. In contemporary literature . . . these foundations are usually referred to as those of Fordism. (p. 177)

Rumble distinguished machine from professional bureaucracy, suggesting that the UK's Open University is an example of the latter. Campion (1995) has argued, following Ritzer (1975), that the professional and the bureaucrat have more in common than Rumble might suspect. Both machine and professional bureaucracy are subsumed into the broader process of rationalization, which is, for Weber, the decisive process of modernity. We seek to locate our argument within the current debate concerning the alleged shift from bureaucratic to post-bureaucratic methods of management rather than grounding it in the distinction between machine and professional bureaucracy. This debate about the future of bureaucracy complements debates about the future of Fordism in our consideration of the mega-universities.

Barker (1993) notes that

> Contemporary writers have unleashed a flood of literature announcing the "coming demise of bureaucracy and hierarchy" (Kanter, 1989, p. 351) and detailing the dawn of a post-bureaucratic age in which

TABLE 11.1 Contrasting the Bureaucratic and Post-Bureaucratic Paradigms

Bureaucracy	*Post-Bureaucracy*
Public interest	Results citizens value
Efficiency	Quality and value
Administration	Production
Control	Winning adherence to norms
Specify functions, authority, and structure	Identify mission, services, customers, and outcomes
Justify costs	Deliver value
Enforce responsibility	Build accountability Strengthen working relationships
Follow rules and procedures	Understand and apply norms Identify and solve problems Continuously improve processes
Operate administrative systems	Separate service from control Build support for norms Expand customer choice Encourage collective action Provide incentives Measure and analyze results Enrich feedback

SOURCE: Barzelay and Armajani, 1992.

control emerges not from rational rules or hierarchy but from the concertive value-based actions of the organisation's members. (p. 411)

In Table 11.1, Barzelay and Armajani (1992, p. 118) juxtapose the rhetorics of the bureaucratic and post-bureaucratic paradigms. The "public interest" is seen by Barzelay and Armajani to be defined by the bureaucrats, whereas "results citizens value" are argued to more genuinely reflect the public's interest. Similar proposals are put forward by other authors, for example, Osborne and Gaebler (1993). It is not just in industry that this message is being relayed; university staff involved in quality assurance processes and in generating mission statements and strategic plans over the past ten years have been thoroughly immersed in the rhetoric of the post-bureaucracy paradigm.

It is, however, crucial to draw a distinction between post- and neo-bureaucratic practices along similar lines to the distinction between post- and neo-Fordism (Campion, 1995). Ramsay and Parker (1992) use the notion neo-bureaucracy but do not distinguish post- from neo-bureaucracy. Such a distinction, that is, between a progressive and a regressive transformation of bureaucracy, is at the heart of our argument. Consequently, readers should bear in mind that many who write of post-bureaucracy are actually referring to what we term neo-bureaucracy. For example, when du Gay (1994, p. 670) criticizes the supporters of the post-bureaucratic paradigm for proposing that public administrators be judged by the standards of the entrepreneur, in our terms, he is criticizing the supporters of neo-bureaucracy.

Organizations such as universities, and organizational activities such as teaching and learning, are reconstructed and come to be governed "along the lines of the commercial firm, with attention focused in particular on its orientation towards the 'sovereign consumer' " (du Gay, 1994, p. 660). We are reminded of the statement of the foundation vice chancellor of the UK Open University, Lord Perry:

> From the outset we foresaw that we would be operating not only an academic establishment, but, in a very real sense a sort of commercial establishment as well. The latter would require a form of government quite different from that which was common in conventional universities. (cited in Keegan, 1980, p. 26)

That concepts drawn from commercial enterprises are influencing the universities seems clear. However, the hard work of distinguishing between processes that increase the regressive nature of the workplace (neo-bureaucratic) and those that have progressive potential (post-bureaucratic) still needs to be done. That work cannot be done here, but we can display a number of continuities between bureaucracy and so-called post-bureaucracy in order to illustrate why the application of the notion post-bureaucracy may, in many cases, be inappropriate:

- The distinction between formal and informal processes
  Blau's classic piece of research found (per Clegg, 1990, p. 48) that key processes that kept bureaucracies rolling were informal and were unlike the formal processes on which Weber had focused. There may be discontinuities between traditionally understood formal bureaucratic processes and so-called post-

bureaucratic processes; however, it may turn out that the informal processes have not changed radically. Moreover, they may all along have been more decisive than the formal.

- Processes of devolution
  Dandeker (1990, p. 211) challenges the widespread assumption that contemporary processes of decentralization and devolution represent a reduction in the vertical nature of bureaucratic power/organization.

- Managerial or concertive control
  Barker's (1993) study of one company's shift from hierarchical bureaucratic management to self-managing teams provides one illustration of how so-called post-bureaucratic processes can produce outcomes that are far from progressive. He found that over a relatively short period, team members/workers became their own masters and slaves by exercising control over one another's actions in ways that the bureaucratic system could not. So members of a workforce previously difficult for management to control came to control each other in a far more effective manner. Casey (1995, p. 192) points to the broader significance of such processes when she concludes that totalizing corporate cultures reduce the space for counter-corporate action.

- Versions of selfhood
  When thinking about peer group control (per Barker et al., 1993), it is crucial that we not ignore the way in which the dominant discourse molds even our perceptions of ourselves. For example, within bureaucratic institutions, individuals or workers who have the ability to conform and use existing routines are highly valued, whereas in post- or neo-bureaucratic institutions proactive entrepreneurial innovators are likely to be more highly valued. The connection between such versions of selfhood and the achievement of societal economic objectives grounded in the dominance of the market has been noted by authors such as Nikolas Rose (1990) and Paul du Gay (1991). The point for educationalists is that organizational forms draw out specific forms of selves.

- Processes of surveillance

  The whole process of quality assurance in universities, and the measurement of outcomes it relies upon, requires a more extensive and intrusive examination of the work of academics than in the past. Like other professionals (Thompson, 1993, p. 194), academics are being incorporated into rule-governed bureaucratic forms of regulation for the first time. In addition, computerized student record systems are increasing in power and reach while all of the supposedly post-bureaucratic features come into play. Dandeker (1990) reminds us of the role of surveillance in bureaucratic processes. The existence, and at times perhaps even intensification, of surveillance activities within supposedly post-bureaucratic organizations is suggestive of continuity, not discontinuity, with bureaucracy.

Having raised these possible areas of continuity, we also need to remember that it is not at all unusual for academics to join others in relishing bureaucracy's demise. Goodsell (1985, p. 145) provides a lucid exposition of how easy and apparently compelling it is to jump aboard the anti-bureaucracy bandwagon. A few words in bureaucracy's defense may therefore be appropriate. First, bureaucracy was crucial to the process through which the work of government was drawn away from aristocratic privilege (Pusey, 1976, p. 15). Second, connections between bureaucracy and democracy are intricate. Efforts to move beyond the former need to be carefully weighed as to their implications for the latter. So we need to be wary about rejecting bureaucracy *in toto*; doing so may further increase the power of the already powerful.

Bureaucracy is, of course, far from fault-free. Bureaucracies frequently marginalize the least powerful, as the critiques from feminist and other perspectives make plain (cf. Burton, 1987, 1991). Yet, paradoxically, bureaucracies may also have some openness to equity orientations. Furthermore, the bureaucratic ideal type may serve as a useful counterfoil or juxtaposition to the limitations of entrepreneurial, neo-bureaucratic approaches. So crucial questions arise as some rush headlong into being anti-bureaucratic per se, availing themselves of every opportunity to dismantle bureaucracy and, moreover, feeling automatically morally virtuous as they do so, and regarding it as an act of conscientiousness that thereby allows them to cut through the red tape and be people-oriented. Note the assumption that to be "for people" is to be anti-bureaucratic: The interests of the two are assumed to be inherently antagonistic.

We would expect an analysis of the processes involved in the mega-universities, given the relatively large size of their student populations, to show them to be either bureaucratic or neo-bureaucratic, and consequently as not opening up the progressive possibilities of post-bureaucracy as we have described them. We need to make it clear that although we defend bureaucracy against proponents of neo-bureaucratic options, we want to be formulating and promoting post-bureaucratic policies.

As attention has been drawn to the intersections between Fordism and bureaucracy, and between these organizational types and modernity, we begin to access the tools necessary for a clearer understanding of how the mega-universities could come to be formulated as pointers to the future. However, if postmodernism better reflects contemporary reality as Albertsen (1988, p. 358) suggests, then it may be that educational institutional forms grounded in post-Fordist and in post-bureaucratic strategies are more appropriate.

CONCLUSION

Although Daniel's triangle of cost, access, and quality does not appear to adequately address some aspects of the more complex reality of how to maintain the local within current globalizing trends, we have no wish to deny the importance of that triangle. We would argue, however, that we can learn from industries that organizational forms that generate economies of scope rather than economies of scale (Badham, 1986) may be both more cost-effective and more likely to better serve the needs of highly differentiated local populations. How, for example, does the idea of educational provision via mega-universities mesh with the suggestion that the local community is the key to educational success (cf. Ordonez, 1996)? Can educational provision from mega-universities save indigenous cultures? How much sense does it make to educate ourselves in mega-universities, given Illich's (1974) notion of the hidden curriculum, if work is increasingly likely to take place in organizations that are no longer bureaucratic or Fordist? (The hidden curriculum consists not of course content, but of the organizational routines that the student has to learn in order to operate effectively within the institution. Where the organizational structure of the educational institution matches the organizational structures of the workplace, this hidden curriculum may, by some, be judged effective. For Illich, of course, such a match is all the more enslaving!) How much sense does it make to educate ourselves in mega-universities if this means that local regions will be deprived of the various talents provided through the professional personnel that might otherwise have been part of local universities?

Technologies and organizational forms currently available present many options in addition to the mega-university option. In our view, these options could prove to be more democratic, participatory, open, flexible, and perhaps even more efficient. We would at least argue that, for the moment, the jury is out on which of these trajectories is to be preferred. Until such time as it comes in, we remain ambivalent.

REFERENCES

Aglietta, M. (1976). *A theory of capitalist regulation*. London: Calmann-Levy.

Albertsen, N. (1988). Postmodernism, post-Fordism, and critical social theory. *Environment and Planning D: Society and Space, 6*, 339-365.

Badham, R. J. (1986). *The challenge of change: Discussion paper 1*. Perth: Western Australian Technology Directorate.

Badham, R., & Mathews, J. (1989 June). The new production systems debate. *Labour and Industry, 2*, 194-246.

Barker, J. R. (1993, September). Tightening the iron cage: Concertive control in self-managing teams. *Administrative Science Quarterly, 38*, 408-437.

Barzelay, M., with Armajani, B. J. (1992). *Breaking through bureaucracy*. Berkeley: University of California Press.

Beilharz, P. (1997). Globalising the antipodes? Australia in the world system, then and now. In M. Booth & T. Hogan (Eds.), *Ambivalence and hope: Social theory and policy making in a globalising, postmodern Australia*. Perth: Institute of Science and Technology Policy, Murdoch University.

Burton, C. (1987, May). Merit and gender: Organisations and the mobilisation of masculine bias. *Australian Journal of Social Issues, 22*, 424-435.

Burton, C. (1991). *The promise and the price—The struggle for equal opportunity in women's employment*. Sydney: Allen & Unwin.

Campion, M. (1995). The supposed demise of bureaucracy: Implications for distance education and open learning—more on the post-Fordism debate. *Distance Education, 16*, 192-216.

Campion, M. (1996). Post-Fordism not a poison either! *Open Learning, 11*, 41-46.

Casey, C. (1995). *Work, self, and society: After industrialism.* London: Routledge.

Clegg, S. (1990). *Modern organizations: Organization studies in the postmodern world.* London: Sage.

Dandeker, C. (1990). *Surveillance, power, and modernity: Bureaucracy and discipline from 1700 to the present day.* Cambridge, UK: Polity.

Du Gay, P. (1991, Spring). Enterprise culture and the ideology of excellence. *New Formations, 13,* 45-61.

Du Gay, P. (1994, December). Making up managers: Bureaucracy, enterprise, and the liberal art of separation. *British Journal of Sociology, 45,* 655-674.

Elam, M. J. (1990). Puzzling out the post-Fordist debate: Technology, markets, and institutions. *Economic and Industrial Democracy, 11,* 9-37.

Evans, T. (1995). Globalisation, post-Fordism, and open and distance education. *Distance Education, 16,* 256-269.

Goodsell, C. T. (1985). *The case for bureaucracy: A public administration polemic* (2nd ed.). Chatham, NJ: Chatham House.

Guy, R. (1991). Distance education and the developing world. In T. Evans & B. King (Eds.), *Beyond the text: Contemporary writing on distance education* (pp. 152-178). Geelong, Australia: Deakin University Press.

Hirst, P. Q. (1994). *Associative democracy: New forms of economic and social governance.* Cambridge, UK: Polity.

Hirst, P., & Thompson, G. (1996). *Globalization in question: The international economy and the possibilities of governance.* Cambridge, UK: Polity.

Illich, I. (1974). *Deschooling society.* Harmondsworth, UK: Penguin Education.

International Centre for Distance Learning (ICDL). (1995). *Mega-universities of the world: The top ten.* Milton Keynes: The Open University, UK.

Kanter, R. M. (1989). *When giants learn to dance.* New York: Simon and Schuster.

Keegan, D. J. (1980). *On the nature of distance education* (ZIFF papiere). Hagan, Germany: Fern Universitat (ZIFF).

Keegan, D. (1986). *The foundations of distance education.* Sydney: Croom Helm.

Kenney, J., & Florida, R. (1989, April). Japan's role in a post-Fordist age. *Futures,* pp. 136-151.

Mathews, J. (1989). *The age of democracy: The politics of post-Fordism.* Melbourne: Oxford University Press.

Mintzberg, H. (1979). *The structuring of organizations: A synthesis of the research.* Englewood Cliffs, NJ: Prentice Hall.

Murray, R. (1991, May). The state after Henry. *Marxism Today,* pp. 22-27.

Ordonez, V. (1996, July). Plenary Session Speech, World Congress of Comparative Education Societies [WCCESS], Sydney, Australia.

Osborne, D., & Gaebler, T. (1993). *Reinventing government: How the entrepreneurial spirit is transforming the public sector.* New York: Plume.

Pusey, M. (1976). *Dynamics of bureaucracy: A case analysis in education.* Sydney: Wiley Australasia.

Ramsay, K., & Parker, M. (1992). Gender, bureaucracy, and organizational culture. In M. Savage & A. Witz (Eds.), *Gender and bureaucracy.* Oxford, UK: Blackwell/The Sociological Review.

Ritzer, G. (1975). Professionalization, bureaucratization, and rationalization: The views of Max Weber. *Social Forces, 54,* 627-634.

Roobeek, A. (1987, April). The crisis of Fordism and the rise of a new technological paradigm. *Futures*, pp. 129-154.

Rose, N. S. (1990). *Governing the soul: The shaping of the private self.* London: Routledge.

Rumble, G. (1995a, February). Labour market theories and distance education 1: Industrialisation and distance education. *Open Learning, 10,* 10-21.

Rumble, G. (1995b, June). Labour market theories and distance education 1: How Fordist is distance education. *Open Learning, 10,* 12-28.

Rumble, G. (1995c, October). Labour market theories and distance education 1: Post-Fordism the way forward? *Open Learning, 10,* 3.

Thompson, P. (1993). Postmodernism: Fatal distraction. In J. Hassard and M. Parker (Eds.), *Postmodernism and organizations* (pp. 183-203). London: Sage.

CHAPTER 12

Globalization, the OECD, and Australian Higher Education

Robert Lingard
Fazal Rizvi

That globalization is having a direct effect on Australian universities is a claim that is often asserted but seldom examined. In its submission to the federal government's current Review of Higher Education Financing and Policy, the Australian Vice Chancellors' Committee (AVCC, 1997) argues, for example, that "Globalization is transforming existing structures of wealth, skills, technology, and production" and that increased national intellectual capacity and universities' role in relation to this is central to Australia's economic future, in which there is "increasing globalization of technology, communications, and commerce" (p. 1). This chapter explores the relationships between the processes of globalization and the development of higher education policies at the level of a nation-state, namely, Australia. We argue that this relationship is not simple or direct but is mediated by a range of complex factors that

AUTHORS' NOTE: Funded by the Australian Research Council, the project on Globalization and Education Policy: An Exploration of the Role of the OECD in Shaping Australian Education (1984-present) is under the direction of F. Rizvi, R. Lingard, S. Taylor, and M. Henry (1995-1997).

are specific to the character of Australian institutions, including its policy community and its universities.

Our analysis is based on a case study of the ways in which recent Australian higher education policies are mediated by the Organization for Economic Cooperation and Development (OECD), of which Australia has been a member since 1971. It draws upon a research project in which we have been involved since 1995. In this chapter, we consider the relationship between globalization, on the one hand, and the OECD and Australian higher education, on the other, by discussing two recent OECD-sponsored conferences on higher education in which Australia has been an important participant. The two conferences are The Transition from Elite to Mass Higher Education held in Sydney, June 15-18, 1993, and sponsored jointly by the OECD and the federal Department of Employment, Education, and Training (DEET), and Internationalisation of Higher Education in the Asia-Pacific Region, held in Melbourne, October 7-9, 1996. Our discussion of the conferences is designed to illustrate the multiple and contradictory ways in which the work of a globalizing agency informs and influences policy at the level of the nation-state.

We suggest that talk of any direct impact of globalization on higher education is fundamentally misleading because, in the construction of policy, globalization works as an ideology just as much as it refers to direct empirical effects (Hall & Harley, 1995). Thus, governments argue that certain policy developments are the only possible options in response to global imperatives. This is a hegemonic policy device, because the way in which policies are stated often "creates" their contexts and already frames problems in particular ways (Seddon, 1994). Increasingly, globalization is a constructed policy context for policy development in Australian education. In focusing on the OECD and higher education, we wish to show how this policy development is mediated by certain ideological discourses of globalization promoted by the OECD.

DEFINING GLOBALIZATION

Globalization could be described as a set of economic, cultural, and political processes that in various ways make supranational connections. In his discussion of a world economy, Hobsbawm

(1994) distinguishes between international and supranational dimensions, the latter being characterized by "a system of economic activities for which state territories and state frontiers are not the basic framework, but merely complicating factors" (p. 277). Hobsbawm suggests that "some time in the early 1970s such a transnational economy became an effective global force." Waters (1995) argues that globalization is most advanced in the domain of instantaneous and stateless financial markets.

According to Giddens (1994), globalization is really about the transformation of time and space—"action at a distance" (p. 4). He suggests that its intensification over recent years owes much "to the emergence of means of instantaneous global communication and mass transportation." Appadurai (1996) emphasizes the significance of the globalization of mass migration and electronic media and the use of the latter to create "diasporic public spheres" across the boundaries of nation-states. Action at a distance then refers to the interconnectedness of economic, political, and cultural activities across the globe, resulting not only in "the creation of large-scale systems" but also in "the transformation of local and even personal contexts of social experience" (Giddens, 1994, pp. 4-5).

Although globalization may be discussed in a number of ways, we wish to stress its political dimensions here. Questions of the extent of political globalization require us to examine the character of the nation-state, the creation par excellence of the modernist project, which grew into its mature form throughout the nineteenth and twentieth centuries. Globalization is placing pressures upon the nation-state. Appadurai (1996) even argues that its era is drawing to a close. As part of the emergence of a postnational politics, he suggests that the hyphen between *nation* and *state* has become somewhat attenuated, each becoming the project of the other.

Supranational organizations such as the European Union (EU), whose membership and decisions transcend nation-states, have emerged even while fragmentation has taken place within other putative nation-states. Many other international bodies, including the OECD, collectively constitute "a complex and ungovernable web of relationships that extends beyond the nation state" (Waters, 1995, p. 113).

The international relations literature tends to dichotomize the impact of globalization on the nation-state between besieged and defiant accounts, with the former overemphasizing the "intrusive and corrosive processes of globalization" and the latter underemphasizing these same effects (Reus-Smit, 1996, p. 163). The stance taken here is that the nation-state remains important but works in different ways and sits in a "mutually constitutive relationship" with "emerging global structures and processes" (Reus-Smit, 1996, p. 163). Without reifying the idea of globalization, we argue that globalizing processes are relevant to an understanding of the ways in which the Australian state is currently being restructured and the work of the OECD has been influential in reshaping public policy discourses.

THE OECD

The OECD can be seen as a globalizing institution while itself being affected by globalizing pressures. It was founded in 1961 as successor to the Organization for European Economic Cooperation, which was established by the United States in the context of the Cold War to channel Marshall Plan money toward the reconstruction of postwar Europe. Unlike, say, the World Bank, the OECD has no prescriptive mandate over its member countries, basically the rich countries of Europe, North America, Australia, New Zealand, and Japan, as well as newer members, Korea, Mexico, and the Czech Republic. Rather, it describes itself as a place for reflection and discussion, research and analysis—a kind of international think tank—"that may often help governments shape policy," exerting influence through processes of "mutual examination by governments, multilateral surveillance and peer pressure to conform or reform" (OECD, undated, p. 10). Its education policy agenda is framed by its formal charter as a "commitment to a market economy and a pluralistic democracy" (OECD, undated, p. 1), with the priority of fostering a "post-industrial age in which . . . OECD economies [can be woven] into a yet more prosperous and increasingly service-oriented world economy" (OECD, undated, p. 6).

Formally, the OECD is an intergovernmental organization, but it connects to member countries at two not necessarily congruent levels—government and research communities. For example, whereas the Education Committee of OECD represents the consensual interests of member nations and sets the broad program for OECD's education work, the Centre for Educational Research and Innovation (CERI) links in nongovernmental fashion to the educational research community. The Institute for Management in Higher Education (IMHE) is a self-funding unit with membership from individual universities within member nations and reports to the Education Committee. Despite the fact that the Higher Education Division of Australia's Department of Employment, Education, Training, and Youth Affairs (DEETYA) has recently become a member, IMHE is largely nongovernmental in character. To some extent, then, the OECD can be described as partially nongovernmental in nature, embracing alternative networks of influence.

While governments see the OECD as their instrument, it can also be viewed as an independent policy actor (Archer, 1994) that, steered by its secretariat, fulfills both research and administrative functions. The secretariat is supposedly the administrative arm of the OECD, acting on behalf of its member countries, but this function is becoming increasingly problematic in the context of globalization. This much is clearly evident in its relationship with nonmember countries and the strengthening of its links with newly emerging nations of the former Eastern bloc. At the same time, however, in the face of common problems confronting many countries, the OECD is becoming aware of the inadequacy of the nation-state as an analytical unit. And thus, in its educational work, it is moving toward more thematic analyses, for example, on issues such as mass higher education and the development and use of educational performance indicators. Such analyses promote relationships with subnational units and individual institutions and have the potential to circumvent national control over policy agendas.

This tendency is reinforced by two other factors. First, in its research capacity, the OECD secretariat is linked into its own pool of consultants as well as governmental forums, often using the former for policy research and advice. How governments choose to use that advice is a moot point, but paradoxically, the OECD's influence and cachet significantly stem from its perceived independence from the vested interests of governments. This tension provides secretariat staff with some freedom to maneuver beyond the constraints of government-set agendas.

Second, the OECD is itself part of another sphere of influence: the network of international organizations including UNESCO, the

World Bank, the International Labor Organization, and the Commonwealth Secretariat—all with an interest in education policy. The inclusion of a representative from the EU—a supranational organization—on the governing council and other forums of the OECD is symbolic of this trend, as is the proclivity for former OECD staffers to take consultancies with other tendering agencies in Europe. Although these organizations have different constituencies and purposes, the congruence of their policy positions on educational issues is notable. This points toward the emergence of a global policy community, constituted by an overlapping membership of globalizing bureaucrats (Sklair, 1996)—senior public servants, policymakers, and advisers.

The basic organizational units within the OECD are the directorates, with education sitting within the Directorate of Education, Employment, Labor, and Social Affairs (DEELSA). Australia connects to the OECD most directly through its formal delegation located in Paris, which also has responsibilities for and with other international agencies in Europe, for example, UNESCO. DEETYA is a member of this delegation.

OECD'S EDUCATION POLICY APPROACHES

Papadopoulos (1994) has documented the tensions between the economic and the social in the OECD's educational policy developments over its first thirty years. He notes that it is primarily the economic conception of benefits that has led to OECD's stress on educational policy. By the mid-1980s, prompted by the impact of globalization pressures on national economies, the economic imperative was taking center stage in OECD thinking about education. These pressures were acknowledged in the first OECD education ministers' conference in 1978, Future Educational Policies in the Changing Social and Economic Context (OECD, 1979), which Papadopoulos (1994) observes was notable "for the force and urgency with which educational change was politically advocated to respond to the new economic imperative, marked by growing country interdependence and competition in the global economy" (p. 171). In such a context, the conference noted, education policy was being framed by factors "largely outside the ambit or control of education" (OECD, 1979, p. 12). Albeit largely framed in economic terms, the social purposes of education continued to be strongly asserted as well, for example, in terms of labor market disadvantage for particular social groups.

A decade later, in 1988, an intergovernmental conference, *Education and the Economy in a Changing Society*, saw the relationship between economic and social purposes of education as explicitly interlinked. The conference theme was the convergence of education and economic functions in the new global context, arguing that the "human factor" is a central element in production: "The skills and qualifications of workers are coming to be viewed as critical determinants of effective performance of enterprises and economies" (OECD, 1989, p. 18). Although the secretary-general insisted that the conference would discuss "much more than conditions of economic efficiency" (p. 8), matters of social equity in fact were framed by a dominant concern with economic efficiency. According to Apple (1992), the significance of the conference lay not so much in the details of the discussion as in "the overall orientation of its analysis and its linguistic strategies in creating a rhetoric of justification for a tighter connection between educational systems and the world economy" (p. 127).

Apart from the conferences and research it sponsors, the OECD pursues its educational work through reviews of national educational systems that are conducted at the request of a particular nation, unlike the yearly reviews of the economies of member nations. More recently, the OECD has conducted some "thematic reviews" across nations. The themes chosen for review and their mode of analysis reveal much about the OECD's distinctive approach to educational policy.

This distinctive OECD approach (Istance, 1996) reflects its character as both governmental and nongovernmental in orientation and its internal organizational principle of horizontality, which seeks interrelationships between social and economic policies (Papadopoulos, 1994). Istance characterizes the OECD approach in the following fashion:

- that educational policy making must be framed at least in part in relation to the other social and labour market policies that address people;
- that focus on people is integral to economic prosperity apart from any social or cultural benefits;

- that academic and political insights should be combined in "policy-relevant" analysis rather than the educational community setting itself up in opposition to "politicians"; and
- that national policies and practices should be informed through reference to those of other countries, learning from their achievements and failures but not blindly copying. (p. 94)

This amalgam of the academic and political, of the empirical and the normative, characterizes the specificity of the OECD policy approach and relates to the way OECD work is used in member nations.

THE OECD AND EDUCATIONAL POLICY MAKING IN AUSTRALIA

The relationship between OECD and educational policy development in member nations is a complex one: It is two-way, rather than top-down, in character. Papadopoulos (1994) describes the OECD's catalytic impact in this way:

> The starting point is the identification of major new policy issues which emerge on the educational horizon, and which might call for priority attention in the countries. . . . These issues are then put together within a structured framework, leading to a number of questions which arise for policy making. Arriving at a convincing statement of such issues and questions, of how and why they arise, and of their implications, is already half the work done. It involves a dialectical process of secretariat and country thinking and exchange, including a strong dose of advice from experts, and provides the basis for subsequent programme planning and implementation. (p. 13)

This raises questions as to whether the OECD leads or is led in policy development.

Taylor (1996), Henry and Taylor (1997), and Vickers (1994) have written about the OECD-Australia relationship in educational policy development. Their research clarifies the complexity of the OECD-nation relationships in policy production, demonstrating that different sorts of relationships worked in different eras of Australian education policy. As Vickers (1994) notes, the key question in policy development, particularly for politicians, is often not so much "what shall we do" as "how shall we get it accepted?" (p. 57). For example, Dawkins as federal education minister used OECD analyses somewhat selectively to create and legitimate his own national educational policy agenda (1987-1991). Commenting on his performance in Paris at the 1988 conference, Education and the Economy in a Changing Society, Vickers (1994) observes that "Upon returning home, Dawkins implemented the most extensive program of reconstruction that has ever been imposed on Australia's higher education sector" (p. 26). In the Foreword to *Higher Education: A Policy Discussion Paper,* Dawkins (1987) stressed the impact of globalization on the Australian economy and the concomitant need for a restructuring of higher education. He also quoted with approval an OECD (1987) report, *Universities Under Scrutiny,* which stressed "the enhanced importance of innovation and knowledge in modern societies and the economic importance of a skilled labour force" (p. 98). Thus, the OECD was used to legitimate policies devised within the Australian political context.

Vickers (1994) uses some of the research on "the politics of knowledge utilisation" to consider more generally the relationship between the OECD, as an international think tank and producer of research and reports, and educational policy developments in member nations. Applying Weiss's (1989) empirical work on the U.S. Congress's use of research (p. 55) to reflect on this relationship and reject a technocratic, rational approach to policy making, she outlines four types of relationships: research as *warning* of problems; as *guidance* for possible policy options; as *enlightenment,* which can lead to the reframing of policy problems; and as a way to *mobilize* support for a politically desired policy option. In our own research, which highlights the two-way Australia-OECD policy relationship, elements of each of these types can be identified in the use of OECD work.

GLOBALIZATION AND THE OECD

Despite the contingent character of the Australia-OECD relationship, Australia has nonetheless been a keen supporter of the OECD's ideological discourse of globalization and has used this discourse to promote and legitimize major educational changes. So while it is possible to say that globalization affects Australia, it is equally true that globalization is affecting the OECD itself, as an international organization, in significant ways.

First, as already pointed out, the EU, a supranational political entity, has membership in the OECD. Important to the future of the OECD is its continued significance to countries that are members of both the OECD and the EU in light of the fact that the latter holds legal and financial mandates over its members.

Second, since the collapse of the Soviet Union and the Eastern bloc, many more countries have met the criteria for OECD membership, that is, a commitment to market economy ideology and to liberal democracy. Consequently, the OECD is involved in the Partners in Transition program with the Czech Republic (which became a full OECD member in 1996), Hungary, Poland, the Slovak Republic, and the Russian Federation (OECD, 1994, pp. 18-19). It also has relations with "the dynamic economies of Asia" and with the "advanced economies of Latin America" (OECD, 1994, p. 18). As stated in its own booklet, "Spurred by the globalisation of the world economy and by the breakup of the Soviet system, as of mid-1994 more than 30 non-OECD economies had expressed interest in OECD membership or some form of structured dialogue with OECD" (OECD, 1994, p. 19). Consequently, questions have been raised concerning the character and purpose of the OECD and the desire of long-standing members that it not lose "its capacity for effective, like-minded discussion of common problems, reinforced, where appropriate, by agreed principles" (OECD, 1994, p. 19).

Third, as globalization is tied to the emergence of new regional trading blocs, questions are now frequently raised as to whether or not, in a post-Cold War era with a more global economy, the OECD in an expanded form can continue to meet the interests of both European and non-European members. Australia, for example, has recognized the need to focus its efforts on the Asia-Pacific Economic Cooperation (APEC)—a "government-led forum for facilitating private sector-led economic integration" (Catley, 1996, p. 205). In an interview with a member of the Australian permanent delegation to the OECD in late 1995, it was argued that the OECD was still important for Australia, but if the membership grew and there were substantial differences between the problems facing member countries, then the OECD might not any longer seem as attractive or as relevant to Australian interests.

Finally, as implied earlier, questions also arise about the extent to which globalization is a new form of Western hegemony, specifically U.S. hegemony in a post-Cold War era, and whether the OECD is an important instrument for achieving this hegemony. For example, the North American Free Trade Agreement (NAFTA)—a new regional trading bloc like Asia-Pacific Economic Cooperation (APEC)—was created apparently in response to globalization by the United States, with Canada and Mexico as co-members. Research interviews provide evidence that the United States pressed for Mexico's membership in the OECD. Equally important, the predecessor to OECD was also a U.S. creation in the context of the Cold War. Research has indicated that it was the United States that lobbied vigorously for a Canadian as the new secretary-general of the OECD and who also pushed for the indicators project in education.

McNeely and Cha (1994, unpaged) suggest that international organizations such as the OECD "have been an important catalyst in spreading world cultural themes and accounts, and research conceptualising them as institutionalising mechanisms can provide important insights." A conception of the OECD as an institutionalizing mechanism of global ideologies, including market liberalism and new managerialism, seems to be a useful one. One of the ways in which the OECD spreads these ideologies is through its sponsorship of conferences: Two such conferences are discussed next to illustrate these globalizing processes at work.

The Conference on Transition From Elite to Mass Higher Education

The conference on Transition From Elite to Mass Higher Education, held in Sydney, June 15-18, 1993, was sponsored by DEET and the OECD. In the Foreword to the conference report, Paul Hickey, at the time, deputy secretary of DEET and member of the Governing Board of CERI, noted two important opportunities provided by this conference. The first was to assist the OECD in focusing the agenda of the Education Committee on higher education in the context of the move to mass higher education and on how nations ought to deal with this demand, given tight budgetary situations—both consequences of globalization. The second was to "contribute to the building of a dialogue between OECD member countries and other countries in the Asia-Pacific region, especially in relation to education and training issues" (p. i).

In his opening address, Dr. Malcolm Skilbeck, then deputy director of DEELSA at OECD, talked about the provenance of the terms that framed the conference, namely, the concepts of *elite* and *mass* higher education. He pointed out their original usage in a 1971 paper written by Martin Trow for OECD (see Trow, 1973). The OECD background paper for the conference, *Higher Education: An Overview of Issues in OECD Countries in Conference Proceedings* (1993), was also produced by Dr. Skilbeck with Eric Esnault. The paper documents the changing context of higher education within member countries, noting the uncertainties contingent upon globalization. Increased social demand for university education is also addressed, as is the nature and our uncertain knowledge, of the links between education and changing labor markets and economies. The paper notes that, whereas "the comparative advantage of OECD countries lies in the availability of high-level skills and competences" (p. 4), this advantage "is under severe challenge from a number of dynamic economies around the world" (p. 4).

The individual conference papers will not be discussed here, but rather consideration will be given to what the conference reveals about the working of the OECD in the context of globalization. Many of the papers are replete with considerations of globalization and what this means for nations providing mass higher education. Australia's joint sponsorship of the conference and attempt to refocus the work of the Education Committee of OECD can be seen as part of the two-way character of agenda setting at the OECD. The conference also displays the international think tank role of the organization. Also, its dual governmental and nongovernmental character is apparent in the use of academics to deliver papers as well as OECD and DEET officials.

Earlier, we referred to Papadopoulos's description of the catalytic role of the OECD in national educational policy development. His first stage—the identification of major new policy issues—can be seen in the sponsorship of this conference. A structured framework stage putting forward a number of policy issues is manifested in the OECD Background Paper, which highlights the developmental role of the conference. It is also present in the opening address by Dr. Skilbeck. He says that conference deliberations will lead to the production of a paper for discussion by OECD's Education Committee, as the beginning of a new phase of the work program. Papadopoulos's (1994, p. 13) "dialectical process of secretariat and country thinking and exchange, including a strong dose of advice from experts" to subsequent "programme planning and implementation" can be seen at work in the conference and subsequent developments.

We also have noted the academic-political, empirical-normative nature of OECD writings about education. This is evident in the OECD papers in the conference publication. Framing the conference with the concepts of elite and mass higher education ensured some commensurability in policy discussions between nations. Ensuring commensurability has been an ongoing role of the OECD, which, in turn, is one factor in policy convergence and borrowing across nations and perhaps in the emergence of a global policy community. While arguing this, we recognize that universities have always striven to be international rather than parochial in their reach. Furthermore, we agree with Papadopoulos (1994) that, despite such convergent pressures, educational policies remain "par excellence national policies reflecting the specific circumstances, traditions, and cultures of individual countries" (p. 13). Thus, because globalization is mediated through the nation-state, the participation in the conference of some APEC-member countries and the establishment of a dialogue between them as one goal of the conference is indicative of an emergent geopolitics contingent upon globalization.

The Conference on the Internationalization of Higher Education

The OECD sees Asia not only in terms of new markets but also as part of a new global configuration of nations. The global flows of technologies, finance, images, and people are now such that they require greater collaboration between regional and economic groupings. International collaboration in education is part of these trends toward globalization. And it is this recognition that led IMHE/OECD to sponsor a conference in Melbourne in October 1996 on the Internationalization of Higher Education in the Asia-Pacific Region.

Building on two previous conferences on this theme, one in Washington, D.C., in 1994 and the other in California in 1995, the aim of the Melbourne conference was to extend the work that IMHE was already doing on developing institutional strategies for internationalization in higher education. It was felt that a dialogue ought to be established with the nations of the Asia-Pacific region, which included the homelands of many international students at European and North American universities. Australia was thought to be an appropriate location for the conference because of its regional links and its commitment to the policies of internationalization of higher education.

The conference was highly structured, following a pattern that the OECD has developed over the past decade; Professor Ken McKinnon opened by raising issues confronting Australian higher education. McKinnon argued that Australia had to overcome a perception that Australian universities were more interested in education as an important source of export revenue, and as a market commodity, than with the mutual benefits of international education within the context of an emerging global economy. A view of internationalization that was narrowly commercial with insufficient recognition of student needs and of the benefits of international education did not serve the nation well, he added, particularly as Australia sought to become a more open, internationally competitive, and globalized economy. The policy of internationalization, he noted, needed to highlight the increasing interdependence among nations, implying an education system that facilitated partnerships and exchange of ideas, skills, staff, and students, within a diverse and sophisticated global environment.

The analysis presented by McKinnon had much in common with an ideology of globalization put forward in position papers by representatives of Hong Kong, Indonesia, Thailand, Malaysia, Singapore, the Philippines, Japan, and Korea. Lively discussions followed the formal presentation of country papers, although what was striking was the degree of consensus. Most of the speakers had assumed that the globalization of the economy implied a particular way of managing higher education. Internationalization of education was thus interpreted as both an expression of and a response to the broader processes of globalization. No attempt was made, however, to analyze these processes: They were taken as self-evident.

Indeed, a particular analysis of global imperatives sets the background against which IMHE experts Jane Knight and Hans de Wit developed a framework for comparative assessment of the range of strategies employed nationally and institutionally in the internationalization of higher education. This framework—a form of benchmarking—was also intended as a forum for discussing current issues and future trends (de Wit, 1995). Insofar as Knight and de Wit's evaluative framework highlights the need for all universities to adopt a similar pattern of organizational development, it assumes a "single idealisation of appropriate organisational behaviour," whereby "organisations must have the capacity to make a flexible response to uncertain market conditions caused by commodity saturation" (de Wit, 1995). This means in part that organizations are now required to become more competitive and develop new "educational products" to stay "ahead of the pack" by creating new markets (Waters, 1995, p. 81). It also implies a particular form of higher education: one that is sensitive to the need to prepare graduates to enter global workplaces, graduates who are confident in their capacity to move across national boundaries and to relate to a diverse range of cultural practices and traditions.

CONCLUSION

The argument of this chapter has been that globalization is a complex process. It involves economic, political, and cultural manifestations that reconstitute the nation-state and rearrange local/global relationships. We would argue that the most substantial effect of the OECD in relation to globalization has been its role as an institutionalizing mechanism for the idea of an integrated global economy underpinned by the ideology of market liberalism. Related to this role has been OECD's support for the new managerialism, which has resulted in the leaner, meaner, and more competitive state apparatuses within nation-states. Within this scenario, the significance of intellectual capital and labor to the economic competitiveness of nations has also been emphasized. Of course, many other active agents around the globe have also been pushing these views. They have worked their way out in universities both directly and indirectly and also through higher education policies developed in response at the national level.

Drawing on Archer's (1994) work on international organizations, we have noted throughout that the OECD is actor, arena, and instrument, so that the relationship between educational agenda setting and policy development in the OECD and within member nations is a complex, two-way process. We have demonstrated this in relation to higher education policy in Australia. We also stress that, whereas the OECD has strongly supported market liberalism, there have been tensions within the organization itself between what those at OECD call the *Anglo-Saxon* and *continental European* models, with the former supporting a harsher version of market liberalism. Moreover, this suggests that the OECD's educational policies and its particular construction of globalization ideologies, as well as educational responses to them, have not been accepted uniformly by the member countries. There has been much debate within Australia, for example, as to whether the OECD's formulations are entirely appropriate. However, what is beyond doubt is that, despite the horizontality principle of connections between sectors within the OECD, its education policy has always had some autonomy from economic policies—to a lesser or greater extent at different policy moments. Overall, the OECD has been a significant mechanism for encouraging the global flows of people, information, and ideology, and, indirectly, of educational policies.

REFERENCES

Appadurai, A. (1996). *Modernity at large: Cultural dimensions of globalization*. Minneapolis: University of Minnesota Press.

Apple, M. (1992). Review of "Education and the Economy in a Changing Society" by the OECD 1989. *Comparative Education Review*, 36(1), 127-129.

Archer, C. (1994). *Organizing Europe: The institutions of integration* (2nd ed.). London: Edward Arnold.

Australian Vice-Chancellors' Committee. (1997). *Shaping Australia's future: Investing in higher education*. The Australian Vice-Chancellors' Committee Submission to the Review of Higher Education Financing and Policy.

Catley, B. (1996). *Globalising Australian capitalism*. Cambridge, UK: Cambridge University Press.

Dawkins, J. (1987). Foreword. In J. Dawkins (Ed.) *Higher education: A policy discussion paper* (pp. iii-iv). Canberra: Australian Government Publishing Service.

De Wit, H. (1995). *Strategies for internationalising higher education*. Paris: OECD.

Giddens, A. (1994). *Beyond left and right: The future of radical politics*. Cambridge, UK: Polity.

Hall, R., & Harley, B. (1995). The Australian response to globalisation: Domestic labour market policy and the case of enterprise bargaining. In P. Gollan (Ed.), *Globalisation and its impact on the world of work* (ACIRRT Working Paper No. 38, pp. 71-96). Sydney: University of Sydney.

Henry, M., & Taylor, S. (1997). Globalisation and national schooling policy in Australia. In B. Lingard & P. Porter (Eds.), *A national approach to schooling in Australia?* (pp. 46-59). Canberra: Australian College of Education.

Hobsbawm, E. (1994). *Age of extremes: The short twentieth century 1914-1991.* London: Michael Joseph.

Istance, D. (1996). Education at the Chateau de la Muette. *Oxford Review of Education,* 22(1), 91-96.

McNeely, C., & Cha, Y. (1994). Worldwide educational convergence through international organisations: Avenues for research. *Educational Policy Analysis Archives,* 2, 14.

Organisation for Economic Co-operation and Development (OECD). (1979). *Future educational policies in the changing social and economic context.* Paris: Author.

OECD. (1987). *Universities under scrutiny.* Paris: Author.

OECD. (1989). *Education and the economy in a changing society.* Paris: Author.

OECD. (1994). *Organization for Economic Cooperation and Development* [Brochure]. Paris: OECD.

OECD. (undated). Brochure outlining the functions and structure of the OECD. Paris: Author.

Papadopoulos, G. (1994). *OECD 1960-1990. The OECD Perspective.* Paris: OECD.

Reus-Smit, C. (1996). Beyond foreign policy: State theory and the changing global order. In P. James (Ed.), *The state in question: Transformations of the Australian state* (pp. 161-195). Sydney: Allen & Unwin.

Seddon, T. (1994). *Context and beyond.* London: Falmer.

Skilbeck, M., & Esnault, E. (1993). *OECD background paper: Higher education: An overview of issues in OECD countries in conference proceedings: The transition from elite to mass higher education.* Canberra: Department of Employment, Education, and Training.

Sklair, L. (1996). Conceptualising and researching the transnational capitalist class in Australia. *The Australian and New Zealand Journal of Sociology,* 32(2), 1-19.

Taylor, S. (1996, December). *The OECD and the politics of education policy-making: An Australian case study.* Paper presented to the Australian Sociological Association Conference.

Trow, M. (1973). *Problems in the transition from elite to mass higher education.* Berkeley, CA: Carnegie Commission on Higher Education.

Vickers, M. (1994). Cross-national exchange, the OECD, and Australian education policy. *Knowledge and Policy,* 7(1), 25-47.

Waters, M. (1995). *Globalization.* London: Routledge.

Weiss, C. (1989). Congressional committees as users of analysis. *Journal of Policy Analysis and Management,* 8(3), 411-431.

CHAPTER 13

Reshaping the Educational Agendas of Mexican Universities

The Impact of NAFTA

Heriberta Castaños-Lomnitz
Axel Didriksson
Janice Newson

On New Year's Day 1994, Chiapas Mexico moved from obscurity to the center of international attention. On this day, the North American Free Trade Agreement (NAFTA) negotiated between Canada, Mexico, and the United States came into effect. Early that morning, an indigenous peasant army based in Chiapas in the southern region of Mexico declared war against NAFTA. Spokespersons for the rebels declared that this trade agreement would bring about their "disappearance"[1] as an ancestral culture.

As word of this anti-NAFTA "rebellion" buzzed around the world, most media commentators characterized it as an echo from the past: a desperate and futile attempt of an old culture to resist the inexorable and overwhelming forces of progress and change. But as the months of 1994 passed, the Chiapas rebellion served as a harbinger of the future rather than an inscription to the past.

After enduring heavy sacrifices in the 1980s in order to restructure the economy, Mexico had high expectations that a new era of commercial success and economic prosperity would begin to unfold on January 1, 1994. The country was poised to enter into a full-blown modernization, and NAFTA was presented to the Mexican people as the doorway to this modernization. Whether animated by their past or seeing clearly into the future, the revolutionary army of peasants could neither take credit for nor be blamed for the economic and political events that took place in the months following their uprising.

Problems with the presidential succession signaled that the prevailing political regime was floundering. The crisis of political leadership intensified as story after story circulated of corruption and criminal activity perpetrated by high-ranking public officials. Early in 1995, Mexico's financial system collapsed. As the peso was devalued, the cost of imported goods sky-rocketed, and the incomes of most Mexicans lost almost 90% of their value practically overnight. International organizations intervened in Mexico's public finances. Even salvation in the form of financial resources from the government of the United States spawned more uneasiness than it quelled. The spiraling effects of the crisis extended beyond Mexico's borders and reverberated throughout the international financial system. It was as though a self-destruct clause had been planted somewhere within the voluminous NAFTA documents, which, like a computer virus, was activated on the day that NAFTA came into effect and proceeded to undermine all of the promise.

Critics of NAFTA and similar regional trade agreements may only see in these events the "proof" that such arrangements don't work. But there is more to learn than this. After all, although it was Mexicans who suffered the brunt of the financial disorder, and the Mexican political leadership that was finally confronted by the Achilles' heel of long-standing political corruption, the other partners to NAFTA and many countries around the world felt the shudder of the Mexican collapse as well. We learn that many of the assumptions and methodologies that are embedded in these economic region-based trade agreements are too simple and crude to transplant into real countries with real histories and with real people who share living cultures. Even though political and economic powers-that-be may impose on citizens and markets the package of arrangements to which they themselves have agreed, we learn that cultures, peoples, histories, and even economies can bite back (Tenner, 1996).

A vast literature is accumulating that describes and analyzes the implications of trade agreements, like NAFTA, that bind several nations together into a common market with no internal trade barriers and with transnational dispute resolution mechanisms to adjudicate and enforce the provisions of the agreements. Even though this chapter takes up a more limited task, it provides a framework for analyzing the relationship between arrangements negotiated by the political leaderships of the countries involved and the various institutional sectors that are expected to facilitate the economic objectives for which the trade agreement was designed. In this respect, this chapter not only speaks to the experience of Mexico, but also contains lessons for other countries in the Caribbean and Latin American region that are now attempting to gain entry into the trade bloc.

On the one hand, we illustrate how the provisions of such agreements fall unevenly on the trading partners and, in domino-like fashion, on disparate sectors and regions within each country. This unevenness becomes particularly problematic in situations like NAFTA, wherein the trading partners have entered into the agreement from histori-cally based relations of economic dependence and even exploitation. On the other hand, we also want to illustrate how cultures, histories, people, and even existing economic arrangements may provide the basis for resisting these regionalizing and globalizing economic ar-rangements. Such resistance may have consequences not only for the trading partner in which it takes place, but also for the other trading partners and nations elsewhere, precisely because of the global inter-connectedness that regional trade agreements bring about.

Focusing on the Mexican experience, we conduct two related examinations into the relationship between the higher education sector and NAFTA. First, we show how the relatively uneven and unequal development of Mexican higher education affects Mexico's ability to supply the workforce and expertise that are required for Mexico's participation in the North American Trade Region. Second, through focusing on a major public university as a case study, we will show how the "new order of business" for higher education that is called for by the trade agreement collides with historically based social, cultural, and political divisions that deeply penetrate the institution in question.

MACROLEVEL INEQUALITIES
IN THE MEXICAN HIGHER
EDUCATION SECTOR

Economic Blocs and the Transfer
of Knowledge and Technology

Developing a new global economic order is the centerpiece of trade agreements such as NAFTA. The life supports of this economic order are the migratory flow of professional and technical workers and the development of international networks that facilitate knowledge and technology transfer. Critical attention is placed, therefore, on labor market issues, particularly in dynamically related industries such as micro-electronics, biotechnology, telecommunications, new materials science and technology, technological fusion, and others.

National systems of higher education are called on to meet the workforce needs of these types of industries, but at any given time, their programs and structures do not simply mirror labor market projections and formulas. They have been shaped as much by their cultural, social, and political histories as by their economic context. Hence, there are important differences among national systems of higher education and in the ways they respond to the demands placed on them. These differences include their institutional frameworks, legislative guidelines and policies, structures of governance, curricular organization, and even the behavioral "codes" and aspirations of the individuals who participate in them. Also, they vary significantly in the extent to which the skills, knowledge, and expertise that they have traditionally emphasized differ from those required in industries that are central to the new economic order.

But especially important to the North American trade bloc partners are differences in the process of economic integration itself, which have been underanalyzed or completely ignored in the economic literature.[2] Yet, economic integration is predicated on and conditioned by the "starting point" of each partner. One such difference relates to the ability of various institutional sectors, such as higher education, to accommodate the new order of business imposed by the trade agreement.

Disadvantages of Mexico's Higher Education System in the Context of North American Integration

Mexico's system of higher education has been handicapped in several ways in meeting the demands of the NAFTA-style economic integration. First, in comparison with the other trading partners, Mexico's professional and technical labor market is underdeveloped. It is smaller, segmented, and concentrated, with a predominant trend toward low salaries. With a population of 90 million (almost four times that of Canada and more than one third of the United States), scarcely more than 4 million people have a college-level education, and only 8.5% of these have received postgraduate training. Moreover, they are concentrated in the urban and industrial centers, where the educational infrastructure is most developed. Most hold administrative positions in the health, social services, food, biomedical, and tourism sectors of the economy. Only 13% are in engineering (Muñoz & Suárez, 1995, pp. 14, 17-18).

Consequently, the existing pool of college and university graduates does not support the labor market demands generated by economic integration in such areas as contracting, international trade exchange, systems analysis, research and development, engineering, and innovative design. Also, because access to professional and technological training is not equally distributed throughout the country,[3] the benefits of new jobs and improved business opportunities in these high demand areas are distributed unevenly, thus aggravating existing inequities among the various regions of the country. Finally, to the extent that it exists, Mexico's internal capacity for technological development and innovative decision making has been displaced by the increasing presence of foreign—especially U.S.—capacity in these areas, thus compounding Mexico's already considerable disadvantages.

Second, in spite of their educational advantages, college- and university-educated Mexicans have not acquired the knowledge and expertise in the areas now under demand. College and university graduates in the United States, Canada, and other highly developed societies are more likely to possess this knowledge and expertise. Moreover, to develop fully integrated and competitive labor markets, NAFTA imposed specific regulations and standards for the accreditation and certification of professional workers,[4] which are designed to guarantee such things as confidence in the enterprise, worker responsibility, competitiveness, and adaptability to market demands. Such criteria are not taken into account in the Mexican labor market. Imposing these regulations and standards—a practice that is deeply rooted in the United States and other developed societies—greatly disadvantages Mexican professionals insofar as it assumes that the Mexican educational system does not guarantee or prepare a "modern" workforce that meets international criteria. In a series of trilateral meetings in 1991 and 1996, the three partners agreed to promote the "harmonization" of standards and to develop evaluation activities and communications relevant to standards and problem resolution.[5] Because Mexico had no previous experience with the standardization and assessment of professional quality, new mechanisms referred to as *integration frames* have been promoted by the government and college-level institutions.[6] Mexican universities and colleges now have the added burden of institutionalizing standards of performance and evaluation that are oriented not to the specific educational needs and requirements of their own population, but rather to conceptions of needs and requirements that are established in other "more developed" societies, especially in the United States.[7]

Third, the Mexican higher education system is less able to adjust to the new workforce demands that are created by the economic activities and enterprises that NAFTA encourages. For example, in the United States, as in Canada and other industrially developed societies, technological changes are reshaping the content and characteristics of many jobs and are thus determining the abilities required of the worker. The employed workforce is becoming more highly educated and specialized. However, a new polarization and segmentation is also emerging in the context of these technology-driven employment patterns; although the skills and training requirements are increasing at the middle and upper levels of the workforce, they are reduced in the lower levels (Mowery & Mowery, 1988).

Mexican data show a similar tendency with regard to job content and workforce polarization (Carrillo, 1995, pp. 270-271). However, compared to the United States, Mexico has fewer institutional supports to ensure that newly required skills, capacities, and technological expertise are being developed in workers to counteract these imbalances between segments of the workforce. For example, the average number of years of formal education in the United States is 12, whereas one in every four Mexican workers has no schooling, and 60% of the economically active population has acquired only elementary schooling. In fact, elementary education in Mexico continues to produce a bottleneck largely based on socioeconomic factors, followed by a second bottleneck between high school and college-level training. In addition, the number of teaching personnel available in Mexico to improve the general level of educational achievement of the population is far less than in the United States. For every college-level professor in Mexico, there are eight in the United States, and whereas Mexico has almost 8,000 postgraduate-level professors, there are 300,000 in the United States (Lovell & Sánchez, 1995, p. 3). About 70% of Mexican professors are employed on a temporary or part-time basis, and 3% of the total have Ph.Ds.[8] By contrast, two thirds of U.S. academic personnel are employed full-time, and over half have Ph.Ds (Lovell & Sánchez, 1995, p. 6).

Moreover, the United States allocates 60 times as much funding to its educational system and constantly increases its allocation. By contrast, Mexico has not increased public funding to education beyond the level reached in the early 1980s. The current level of U.S. investment in research and development is 2.7% of the gross national product (GNP)—one of the highest percentages in the world—whereas from 1992 to 1994, Mexican investment in research and development fell from 0.5% to 0.3% of the GNP. Although the United States and Canada have also suffered cuts in public funding to science and technology in recent years, the cuts in Mexico have been much larger because of the devaluation and reduction in public resources that occurred in the 1995 financial crisis. Whereas private funding for these activities in Mexico is so minimal as to be barely worth mentioning, it has been constantly increasing in the United States.

In sum, Mexico's economic integration into the trade bloc has been hampered by a higher education system less equipped than its trading partners to respond to the new order of business imposed on it by the trade agreement. Also, economic integration itself has exacerbated existing asymmetries within Mexico's education sector and between its higher education system and those of the other trading partners. In many respects, Mexico may be less able to compete with its trading partners than it was in 1992 when NAFTA was signed. Small wonder, then, that protests and acts of resistance against the NAFTA have arisen not only from the poorer southern peasant populations but also from urban-based professional workers. As members of the middle class, these workers have borne the brunt of the post-1994 financial crisis. Those who work within higher education specifically have experienced firsthand the impositions of the new order of business: the demands to change curricula and traditionally valued knowledge, the devaluing of their educational certification, the disruption of their career paths, and the displacement of their professional competence by foreign know-how and expertise that either is deemed to be more suited to the new global economic order or is able to compete more effectively for the new positions and opportunities that economic integration has made available.

UNAM: A CASE STUDY IN RESISTING NAFTA'S NEW "ORDER OF BUSINESS" FOR UNIVERSITIES

The problems described in the previous section form part of the context in which institutions of higher education and their related constituencies either accommodate and participate in the new order of business arising out of NAFTA's agenda or resist it. But universities and colleges are complex institutions. Those who have influence over them hold diverse and often contradictory conceptions of their roles and missions, reflecting the social, political, and economic milieu of the historical periods in which they have arisen. In spite of the apparently homogenizing and harmonizing tendencies of trade agreements and their designs for transcending and overcoming national and local differences, historically based vicissitudes and relationships—institutional, municipal, regional, national—also significantly shape specific institutions' responses to the demands and expectations for change.

This important point is illustrated in interviews[9] conducted with representatives of three key constituencies—academia, industry, and government—whose outlooks have been influenced by the continuing development of the National Autonomous University of Mexico (UNAM). The initially surprising finding concerning these interviews is that none favored technology transfer or any other formal cooperation between the university and industry, even though, since 1982, an apparent consensus has existed on the need for increased cooperation and integration of academic research with industrial production needs.

The discourses and perspectives employed in the interviews are infused with the legacy of the past (Schiffrin, 1987). They are rooted in the cultural, social, political, and economic relations in which UNAM has been historically embedded. In the context of the present, however, they constitute a stalemate—a collective resistance to institutional reform that inhibits meaningful or effective engagement with the new order of business described in the previous section. By looking to the recent and more distant history of UNAM, a deeper understanding can be gained of why the high expectations for NAFTA prior to January 1, 1994, have not been fulfilled.

UNAM in Historical Context

Two competing interpretations exist of higher education in Mexico. One postulates a crisis in Mexican universities arising at least since 1968, when a student movement originating in UNAM was bloodily repressed by the government. The problems of higher education, in this view, stem mainly from politics. This interpretation is not necessarily restricted to the political left or to New Age critics. Even in 1944, the moderate conservative Rector Alfonso Caso (1944/1976), in proclaiming the new Act of Governance that excluded industrially focused research as a primary objective of UNAM, proposed that the problems of the university were due to certain legal strictures that "force it to have an eminently political character."

A second story, with variants, contradicts the first. One version is that public universities are in crisis because they have been unable to supply the qualified professional and technical personnel that are required to fuel Mexico's industrial takeoff. Another offered by David Lorey (1993) argues that there is no crisis in higher education itself. Nor has there been substantial disagreement between UNAM and the Mexican state. The problems belong more to the economy and society in general: Universities have consistently produced more skilled labor power than the country could reasonably use (Lorey, 1993). In historical context, these are not entirely incompatible stories: UNAM has always been a tool of politics, its development marked by its relationship to the ruling regime. But at the same time, this relationship has fluctuated with the economic and sociocultural development of Mexico as a whole.

The Colonial Period[10]

From the time that the royal charter was granted in 1547, the University of Mexico was designed to serve the specific political ends of the Spanish colonial regime: that is, to be a bulwark of scholastic philosophy, erected by the King of Spain and the Pope, against the Protestant heresy from northern Europe. A complicated apartheid system known as the *Leyes de Casta* placed the Spaniards at the top of the social ladder, with the Indians and Blacks at the bottom. One rung below the pure Spaniards were the Criollos, or white people born in Mexico of Spanish parentage.

The Royal and Pontifical University of Mexico quickly became an exclusive preserve of the Criollos. Few Indians were recipients of the 30,000 degrees—of which 1,403 were doctorates—awarded during the three centuries of colonial rule from 1521 to 1821. When independence from Spain was finally achieved, the Liberals closed down the university, only to reopen it in 1910 as the National University of Mexico, just a few months prior to the outbreak of the Mexican Revolution.

Postrevolutionary UNAM

Newly named by the liberals just prior to the revolution, the National University of Mexico became the centerpiece of an ambitious postrevolutionary national project. José Vasconcelos, the first rector of the university in the postrevolutionary period and first secretary of education of the revolutionary regime (1920-1923), reorganized the educational system of Mexico, guided by a vision of Mexico as a new kind of society. As a political scientist, he foresaw the trend toward a modern nationhood based on ethnicity, as well as the need for revolutionary regimes (including the one in Mexico) to evolve toward democratic parliamentary systems akin to the American system. His alternation between admiration and loathing for the

United States was not unusual among Mexican intellectuals. But none has gone further in promoting the idea of a Latin American spiritual supremacy. He defined the Mexican people as the "Cosmic Race" born out of centuries of intermarriage and miscegenation, resulting (he felt) in an ethnic community featuring the best of all the world's populations.

The National University of Mexico had an important—even central—role in this project. The motto that Vasconcelos devised for it included the task of defining the character of Mexican culture and inspiring "our race" to "give rise to a culture with new, essentially spiritual and utterly free tendencies" (Valadés, 1974, p. 5).

But Vasconcelos lost political influence in 1928 and was effectively barred from political office with the creation of the government party, the PRI. In 1929, a student movement arose at UNAM that was widely interpreted as supporting Vasconcelos. In response, President Portos Gil granted autonomy to the university, hoping to destroy it by cutting it loose, so to speak, from the source of its economic stability. The dissension that emerged at this point between the university and the ruling regime has marked UNAM's evolution through much of this century. Its recurring themes were present in the speeches made by some politicians during the 1929 conflict. Examples translated from the records of the congressional debate follow:

> That is a great truth we have just heard from the Secretary of Educa-
> tion. The intellectual classes in this country have lived in a situation
> where they have been divorced from the people. I want the University
> to mend its ways. The Revolution expects the University and our
> precious students to be capable of taking care of themselves. She
> demands of them not to shut themselves up in the ivory tower of their
> wisdom, but rather always to go out to the people, who have to sweat
> the money to be used for university teaching [Applause].
>
> *Rep. Federico V. Medrano: Congressional Record, June 4, 1929.*

> Of course I must tell you that the youngsters have demanded the
> removal of the Secretary of Education, of the Rector of the University,
> of the Chief of Police, and it's a wonder they did not ask for Mount
> Popocatépetl to bring forth *chalupas* and for the water in Xochimilco
> to turn into *tepache*,[11] to put a flourish into their strike. But the President

of Mexico has called their bluff, and he has told them: "Here, take the autonomy of the National University."

The Hon. Senator Caloca: Congressional Record, June, 5 1929

Because the university had become the stronghold of the new middle class of mestizo administrators and politicians in the post-revolutionary period, UNAM was able to stand its ground, even though it endured serious economic hardships from 1929 to 1944. But the granting of autonomy began a related struggle over the extent to which the university should be drawn into the economic and political projects of the government.[12] A camp led by Vicente Lombardo Toledano proposed to turn UNAM into a socialist university where Marxism would be taught to the exclusion of other doctrines. The university would be "revolutionary, proletarian, politically committed and anti-imperialistic." It would make sure that all production in the country was state-controlled.[13] A second camp headed by Antonio Caso, which championed freedom of thought, eventually won out. When Antonio's brother, Alfonso Caso, became the rector of UNAM in 1944, he insisted that the university should have nothing to do with politics or with industrial development: "The Law and the Statutes must make sure that nothing can come between us and the purposes of education and research, these being the only valid ones" (Caso, 1944/1976, p. 85). Caso was so adamant in rejecting a specific role for UNAM in economic development that President Cárdenas had to create the National Polytechnic Institute to fill this void.[14]

From 1945 until the 1960s, tension between the university and the political regime and internal divisions over the appropriateness of the university's involvement in economic matters were less prevalent. The economic boom and the availability of jobs in the expanding civil service fed the growth of the middle class. But modernization of the industrial structure was neglected, and rapid population increase nullified economic advances. Mexico soon entered into a lingering recession. Thus, labor conflicts and student unrest once again prevailed in the 1960s, and the dissension was rekindled between the university and the government. In 1968, a minor student conflict escalated into a popular protest movement against the authoritarian political regime. The campus was eventually occupied by the military. On October 2, 1968, several hundred unarmed protesters were massacred. In Mexico today, the 1968 Movement is interpreted as a pivotal moment in Mexican history.

UNAM Today

The history just recited provides a basis for understanding why, in the context of the new order of business being placed upon UNAM by economic integration, informants from academia, industry, and government privately expressed opposition to technology transfer and university-industry cooperation, contrary to the public position on these issues. It tells us, first, that the issue of the university's relations with industry is a delicate matter, touching as it does on the long-standing dissension between the university, supported by its middle-class constituency, and the ruling political regime. Albeit in contemporary form, themes resurfaced in the interview transcripts (see Note 9) that had emerged in the struggles of the past.

For example, industrialists sneered at academic research (UNAM is the largest purveyor of scientific research in the country) and suspected state universities of conniving with the government in an attempt to saddle industry with the bill for higher education. The academics claimed industry was technologically backward so that a partnership with higher education was hopeless. Finally, government officials explained that industrialists and academics needed each other but refused to acknowledge this out of selfish motives. Only the government was farsighted and patriotic enough to bring them together. The idea of selling technology to industry, they suggested, was probably a gambit of the state universities for wheedling some financing out of development banking.

Second, two conflicting discourses on technology, appearing in the transcripts, can be traced to different periods of history. One discourse, which devalues technology and views it as socially demeaning, can be detected in the mistrust of academics and the reluctance of university graduates to develop manual or practical skills. Informants from industry confirmed that graduates of state universities preferred desk jobs and tended to set themselves apart from foremen by their code of dress. This perception of the technical as inferior is reflected in UNAM's academic practices as well: Laboratory or field courses tend to be taught by low-level assistants, while the professors stick to theory.

This discourse can be traced to the colonial period, when the university mainly served, and reflected the interests and culture of, the moneyed elite of the Criollo caste. Members of this caste—and white people in general—were attended to by servants and were raised to avoid the slightest physical exertion. Technology as manual craft was devalued and despised. It was in the domain of the non-White lower castes. The university of the time reinforced this mental association by stressing information and wisdom found in certain authorized texts at the expense of direct personal investigation. Although the Caste Laws were abolished in Mexico before 1821, a persistent fear remains among middle-class university graduates that they will be taken for members of the lower classes if they show too much familiarity with the technical. Such familiarity may betray a lowly social origin, because manual labor was reserved for Indians, Blacks, and mestizos.

This prejudice against manual and technical work in the colonial period was imported into the new postrevolutionary class structure. For example, in the postrevolutionary period, most graduates of UNAM went into politics, the civil service, and the liberal professions—not into industry. After research oriented toward industrial development was excluded as a primary objective of UNAM in 1944, the National Polytechnic Institute was established by the government that same year for this purpose.

A corresponding prejudice was expressed by industrialist informants. Their comments were raucously anti-academic and rejected a role for public universities in technological training and development. Business leaders said, "if we ever need technology, we'll let the universities know." Personnel managers claimed that graduates from the public universities are poorly trained and have to be retrained by companies at their expense. Although not necessarily better trained, graduates from private universities—mostly from business families—"understand what business is all about," whereas graduates from public universities "don't believe in technical solutions; their reaction is wanting to change the system. All they ever think about is politics. Pretty soon they want to run the company."

Thus, in spite of current economic pressures on Mexico to modernize its scientific and technological capacities to integrate with the new globalized economic order, the long-standing symbolic meaning of technology and "the technical" continues to permeate middle-class Mexican culture and to affect relations between business, academic, and government elites (Gee, 1991). In fact, it gives rise to telling contradictions. Whereas foreign industrialists readily commend the skill and inventiveness of Mexican workers when they are provided with incentives and opportunity, middle-class Mexicans regularly employ ironic or self-deprecating expressions about Mexico's supposed technological inferiority. For example, some clever gadget is apt to be referred to as "white man's technology," even though it is often Japanese.[15] Paradoxically, technology becomes respectable only when it is imported and glossy—especially when it can be shown off to impress visitors. Implied in this double standard is a definite preference for "turnkey" installations that can be maintained from abroad.

The second technological discourse has been introduced more recently by foreign-based manufacturers, and it incorporates the ideology of science and technology familiar in industrial nations such as the United States, Europe, and Japan (Habermas, 1980). In Mexico, this discourse has permeated the official stance on the role of higher education. Informants in all three sectors—academia, industry, and government—paid lip service to this "official" discourse, and in this context, they strenuously denied Mexican technical inferiority.

The juxtaposition of these contradictory discourses is perplexing. Are these decision makers unaware of the contradiction between their private and public stances? Perhaps not. While justifying their own stance, representatives of each of the sectors blamed each other, as though they were attempting to account for the fact that the much-touted cooperation between the university and industry has yet to be realized. In so doing, however, they drew upon the symbolic meanings of the past and wove them into the cultural and political divisions of the present. It appears, then, that a widespread colonial discourse is used in modern-day Mexico. Even if obsolete, the symbolic values embedded in this colonial discourse have considerable efficacy in the present, even in the face of high expectations for economic payoffs that are tied to relinquishing an attachment to these meanings. Moreover, the survival of these symbolic meanings—indeed, their recirculation—may be due to their continued usefulness to the political positions and counterpositions adopted by each sector in relation to the pressures for change that are presently at work in Mexico.

CONCLUSION

To account for why Mexico appears not to be meeting the high expectations for its economic integration into the North American trade bloc, we first displayed in the first part of this chapter not only the relative disadvantages of Mexico's higher education sector in the North American trade bloc, but also how economic integration itself has exacerbated these disadvantages. The second part has provided a penetrating gloss on the first. It raises further questions about who or what may underlie Mexico's apparent failure to achieve more than a facade of modernization,[16] and it points us toward a sociologically complex answer. The case study of UNAM suggests that more is involved than simply the inequalities, lack of capacity, or structural peculiarities of the national system of higher education; historically based social, political, and cultural factors are deeply at play.

The NAFTA provisions conceive of development primarily in terms of economic processes and thus treat historically distinct social, cultural, and political issues as obstacles needing to be overcome. Foreign commentators and analysts of the Mexican situation have also tended to overlook or reject these issues as relevant. A 1993 study by David Lorey of UCLA and a 1994 study conducted by the Organization for Economic Cooperation and Development (OECD) are two recent examples. Lorey proposes that the problems of the university arise fundamentally from an economic misfit. Since about 1958, he says, Mexican higher education has bestowed on its graduates social status instead of job opportunities; "reformist or radical ideologies" that the students imbibe at public universities represent a valuable psychological crutch that helps students overcome their guilt feelings about being unable to land a suitable job. He rejects the idea that the political activism of university students might stem from opposition to the regime.[17] The OECD review panel argued somewhat differently that the peculiarly Mexican system of university autonomy has rendered state universities insensitive to national needs.[18]

Notwithstanding Mexico's various inequalities in relation to trading partners such as the United States and Canada, Mexicans themselves are significant players in the integration drama, and they do not base their actions on interpretations such as those presented by Lorey and the OECD. Within Mexico, the dissension between UNAM and the ruling political regime has always found expression along political lines. When the government was leftist or populist, UNAM was conservative. When the government veered to the right, UNAM turned to the left. Today, many members of the academic community sympathize with the opposition parties, particularly with the Party of the Democratic Revolution. Because the ruling PRI party has staked its political future on the modernization project tied to NAFTA, it stands to reason that resistance to NAFTA-style integration arises at least in part—and significantly—from political resistance to the regime.

The public university in Mexico has evolved historically—often in the context of dictatorial regimes—as an instrument and repository of various social and cultural projects. It has been and continues to be an important site of politics. Transnational trade agreements that ignore this are at risk from the "biting back" of real cultures, of lived histories, and even of economically motivated actions.

NOTES

1. *Disappeared* and *disappearance* have special meaning in the experiences of indigenous peoples in this area of the world.

2. Marketing and production issues have been the major foci of analysis.

3. By comparison, for every eight persons qualified in the United States, Mexico has one qualified person to fill these new areas of labor market demand. It is estimated that the ideal proportion of engineers to a population of 10,000 should be 100 to 200 in order to reach a sustained industrial and technological takeoff, whereas in Mexico at present, the proportion is 13 to 10,000—and only 1 of the 13 has a postgraduate degree. (Carrillo, 1995, p. 261).

4. See the chapter on "Transborder Services Trade Exchange," mainly article 1210, "Granting Licenses and Certificates" as well as annex 1210.05, "Professional Services."

5. The Forum of North American Trilateral Standardization was formed with the participation of the American National Standards Institute (ANSI-US), the national Chamber of Transformation Industry (CANACINTRA), and the Standards Council of Canada (SCC).

6. One such mechanism adopted in 1993 is the General Examination for Professional Quality, which has been applied since 1994 under the supervision of the Centre for the Evaluation of College Level Education (CENEVAL), a body created specifically for this purpose. A second mechanism, created in 1995, is the Normalization System of Labor Competences.

7. The U.S. model of higher education is increasingly urged upon nations by other supranational bodies as well. See World Bank, 1994.

8. Lovell and Sánchez (1995, p. 10) report dramatic differences in salary as well.

9. This was drawn from 43 tape-recorded interviews conducted by Heriberta Castaños (1991, 1995) with decision makers in academia, industry, and government.

10. For an expanded history of UNAM during this period, see Revilla (1794) and Humboldt (1822).

11. *Chalupas* is a kind of Mexican popular food. *Tepache* is a popular refreshment made of fermented pineapple juice.

12. UNAM's meager endowment of 10 million pesos was supplemented by under-the-table subsidies that involved political concessions.

13. This position differed little from the government's original populist and authoritarian project for higher education.

14. Significantly, the Polytechnic was denied autonomy and still depends on the Department of Education. Its rector is a government appointee.

15. During colonial rule, all prestigious artifacts were imported from Europe.

16. Unger (1995, pp. 53-54 and 76-77) argues that modernization is largely an appearance rather than an actual achievement, reinforced by phantom franchises and the dramatic increase in imported manufactured goods, particularly in products with a high value-added knowledge and technology component such as automobiles, electronic equipment, and chemicals. Mexican enterprises that have gained a comparative advantage from economic integration are those that benefit from the absolute advantage of transnational companies that have access to Mexican markets and increased opportunities for foreign investment.

17. We know of no evidence to support this overly psychoanalytic theory of why student activists embraced radical ideologies. We do know that many leaders of the 1968 movement are now active in national politics, usually in the opposition. Such a stubborn insistence on having been right thirty years ago seems hard to reconcile with explanations in terms of denied job opportunities, or feelings of inferiority. There are several additional problems with Lorey's reasoning that we can't elaborate on here. (See Castaños, 1995.)

18. It equated the autonomy of UNAM and other state universities with lack of accountability, even though similar problems exist at the National Polytechnic Institute—which is not autonomous—and even though UNAM is at least as well audited as is the National Polytechnic Institute. Ironically, without acknowledging the role of politics, the review panel implicated itself in the politics of the situation. How else could the bias against autonomy have been fed to the foreign reviewers, except by Mexican government officials who shepherded them throughout their brief visit?

REFERENCES

Carrillo, F. J. (1995). La Identificación, Capacitación y Motivación de los Recursos Humanos Técnicos. In Pablo del Pozo Mulás (Ed.), *Aspectos tecnolúlogicos de la modernización industrial de México* (pp. 248-295). México City: Fondo de Cultura Econúmica, Academía de la Investigaciún Científica, Academia Nacional Ingenieríe.

Caso, A. (1976). Exposiciún de Motivos, en Ley Orgánica de la Universidad Nacional Autúnoma de México. In E. Hurtado Márquez (Ed.), *Comision tecnica de estudios yu projectos legislativos* (Vol. 4). Mexico City: UNAM Press. (Original work published 1944)

Castaños, H. (1991). *Vinculaciún Universidad-Industria?* Unpublished doctoral dissertation, Universidad Autónoma Nacional de México, Mexico, D.F.

Castaños, H. (1995). Technology transfer in Mexico: The issue of higher education and industrial development. *Science and Public Policy, 22,* 325-332.

Gee, J. P. (1991). *Social linguistics and literacies: Ideology in discourses.* London: Falmer.

Habermas, J. (1980). Technik und Wissenschaft als Ideologie. In B. Barnes et al. (Eds.), *Estudio sobre la sociología de la ciencia*. Madrid: Alianza Universidad.

Humboldt, A. (1941). *Essai politique sur le royaume de la Nouvelle-Espagne*, 5 vols. (V. González Arnau, Trans.). Mexico: P. Robredo. (Original work published in 1822)

Lorey, D. E. (1993). *The university system: Economic development in Mexico since 1929*. Palo Alto, CA: Stanford University Press.

Lovell, C. D., & Sánchez, M. D. (1995). *Higher education faculty in Mexico and the United States: Characteristics and policy issues* (Working Chapter No. 2). Tucson, AZ: Western Interstate Commission for Higher Education (WICHE).

Mowery, R., & Mowery, D. (1988). *The impact of technological change on employment and growth*. Cambridge, MA: Ballinger.

Muñoz, H., & Suárez, M. H. (1995). Los que tienen educaciún Superior. In M. García & R. R. Gúmez (Eds.), *Escenarios para la universidad contemporánea* (pp. 11-32). Mexico: CESU, Universidad Autúnoma Nacional de México.

Organization for Economic Cooperation and Development (OECD). (1994). *Reviews of national science and technology policy, Mexico*. Paris: Author.

Revilla, G., 2nd. Count. (1966). Instrucciún reservada al Marqués de Branciforte. In *Colecciún México Heroico*, Vol. 50. Mexico: Jus. (Original work published 1794)

Schiffrin, D. (1987). *Discourse markers*. Cambridge, UK: Cambridge University Press.

Tenner, E. (1996). *Things that fight back: Technology and the revenge of unintended consequences*. New York: Random House.

Unger, K. (1995). El desarrollo industrial y tecnolúgico Mexicano: Estado actual de la integraciún industrial y tecnolúgica. In P. Mulás del Pozo (Ed.), *Aspectos tecnolúgicos de la modernizaciún industrial de México* (pp. 44-80). Mexico: Fondo de Cultura Econúmica, Academía de la Investigaciún Científica, Academia Nacional de Ingeniería.

Valadés, D. (1974). La universidad nacional autúnoma de México. In E. Hurtado Márquez (Ed.), *Comision tecnica de estudios yu projectos legislativos* (Vol. 4). Mexico City: UNAM Press.

World Bank. (1994). *Higher education: The lessons of experience*. Washington, DC: Author.

CHAPTER 14

Conclusion

Repositioning the Local Through Alternative Responses to Globalization

Janice Newson

Just as I started to write this closing chapter, I found myself in the middle of a strike at York University, in Toronto, Canada. The strike lasted for eight weeks—the longest university-based academic staff strike in English Canada. When it began on March 20, 1997, the issues in dispute between the union and the administration would have appeared neither unusual nor surprising to many observers, particularly in a collective bargaining context: demands for salary increases arising from a government-imposed wage freeze in 1993, pay equity for women faculty, retirement policy, workload, and technological changes affecting academic activities.

However, three weeks into the strike, it became evident that the support, which grew stronger with every week, was being driven by a much broader range of concerns than the issues of dispute in bargaining—concerns not formulated as "strike issues" when it began. Once the faculty and professional librarians became "the striking faculty and professional librarians" and found themselves walking the picket lines and gathering around fire bins to chat while drinking hot coffee and eating doughnuts delivered by concession vans, the strike exploded into a remarkable release of energy, as though a prolonged collective catharsis had taken over.

Anger toward the university administration sizzled across electronic circuits in the evenings, when the union's e-mail server processed hundreds of exchanges about the events of the day. It had been enough to provoke the faculty and librarians to support strike action, in the first place, that the previous sixteen months of unproductive and frustrating negotiations, punctuated by the administration's unprecedented action of abrogating the collective agreement that was in force and imposing its own terms, appeared as a deliberately chosen strategy to destroy the union and do away with the collective bargaining arrangements of the previous twenty years. But as the strike progressed, the anger that gained momentum each day was anger that had been accumulating over the previous decade for a litany of administration "sins": mismanaging scarce resources and directing them away from academic needs to expand and enrich the senior administration; failing to show leadership in the face of government funding cuts; imposing new technologies that disrupted library services and drove students, staff, and faculty alike into fits of rage during registration periods; and, perhaps most egregious of all, selling out the university to the "corporate agenda."

When striking academic staff members began to voice their concerns about an overbearing and overly corporate-style management, the increasing commercialization of campus culture, and corporate influence over research and teaching programs, I was struck by the special irony of my situation. While I was facing an impossible-to-meet deadline for my contributions to this book and struggling unsuccessfully to draft a chapter on repositioning the local through alternative strategies, I was becoming engaged in an alternative-in-the-making—a locally based political struggle that began to map out some alternatives to the very changes in universities that are described in this book.

But the irony of my situation does not end here. As outlined in the Preface, I first became involved in research and writing about the growing influence of managerialism and corporatism in the university through my involvement in the unionization of faculty associations that took place in Canada from the 1970s to the early 1980s. From 1985 onward, I began documenting and developing a critical scholarly analysis of significant policy and infrastructural initiatives that were leading universities toward intensified collaborations with the corporate sector (see Buchbinder & Newson, 1990; Newson, 1992;

Newson & Buchbinder, 1988). This policy of linking universities and university researchers with the domestic corporate sector to enhance national economic competitiveness—strongly promoted in Canada by such organizations as the Business Council on National Issues (BCNI), the Canadian Manufacturers Association (CMA), the Corporate Higher-Education Forum (CHEF), and the now-defunct Science Council of Canada (SCC)— has been a crucial initial step in drawing universities across the world into the globalizing processes described by many chapters in this collection.

A main objective of my research and writing was to promote greater public awareness of the serious implications of this new "order of business," which, without being subject to any public debate, was being advocated and implemented in Canadian universities throughout the 1980s.[1] Along with a small band of Canadian academics who had similar concerns, I was convinced that participating in this new order of business was undermining important ways that universities serve the public interest, such as creating and disseminating knowledge that is broadly accessible and sustaining democratic life (Newson, 1994). I made a number of efforts—without much success—to interest journalists in reporting on the changing circumstances of universities and these underlying issues.

But I directed my writing primarily to academics themselves, who, in my view, bear the primary responsibility for giving direction to universities and who, in spite of the increased powers of central administrations, retain sufficient influence and authority to intervene in the affairs of universities. Moreover, my interest in the dynamics of the *corporatization* of universities included a concern with the way that academics themselves were being drawn into the corporatization project[2] at the same time as they were also becoming more peripheral to the decision making of their own institutions and the conditions of their work were deteriorating in the ways described by Vidovich and Currie (Chapter 9). I believed that a greater awareness and understanding of the changes taking place in universities and of their implications might disrupt academics' complicity and inspire a more challenging intervention.

I cannot say that my writing nor the writing of other colleagues concerned about these issues had a significant effect on the political consciousness of academics, either in my own university or in other universities. But by the mid 1990s, the changes in policies, practices,

and infrastructures accomplished in the 1980s were bearing consequences that could not be easily ignored. At York University, as at
other universities, these included repeated budget-cutting cycles
combined with deteriorating salaries and working conditions, even
while areas and programs of the university that the administration
believed to be, or to have the potential to be, more "profitable" were
gaining resources; a more "corporate style" approach to the management of the university, along with a decreasing involvement of
faculty members and librarians in university decision making; and
visible manifestations of corporate-linking and the commercialization of university activities in such things as corporate names and
logos on university buildings and teaching materials, advertisements
on the walls of washrooms, the presence of private research companies in university facilities, the appearance of shopping malls centrally located on campus, and so on.

As visible as many of these issues had become, it was not until the
strike pulled the faculty and librarians out of university buildings
and they reconstituted themselves, not as members of departments
and programs, but of picket "gates," that they became the focus of
concern and fueled support for the strike. It was as though the
gradual process of accommodation to what the university was becoming over the previous decade or more—to incremental rather
than dramatic changes in routines, language, patterns of connecting
to colleagues, justifications for decisions, and a myriad of other things
that make up day-to-day academic work life—prevented them
from seeing the deeper implications for themselves as academics
and the university as they conceived it. Prevented them, that is, until
the sudden and dramatic shift of perspective that came from leaving
the buildings and walking on picket lines: a shift of perspective that
writing about these issues did not achieve itself.

Moreover, through the strike, I found myself in a unique position
to shape public perceptions of what the strike was about. Although
I had not held an official position in the faculty union for several
years, I was quickly drawn into the daily process of planning strike
strategy and especially of dealing with the media, whose initial
coverage was hypercritical of the striking faculty and librarians. For
the first time since I began my scholarly work on the transformation
of universities through budget-based rationalization and corporate
linking, it became possible to focus media attention and to get a

public airing on what was happening inside universities from the point of view of the frontline academic staff. It was even possible to get reporters to report on something other than the greed and self-indulgence of privileged academics—although there certainly were enough stories that repeated those as reasons for the strike as well. Equally important, my own colleagues—hundreds of them, not just a dozen or two—were coming to an awareness of the conditions underlying their alienation from the university and their failing efforts to make good on the objectives and values that had originally inspired their choice of vocation. At a rally held in downtown Toronto at the City Hall Square, twelve members of the academic staff spoke passionately and eloquently about why they had chosen an academic career and what they believed the purpose of a university to be. All of them referred to the underlying conditions that were impediments to achieving these purposes.

Ironically, then, this strike—this entering into a mode of action about which many professional workers, including academics, feel ambivalent if not intensely uncomfortable; this forced engagement at picket lines with "clients" (students in this case) who were hostile or upset about the disruption of their final weeks of the academic term; this political polarization that isolated the administration in the ninth floor of a university building while faculty members and librarians took over the grounds and entrances, holding support rallies, organizing information sessions for students, and participating in solidarity picket; this temporary, media-mediated "diaspora" of a university's academic staff captured in news clips as the roving[3] convocation in downtown Toronto or as vigil-antes[4] paying evening visits to the homes of the incoming university president, members of the Board of Governors, and key members of the administration—this strike, this dramatic break with routine has made meaningful, even useful, the analysis of the transformation of the university to which the authors of this volume have contributed.

Two general observations can be made to integrate this story about a particular struggle at a single university into the conclusion of a book about universities and globalization. The first is that this is a decidedly local story. It concerns an event in which a geographically bound university community entered into an intense, politically transformative experience that is hard to convey to anyone who was not physically present. Moreover, the policies and actions that were being challenged by the striking academics were implemented by local and national, not transnational or supranational, bodies (as Richard DeAngelis's Chapter 6 urges us to notice).

Yet it is also a story that resonates globally. Colleagues and academic associations not only in Canada but from around the world heard about this strike, primarily through e-mail communication, and became intensely interested in its outcome. Many sent messages of support and affirmed that the issues that the York strike had confronted were also being confronted at their own local universities. Also, although local, this strike was not an isolated response to the condition of the university in the 1990s. Over the past year, academic staff strikes prompted by similar issues have taken place at several Canadian universities and at universities in other parts of the world. They have drawn attention beyond their own national boundaries[5] and have been accounted for in terms of globalization. Notably, the new forms of communication that are assigned a key role in promoting globalization have become, at the same time, the instruments for engaging a wider constituency in these locally based political struggles. So, although as some have argued, globalization gives reign to social, political, and economic forces that undermine and disempower the local, globalization also amplifies local responses and makes it possible to create a broader base of political support for them and the social, political, and economic projects[6] that *these responses* represent.

The second thing that can be said about the story of the York strike is that the transformation of political consciousness was not limited to the period of the strike. Nor did it consist only of anger toward the university administration and resistance to changes that have been attributed in these chapters to globalization. When the strike ended, the "roving convocation" of academic staff members, along with student supporters, marched back into the university in unison under slogans of "reclaiming the university," "not business as usual," and "the struggle continues." Over ensuing weeks, coordinated efforts were made to renew and recover the influence of the academic staff in university governing bodies, such as the academic senate, faculty councils, and departments, and various actions have focused on exposing and challenging the corporate connections and commercial interests that are embedded in several university projects.

Most important, throughout the strike and after, there has been a remarkable burst of creativity and renewed energy for reimagining the university as an intellectual community and as a locus of intellectual life that is responsive to the changed political, social, and economic conditions of the 1990s. Made possible during the strike by the mix of disciplines assigned to picket gates and the intensive use of the union's e-mail server, discussions of intellectual interests and pedagogical methods traversed the usual lines of communication and brought together, for example, colleagues in dance, theater, and visual art with colleagues in the natural sciences. Talk advanced on plans to open a "free university" and to institute cross-disciplinary courses and programs that are more coherent with the times. After the strike, much energy poured into creating structures that will keep these lines of communication open. Thus, rather than simply refusing the negative consequences of the changed circumstances of universities, this local academic community is attempting to define and capture the creative possibilities in these changed circumstances and to discover anew the role that the university needs to play in them.

I am not arguing that strikes are the only or even the primary way of pursuing alternatives to the negative changes in universities attributed in this volume to globalization. In fact, there are two important limitations to strikes and other collective bargaining strategies in this regard. First, if bargaining strategies focus only on preserving the professional benefits and status of the academic staff, they may have little effect at all on the changes taking place in universities. In a soon-to-be-published book on faculty strikes and collective bargaining in universities, Neil Tudiver of the University of Manitoba argues that full-time, tenure-track professors have been relatively successful over the past decade or so at protecting their jobs from the layoffs that have taken place in other public and private sector workplaces as a consequence of restructuring and globalizing processes. In other words, the profession of academics may survive while the university does not—at least as the public-serving institution that it has been. In fact, combining Tudiver's point with Dominelli and Hoogvelt's (1996) analyses of intellectuals' adaptations to the "introduction of market discipline into the public sector," it is clear that these adaptations constitute new ways for intellectuals to maintain professional position and status in changed conditions, even though the institutions in which they work—universities, for example—are being fundamentally transformed. Dominelli and Hoogvelt go so far as to argue that some university-based intellectuals "through their adaptive response, play midwife to a new social and political formation" (p. 92).

The second limitation of strikes and other collective bargaining strategies is that they may only reinforce the institutional stalemate between survival and resistance[7] that seriously inhibits the mobilization of a strong political challenge to the imposition of changes that arise from globalizing pressures. Several chapters in this collection (e.g., Chapter 4, by Fisher and Rubenson; Chapter 7, by Currie and Vidovich; Chapter 10, by Berman) have pointed to the emergence in universities of an assertive, corporate-styled management that has become a crucial organizational tool for overseeing and implementing such things as restructuring and corporate-linking projects. A common orientation of these managements is to accommodate the funding policies passed down by governments and the new financial climate that encourages privatization, corporate linking, and the commercialization of university activities and services. In contrast, as illustrated by the York strike, faculty associations and academic staff unions offer an organized means of resisting the actions of management that they see as facilitating the transformation of their work and workplaces. This polarization at the local level has seriously impeded the development of an effective and united *sectoral* challenge to the instigators of the changes in universities that have been described—that is, to governments, corporate elites, and various "third-party"[8] lobbying groups.

Notwithstanding these limitations, collective bargaining strategies can promote a political consciousness about the implications to the university of these changes and a renewed commitment to its public-serving purposes. They can thus encourage and enable resistance to the pressures that are represented as "imperatives" of globalization and also be a means of reshaping local institutions in ways that respond to social, political, and economic agendas other than, and in contrast to, these pressures. For example, several writers represented in this book described the way that the microreform of universities that is justified in terms of the globalization imperative creates new and exacerbates old inequities in workload, salary, and contract status of academic staff in universities (e.g., Fisher and Rubenson, Chapter 4; Currie and Vidovich, Chapter 7; Berman, Chapter 10; Campion and Freeman, Chapter 11). The York strike produced a heightened awareness of these inequities,[9] leading to the creation of a standing equity committee within the union to ensure that equity issues are addressed in all facets of the union's activities, including in the development of its bargaining proposals. Another possibility is that academic unions will begin to exercise financial power of their own—particularly if they band their resources together. For example, they could invest their pension funds in businesses and economic projects that strengthen their local economies or that promote social, cultural, and political values that are counter to the single-focus economic growth orientation of the dominant global discourse.

These alternatives are not only useful for counteracting the negative effects of globalization in the university. Precisely because of the relatively high professional status and authority of university-based intellectuals, resisting the downgrading and restructuring of academic work *in alliances with* unions in other sectors can help foster resistance to similar changes in the working conditions of less privileged and less powerful worker groups.[10]

Setting aside my skepticism about the effectiveness of academic writing for generating a heightened political consciousness, I suggest that the chapters of this book are another route to alternative responses to globalization; they are a rich resource for developing political interventions that can modify, reshape, and even reverse the "single-path" model of globalism that is implied in much of the "global talk."[11] Although identified as *critical* studies of globalization, the chapters are by no means mere polemic. In fact, they represent an effort to use academic skills—careful, systematic analysis and examination of evidence—to provide a more nuanced and diverse representation of globalization than is employed by most advocates and too many critics: that is, a representation of globalization as a single path of converging forces imposing themselves on local, regional, and national communities.

The single-path conception reinforces a sense of inevitability to the changes associated with globalism and thus discourages any and all interventions except adaptation and accommodation. However, Chapters 2, 3, and 6 (by Dudley, Slaughter, and DeAngelis, respectively) help to deconstruct this conception by exposing the particular interests it serves and the particular agents promoting it. This model of globalization is thus displayed as a politically and economically directed project, rather than as the inevitable and necessary unfolding of history. By showing that it is based on the cooperation and articulation of a broad range of national and local institutions, including whole systems of higher education and locally administered universities, the simple or automatic accomplishment of this project is called into question. Assigning human agency to the "forces" promoting this model of globalization and exposing in particular their relationship to changes being implemented in institutions of higher education encourage political interventions and empower those who want to modify or reverse their "effects."

In this regard, a key strategy adopted in the York strike was to place the issues in dispute between the union and the administration in a political and economic context broader than the context of bargaining over terms and conditions of employment, in order to promote a more general awareness of the implications of the strike for universities as publicly funded institutions. Names and faces were given to the agents who were promoting the changes that the academic staff were struggling against, to make visible their interests, and to apply political pressure to them. For example, the corporate involvement of specific members of the Board of Governors in the manufacture and distribution of information-processing technologies and software was identified and linked to the on-campus projects for developing and commercializing software-driven courses. This linking supported the union's public claim that the resistance of the administration to the proposal that faculty members have the right to determine whether and how technologies are to be used in their courses was based on the economic benefits that these board members might accrue from the commercial distribution of such technologies, rather than on any particular educational philosophy or sense of fiscal responsibility to the public.

Several chapters also help to recover, rather than annihilate, locality, regionality, and the nation as meaningful and effective sites of social, cultural, political, and economic inventiveness in the face of globalization.(e.g., Tjeldvoll, Chapter 5; DeAngelis, Chapter 6; Lingard and Rizvi, Chapter 12; Castaños-Lomnitz, Didriksson, and Newson, Chapter 13). They eschew abstract constructions of globalization that reinforce its inescapably homogenizing effects, and they focus instead on the experiences of concrete, historically based societies and institutions. The detailed examinations of how specific societies and local institutions are responding to and interacting with this change process not only contribute to intellectual understandings of the phenomena, but also provide strategically valuable information. For example, without ignoring or underestimating the broad sweep of globalization, these studies show how the processes of change in which "real" societies and institutions are engaged are contingent, unfolding, and indeterminate, and thus open up renewed possibilities for world building. They show how globalization can take various forms and can be accomplished in a variety of ways, and they expose points at which crucial choices are being made where political pressure can be applied and alternatives pursued. In other words, rather than simply representing national, regional, and local diversity as that which is being reconstructed by globalization, globalization is highlighted as a process that is and can be contoured by national, regional, and local variations.

Finally, these chapters provide a strategic map of the key places, key issues, and key mechanisms through which globalization is being accomplished. Several chapters (Polster and Newson, Chapter 8; Vidovich and Currie, Chapter 9; Lingard and Rizvi, Chapter 12) identify organizational and conceptual "devices" that help in constructing globalized networks as sites of influence over and within higher education systems—instruments such as performance indicators, quality assurance, interlocking conferences, educational profiling, strategic planning, vision/mission statements, and so on. On the surface and in the day-to-day functioning of universities, these organizational and conceptual devices may appear innocuous and even helpful for alleviating the effects of underfunding, public distrust, institutional malaise, irrelevance to changing societal needs, and so on. But rather than accepting as unproblematic the intended roles assigned to them in policy documents, position statements, academic commentaries, and the like, these chapters probe beneath what is often taken-for-granted and explore the covert consequences and functions of these devices. In so doing, they offer two useful intellectual insights for plotting alternative courses of action.

First, by exposing internal inconsistencies and contradictions between and among the intended roles and consequences of these devices, this volume challenges a common perception of globalization as a logically coherent, organizationally unproblematic, and thus difficult-to-challenge package of changes. These inconsistencies and contradictions are critical points for political intervention and contestation.[12] Second, the authors' interpretations of the links between university changes and globalization are more open and fluid. They strongly suggest that the organizational devices that facilitate globalizing processes are two-way rather than one-way conduits of influence among local, national, and supranational sites of political activity. The authors call for critical intellectual interrogation, vigilance, and a broadened base of political engagement in relation to the construction, application, and workings of these devices.

In addition to the chapters in this collection, critical inquiries into the economic, political, social, and cultural changes attributed to globalization that have been accumulating in recent years also open the door to alternative courses of action. They counteract the overly optimistic, overly simple, and overly coercive character of the global talk that infuses contemporary higher education policy discourse. Rather than assuming that the endpoint of these changes is already knowable and the necessary decisions have already been made, these explorations offer valuable information about, and understandings of how and where, important changes are taking place or need to take place, to accomplish a fully globalized reordering and restructuring of national economies, social and educational programs and institutions, governance structures, and so on. The information and intellectual understandings put forward in these inquiries are useful for developing strategically based interventions and pursuing alternative paths within the context of these changes.

For example, Bob Jessop's (1993) frequently cited "speculative" paper on globalization and post-Fordism presents a relatively detailed, political economy of globalization-as-a-process-in-motion. He explores several broadly conceived trends or trajectories evident in changes in political economies at national and international levels. For each trajectory, he identifies problems that need solutions if the trends are to evolve into full-blown resolutions to the inconsistencies and contradictions that have arisen out of the changes thus far. Based on this examination, he speculates on the specific economic, social, and political alternatives that will most likely be adopted at the global and national levels as responses to these trends.

Jessop (1993) thus identifies a range of problems that need addressing, even as the solutions to them are being framed. If globalization is to proceed, for example, an international framework needs to be constructed within which economic processes will occur. This requires "establishing new legal forms for cross-national cooperation and strategic alliances, re-regulating the international currency and credit systems, promoting technology transfer, managing trade disputes, defining a new international intellectual property regime, and developing new forms of regulation for labour migration" (p. 14). Campion and Freeman's (Chapter 11) *mega-universities* could be added to this list. Critical research into any of these issues—in the genre of

Susan George and Fabrizio Sabelli's (1994) critical studies of the practices and operations of the World Bank—would constitute intervention in itself and provide the grounds for modifying and shaping resolutions to issues that will significantly affect the form that globalization will take.

In this vein as well, an intellectual initiative of particular significance to the relation between globalization and higher education is being undertaken by Claire Polster of the University of Regina in Canada. Polster's work focuses on the increasing international activity around intellectual property rights regimes (IPRs), such as the intellectual property instruments that are being inserted into trade agreements such as the GATT and NAFTA (Polster, 1997b). The institutionalization of intellectual property rights over the past two decades is especially relevant to the changes that have been taking place in higher education. For example, it has been a primary impetus behind policies that promote linkages between universities as sources of new knowledge and corporations that exploit this knowledge to develop value-added, knowledge-based products and processes that they believe will improve their competitive edge in global markets. In anticipation of their entry into world trade blocs, many national governments have made changes to patent legislation, facilitating private sector ownership of the knowledge produced in universities. Also, they have opened doors wide to private sector corporations' donations to (investments in) universities to facilitate their joint participation in publicly funded university research[13] and various types of commercially oriented endeavors. As part and parcel of these initiatives, the higher education sector has become drawn into and subsumed by domestic, international, and globalized economic activity.

Polster's (1997a) work is not only oriented toward understanding how the specific provisions of IPRs help to reorder the social relations of academic work. It also offers strategies for intervening in the political arena in which these regimes are being shaped. She proposes that universities reverse the dual trend toward, on the one hand, increasing their reliance on corporations as the purchasers of research activities and teaching programs and, on the other, competing with private sector knowledge providers by commercializing their own activities. Instead, she proposes two related strategies—community economic development (CED) and the "science shop" concept— to accomplish a double purpose. First and most important, these strategies would enable universities locally and on a national and international level to ally themselves with an increasing number of concerned groups and organizations (including nongovernmental organizations [NGOs]) to preserve the "knowledge commons" in the face of increasing pressures toward the ownership of the world's knowledge resources by commercially motivated private sector corporations. Second, these strategies would enable locally based universities to become genuinely engaged in "serving" the broader needs of society at large.[14]

As an alternative to increased private funding, CED effectively uses the limited public funds available to universities and, at the same time, contributes toward the social and economic development of their own local communities.[15] This is a way for universities to counteract globalizing pressures that would otherwise absorb them into a globalized knowledge industry and, at the same time, to open themselves to creative new ways of engaging with the "outside" world.

Relatedly, the European model of "science shops" allows universities to make their research resources available to local communities and groups that could not otherwise afford such resources.[16] Science shops and community-based research centers allow universities to respond to the changing social, political, and economic needs of society at large, but rather than limiting this activity to private or public sector corporate entities that have the funds to purchase their services—as is currently encouraged by the matched funding approach to support for academic research—they can make them available to less-resourced communities and organizations and address needs other than economic growth alone. Universities can thus assist their local communities in maintaining vibrancy and developing sustainability to offset the tendency in current globalization trends toward the disappearance, fragmentation, or homogenization of locally based social, economic, and political life.

The alternatives presented thus far constitute a basis for universities to selectively resist globalizing pressures and to use their research and teaching resources in ways that are creatively responsive to the changing times without merely accommodating them. However, the final note on alternatives returns us to the idea of the university: that is, to *the idea* of a center of intellectual life that sustains a lively, self-reflective relation to the world at large. This conception of the university preserves a space within—not outside—society for generating insight, for refining critical judgment, and for encouraging disciplined, inspirational, visionary thinking that can substantially enliven and give direction to social, political, and economic institutions.

It is ironic as well as disappointing, then, that in the main, universities have willingly accommodated and adjusted to the globalization discourse of these times rather than challenging its taken-for-granted assumptions and constructing paths of their own through the changing landscape. Globalization discourse emphasizes the importance and value of universities in achieving its purposes, and this could serve well as a lever for universities to play a much stronger role in, and exert much more influence over, these forces of change, based on their unique intellectual purposes, their traditional commitment to developing and disseminating knowledge as a public (rather than private) resource, and their historic association with democratic life and values. Instead of being an influential agent and a voice of lively self-reflection, the university as conveyed in the chapters of this book appears to have been ravaged by the force of these changes—reoriented, restructured, reconfigured—even while, and perhaps because, it has adjusted its goals and its *modus operandi* to them.

But the endpoint of globalization has not yet been reached, the situation remains open, and the university still has a very important responsibility to "serve the public interest." It is not possible to expand at length on the many ways that the university might take up this responsibility, but two related issues are worth noting. Globalization discourse places high dividends on notions of accountability and empowerment. These terms are frequently employed to legitimate sweeping changes to social practices, social institutions, and whole societies in order to support the form of globalism that the discourse advances. Much in this volume exposes the disingenuousness of employing these terms in this way. For example, the call for accountability does not resound in meeting rooms wherein trade agreements are drafted that establish publicly *un*accountable bodies and assign them powers that supersede those of elected governments. *Empowerment* is the last word to apply to the experiences of workers whose jobs are restructured out of existence by managers guided by strategic plans, or to apply to whole communities whose economies are swept away by multinational corporations that absorb local industries and small businesses into their latest mergers.

Accountability and empowerment belong to discourses that are or should be taken up within the university on an ongoing basis. They especially belong to the university's role in promoting democratic life, meaning not only its role in facilitating social mobility and extending access to economic prosperity but also its role in developing democratic sensibilities and the knowledge and skills that enable citizens to be thoughtfully influential over the affairs of the world. Gordon Laxer (1995) refers to democracy as the "neglected aspect of globalisation" (p. 296). Rather than ignoring or remaining silent about this neglect, the university is one place, perhaps one of the only places left, where democratic values, democratic practices, and a democratic vision can be put forward insistently as the underlying guiding principle of the "new world order" building that is taking place.

Moreover, as the knowledge produced in university laboratories and research units becomes the tool for economic, ecological, and human resource exploitation on a global scale, the university is pressed to examine its conscience and to take a position on the uses to which this knowledge is being put. Given the challenges currently facing the world, it is unconscionable for the university to try to function as the community of "objective" intellectuals and to claim neutrality when biotechnology successes that are developed in university labs are put to work for agribusinesses and multinational pharmaceutical companies, forcing small farmers out of business and peasant villages into starvation. The university-in-the-midst-of-globalization is in a unique position to be an outspoken advocate for revitalizing democracy and for pursuing social justice in the face of changes that threaten both. There still is time to make its voice heard.

NOTES

1. I am drawing on the Canadian experience here. Although different in pacing and details, the broad strokes of this policy direction were adopted during the same time period in Britain, Australia, Mexico, the United States, and other countries as well.

2. An interesting and insightful analysis of the responses of academics to their changing circumstances is in Dominelli and Hoogvelt (1996, especially pp. 89-96).

3. A synonym for "roving" is "on the move."

4. Carole Yawney, a social anthropologist and political prisoner activist at York's Atkinson College, gave the name "vigil-antes" to the picketers who conducted these candlelight vigils in the evenings.

5. For example, a strike of teaching assistants in 1996 at Yale University in the United States also attracted global interest.

6. It is important to recognize that local struggles, such as the York strike, may be means of implementing social, political, and economic objectives of their own.

7. I am indebted for this point to Amy Rossiter in the Department of Social Work, Atkinson College, York University.

8. Such groups vary across nations, but in several of the countries discussed in this book, organizations have been created over the past decade and a half that bring together university presidents, as the "CEOs" of their institutions, and the CEOs of the major national corporations. Such organizations were formed in 1979, in the United States, called The Business–Higher Education Forum; and in 1983, in Canada, called The Corporate–Higher Education Forum. Through written reports and other activities, these organizations shape public policy and use their political influence within the university sector to bring about many of the changes that have been critically examined here. Other third-party bodies in Canada, for example, include the Business Council on National Issues.

9. Some of these inequities have a long history, such as the gender discount at the point of hiring. However, restructuring and global competitiveness lead to disparities in salaries and other working conditions among people in the disciplines or research areas that are deemed by the administration to differentially enhance the university's competitive position.

10. I cannot further develop it here, but this point responds to the argument that university professors are "privileged" professionals whose struggles around their terms and conditions of employment cannot be linked to the struggles of the "real" working class.

11. Gordon Laxer (1995) coined the term *global talk* to refer to a discourse constructed largely by the New Right and multinational actors, which builds on some but not all (not the best parts) of Enlightenment thinking. It is a kind of talk that "uses inflated language about a radical rupture in human history, including the universal loss of national sovereignty and claims about the newness of global economic integration" (p. 248).

12. For a more detailed, theoretically grounded attempt to map the transformative possibilities as well as contradictions and inconsistencies in globalisation trends, see Jessop (1993).

13. In many national domains, publicly funded research-granting bodies have adopted matched grants programs that tie public support for research to support from corporate partners. These corporate partners are able to acquire the patent rights to research discoveries to apply them to commercial uses. In some cases, this approach to funding research in public universities has also led to a shifting of funds from the traditional research-granting bodies themselves to newly created bodies that are less accountable to the academic research community and allow for a greater degree of influence over research by the corporate sector. For example, the Canadian govern-

ment's 1996 budget created an almost $1 billion Canada Foundation for Innovation Fund to fund academic research and infrastructure, to be allocated by a board constituted of a majority of industrial representatives. This board will have the authority to determine its own priorities in ways that the research councils do not. For a more detailed discussion of how federal government monies allocated to academic research have been redistributed into programs that involve a greater degree of corporate sector input, see Polster (1996, pp. 108-111).

14. Current rhetoric about the service university concept notwithstanding (see Tjeldvoll's Chapter 5), the policies adopted by governments and institutions to increase the "service" profile of universities focus almost exclusively on providing services to corporations, either as producers of goods or as employers, and to government agencies that contract research services. In fact, service to corporations and government is seen to be synonomous with serving "society." Students are part of the constituency to be served but largely and primarily as potential employees, not as citizens.

15. In a report written by two York University environmental studies students, *Sustaining Ourselves: Community Economic Development at York University*, Dean Markey and Matt Price provide a detailed proposal for the way York University could increase its self-determination in the face of budget cuts and restructuring pressures by using principles of community economic development. (Report is available through the Environmental Studies Faculty of York University, North York, Ontario, Canada.)

16. The idea of science shops first emerged in European countries and has been extensively developed in the Netherlands (Dickson, 1984). It has recently been promoted by the Humanities and Social Science Federation of Canada. Also, the idea of setting up a national network of community-based science centers is being promoted in the United States by Richard Sclove through the World Wide Web Loka Institute's Science Shop homepage: URL:http://www2.nscu.edu/unity/users/p/pwhmds/scishop. html. See also Sclove (1995).

REFERENCES

Buchbinder, H., & Newson, J. (1990). Corporate-university linkages in Canada: Transforming a public institution. *Higher Education, 20*, 355-379.

Dickson, D. (1984). *The new politics of science.* Chicago: University of Chicago Press.

Dominelli, L., & Hoogvelt, A. (1996). Globalization, contract government, and the Taylorization of intellectual labour in academia. *Studies in Political Economy, 49*, 71-100.

George, S., & Sabelli, F. (1994). *Faith and credit: The World Bank's secular empire.* London: Penguin.

Jessop, B. (1993, Spring). Towards a Schumpeterian workfare state? Preliminary remarks on post-Fordist political economy. *Studies in Political Economy, 40*, 7-39.

Laxer, G. (1995). Social solidarity, democracy, and global capitalism. *The Canadian Review of Sociology and Anthropology, 32*(3), 287-313.

Newson, J. (1992). The decline of faculty influence: Confronting the effects of the corporate agenda. In W. Carroll, L. Christiansen-Rufman, R. Currie, & D. Harrison

(Eds.), *Fragile truths: 25 years of sociology and anthropology in Canada* (pp. 227-246). Ottawa: Carleton University Press.

Newson, J. (1994). Subordinating democracy: The effects of fiscal retrenchment and university-business partnerships on knowledge creation and knowledge dissemination in universities. *Higher Education, 27,* 141-161.

Newson, J., & Buchbinder, H. (1988). *The university means business: Universities, corporations, and academic work.* Toronto: Garamond.

Polster, C. (1996). Dismantling the liberal university: The state's new approach to academic research. In R. Brecher, O. Fleischman, & J. Halliday (Eds.), *University in a liberal state* (pp. 106-121). Aldershot: Avebury.

Polster, C. (1997a, May). *From option to necessity? International property rights, community economic development, and the future of the liberal university.* Paper presented to the Department of Sociology and Social Studies Colloquium, University of Regina, Canada.

Polster, C. (1997b, July). *How the law works: Exploring the implications of emerging intellectual property rights regimes for knowledge, economy, and society.* Paper presented to the International Conference on Knowledge, Economy, and Society, Montreal, Quebec.

Sclove, R. (1995, March 31). Putting science to work in communities. *The Chronicle of Higher Education, 41,* B1-B3.

Glossary of Acronyms

Accord   A series of agreements between the ACTU and
                 the Australian Labor Government to control
                 wages and deliver more social benefits during
                 the Hawke and Keating governments
                 (1983-1995)

ACTU   Australian Council of Trade Unions

APEC   Asia-Pacific Economic Corporation

BCLFDB   British Columbia Labour Force Development Board
                 (Canada)

BCNI   Business Council on National Issues (Canada)

CAE   College of Advanced Education in Australia

CAUT   Canadian Association of University Teachers

CCP   Chinese Communist Party

CED   Community Economic Development

CERI   Centre for Educational Research and Innovation

CHEF   Corporate Higher-Education Forum

CHST   Canadian Health and Social Transfer

CJS	Canadian Job Strategy
CMA	Canadian Manufacturers Association
CTEC	Commonwealth Tertiary Education Commission in Australia
DE	Distance education
DEELSA	Directorate of Education, Employment, Labour, and Social Affairs (OECD)
DEET	Department of Employment, Education, and Training, Australia
DEETYA	Department of Employment, Education, and Training and Youth Affairs, Australia
DES	Department of Education and Science, Great Britain
EPF	Established Programs Fund (Canada)
EU	European Union
FTA	Canada–United States Free Trade Agreement
GATT	General Agreement on Trade and Tariffs
GDP	Gross domestic product
GNP	Gross national product
HEC	Higher Education Council, Australia
HECS	Higher Education Contribution Scheme, Australia
ICDE	International Centre for Distance Education
IMF	International Monetary Fund
IMHE	Institute for Management in Higher Education (OECD)
IPRs	Intellectual property rights regimes
KUF	Ministry of Church, Education, and Research (Norway)

LFDB	Labour Force Development Board (Canada)
LFDS	Labour Force Development Strategy (Canada)
MNCs	Multinational companies
NAFTA	North American Free Trade Agreement
NICs	Newly industrialized countries located in Asia (These include Singapore, Taiwan, Hong Kong, Malaysia, and South Korea.)
NRC	National Research Council (Canada)
NSERCC	Natural Sciences and Engineering Research Council of Canada
OCUFA	Ontario Confederation of University Faculty Associations (Canada)
OECD	Organization of Economic Cooperation and Development (OECD countries include all European countries, Canada, United States, Australia, New Zealand, Japan, and South Korea.)
OPEC	Organization of Petroleum Exporting Countries
SCC	Science Council of Canada
SFU	Simon Fraser University (Canada)
SSHRCC	Social Sciences and Humanities Research Council of Canada
TNCs	Transnational companies
UBC	University of British Columbia (Canada)
UNAM	National Autonomous University of Mexico
UO	University of Oslo (Norway)
UVic	University of Victoria (Canada)

Index

About the Authors

Edward H. Berman, Ph.D., Professor of Education at the University of Louisville, is author of *African Reactions to Missionary Education* (1975) and *The Ideology of Philanthropy* (1983). He has also written widely in professional journals on such topics as development aid in Third World countries, the history of higher education, and the political economy of education in comparative perspective.

Mick Campion, Ph.D., is Associate Professor in Sociology at Murdoch University in Western Australia. In recent years, his research has focused on the application of ideas from industrial sociology to distance higher education. He has published widely in the area of distance education and open learning and, in 1995, was guest editor of a special issue of the international journal *Distance Education* that was devoted to the debate about post-Fordism. His previous major publication was *Worry: A Maieutic Analysis*.

Heriberta Castaños-Lomnitz, Ph.D., is Research Professor in Sociology at The Institute of Research in Economics at the National and Autonomous University of Mexico (UNAM) in Mexico City. She specializes in the sociology of higher education, particularly focusing on university-industry relations, higher education policy, and the brain drain. She is the author of *The Tower and the Street: Discourse and Sign of the University in the Face of the New Realities*. She also has

335

published papers on university-industry links in Mexico and on Mexico and globalization.

Jan Currie, Ph.D., is Associate Professor in Education, Murdoch University, specializing in comparative education and sociology of education. Her research interests include gender and work and higher education policy. She has recently published in the *Melbourne Studies in Education, Australian Educational Researcher, Discourse, Australian Universities' Review,* and *Women's Studies International Forum.* She has received three grants in the past five years on Award Restructuring and Disadvantaged Workers, Changing Nature of Academic Work, and Gender and Organizational Culture.

Richard DeAngelis, Ph.D., is Senior Lecturer in Western European and Comparative Political Sociology at Flinders University of South Australia. He has also been a student or teacher at universities in the United States (Chicago, Harvard, San Diego State), Nigeria (Ahmadu Bello), France (Nancy II, Sciences Po/Paris), and Italy (Johns Hopkins/SAIS/Bologna). He has written several articles on comparative higher education reforms, especially in Australia and Western Europe, and is working on a comparison of France and Australian reform efforts.

Axel Didriksson, Ph.D., is Research Professor at the National and Autonomous University of Mexico (UNAM) in Mexico City. As an economist, he specializes in higher education policy and planning, and he coordinates the Prospective in Science and Technology Project at UNAM. He has written and cowritten numerous articles and books, including *La Universidad del Futuro: Un Estudio sobre las Relaciones entre la Educación Superior, la Ciencia y la Tecnologia en Estados Unidos, Japon, Suecia Mexico* (1993). He is an advisory member of UNESCO's Regional Coordination for Higher Education in Latin America and the Caribbean.

Janice Dudley, B. Sc. (Honours), B. Ed. (Honours), is a doctoral student and is Lecturer in the School of Social Sciences and Psychology at Murdoch University, Western Australia. Her research interests are Australian education policy at the Commonwealth level, environmental politics, and the reconstruction of political ideas of citizenship. She is the coauthor with Lesley Vidovich of *The Politics of Education: Commonwealth Schools Policy 1973-1995* (1995).

Donald Fisher, Ph.D., is Professor of Sociology in the Department of Educational Studies and Associate Director of the Centre for Policy Studies in Education at the University of British Columbia. His research on philanthropy, university education, the social sciences, and academic-industry relations is supported by the Social Sciences and Humanities Research Council of Canada. His recent publications include *Fundamental Development of the Social Sciences: Rockefeller Philanthropy and the United States Social Science Research Council* (1993) and, with Kjell Rubenson and Hans Schuetze, *The Role of the University in Preparing the Labour Force: A Background Analysis* (1994).

David Freeman is a doctoral student at La Trobe University in Melbourne. He earned an honours degree at Murdoch University for his work analyzing issues related to workplace democracy. He has been a research assistant at Murdoch University and a research project officer for the Public Sector Administration Industry Employment and Training Council (Perth), and has engaged in consultancies for the Western Australian Council for Social Services.

Robert Lingard, Ph.D., is Associate Professor in the Graduate School of Education at the University of Queensland, where he teaches and researches educational policy. He is working on an Australian Research Council–funded project on the Organization for Economic Cooperation and Development and educational policy making in Australia in the context of globalization. His most recent coauthored book is *Educational Policy and the Politics of Change* (1997) and most recent coedited book is *A National Approach to Schooling in Australia* (1997).

Janice Newson, Ph.D., is Associate Professor of Sociology in the Faculty of Arts of York University in Toronto, Ontario, Canada. She studies universities as workplaces, as instruments of public policy, and as sites of social transformation, especially focusing on the development of the corporate-linked university and its implications for creating and disseminating knowledge as a widely accessible public good in democratically oriented societies. She has been politically active in her own Faculty Union and the Faculty Association movement in Canada and was recently the president of the Canadian Sociology and Anthropology Association. She coauthored *The University Means Business: Universities, Corporations, and Academic Work* (1988) and has published and presented numerous papers.

Claire Polster, Ph.D., is Assistant Professor of Sociology at the University of Regina in Regina, Saskatchewan, Canada. From 1994 to 1996, she held a postdoctorate award from the Social Sciences and Humanities Research Council of Canada, during which she began her work on the intellectual property rights instruments of trade agreements. In addition to her doctoral dissertation, *Compromising Positions: The Federal Government and the Reorganisation of the Social Relations of Canadian Academic Research* (1994), she has published and presented several papers. She is particularly interested in developing alternative ways of organically integrating universities into local communities.

Fazal Rizvi, Ph.D., is Professor of Education at Monash University, having previously worked at the University of Queensland and Deakin University in Australia. He is also the president of the Australian Association for Research in Education. He has written extensively on the cultural politics of education, racism, and multiculturalism, as well as problems of democratic reforms in education. He is working on issues of globalization and educational policy. His most recent books include a coauthored volume, *Education Policy and the Politics of Change* (1997), and a coedited collection, *Disability and the Dilemmas of Justice and Education* (1996).

Kjell Rubenson, Ph.D., is Professor in the Department of Educational Studies and Director for Policy Studies in Education at the University of British Columbia, Vancouver, Canada. Previously, he held a chair in adult education at the University of Link-ping, Sweden, where he still is an adjunct professor. His most recent publications are *The Role of Popular Adult Education: Reflections in Connection and an Analysis of Surveys on Living Conditions, 1975 to 1995* (1996) and *An Analysis of Statistics Canada's 1994 Adult Education and Training Survey* (1996).

Sheila Slaughter, Ph.D., is Professor of Higher Education at the Center for the Study of Higher Education, University of Arizona. She studies the political economy of academic science and technology, higher education policy, and women in higher education. She is coauthor, with Larry L. Leslie, of *Academic Capitalism: Politics, Policies, and the Entrepreneurial University* (1997), and of recent articles appearing in the *Journal of Curriculm Studies* (1996) and *Science, Technology, and Human Values* (1996).

Arild Tjeldvoll, Ph.D., is Professor of Comparative Education at the University of Oslo. He has been a visiting professor at a number of institutions, including Cambridge University and Harvard University. He is author of *Education and the Welfare State in the Year 2000* (1996) and coeditor with Peter Nagy of *Democracy or Nationalism? Education in Post-Communist Europe* (1996). He has also written numerous articles and book chapters.

Lesley Vidovich, M. Ed. (Honours), is a doctoral student at Murdoch University. She began her career as a secondary school science teacher and curriculum developer. She moved to the university sector in the early 1990s, where she has been teaching in the area of politics and sociology of education. Her master's dissertation was on education policy analysis. She is couthor (with Janice Dudley) of *The Politics of Education* (1995).